SEEK KNOWLEDGE

Thought and Travel in the House of Islam

Other Books by Ian Richard Netton

Al-Farabi and His School

Allah Transcendent: Studies in the Structure and Semiotics of Islamic Philosophy, Theology and Cosmology

Arabia and the Gulf: From Traditional Society to Modern States (editor)

Golden Roads: Migration, Pilgrimage and Travel in Mediaeval and Modern Islam (editor)

Middle East Materials in United Kingdom and Irish Libraries: A Directory

Muslim Neoplatonists: An Introduction to the Thought of the Brethren of Purity (Ikhwan al-Safa')

A Popular Dictionary of Islam

Text and Trauma: An East–West Primer

SEEK KNOWLEDGE

Thought and Travel in the House of Islam

IAN RICHARD NETTON

CURZON
PRESS

For Professor C.F. Beckingham FBA,
teacher and friend,
with respect and affection

First Published in 1996
by Curzon Press
St John's Studios, Church Road, Richmond
Surrey, TW9 2QA

Typeset in Times by LaserScript Ltd, Mitcham
Printed and bound in Great Britain by
Biddles Limited, Guildford and King's Lynn

British Library Cataloguing in Publication Data
A catalogue record of this book is available from the British Library

Library of Congress Cataloguing in Publication Data
A catalog record for this book has been requested

ISBN 0–7007–0339–X (hbk)
ISBN 0–7007–0340–3 (pbk)

CONTENTS

PREFACE AND ACKNOWLEDGEMENTS

A love of knowledge and learning has been a *leitmotiv* of Islam from its earliest days. The Holy Qur'ān instructs the believer to ask the Lord to increase him in knowledge (Q.20:114); while in a very famous *ḥadīth*, the Prophet Muḥammad instructed his followers *to seek knowledge even as far as China*. Travel (*riḥla*) in search of knowledge (*ṭalab al-'ilm*) became a cliché of mediaeval Islamic intellectual life. The Second Edition of the *Encyclopaedia of Islam* comments:

> It is true that in the expression *ṭalab al'ilm* the last word was regarded by the majority of Muslims as meaning "traditions" the search for which had involved long journeys, but it is doubtful whether the Prophet intended simply to allude to this activity in the numerous *ḥadīths* exhorting the faithful to seek for *'ilm* ("even in China"); therefore in the traditions in question this word should be translated by "knowledge" just as it should be given the meaning of "learning" in texts dating from the first centuries of Islam.[1]

Franz Rosenthal reminds us that "*'ilm* is one of those concepts that have dominated Islam and given Muslim civilization its distinctive shape and complexion. In fact, there is no other concept that has been operative as a determinant of Muslim civilization in all its aspects to the same extent as *'ilm* . . . There is no branch of Muslim intellectual life, of Muslim religious and political life, and of the daily life of the average Muslim that remained untouched by the all pervasive attitude towards "knowledge" as something of supreme value for Muslim being. *'Ilm* is Islam, even if the theologians have been hesitant to accept the technical correctness of this equation".[2]

The ten essays collected in this volume all explore, in one way or another, various facets of the Islamic search for knowledge, or the multifarious dimensions of that knowledge or, by neat contrast, especially in the first essay, the search for knowledge about Islam. They are divided into two main sections, *Thought* and *Travel*, but all are linked by this common theme of questing for knowledge, whether *'ilm* or the more intuitive *ma'rifa*,[3] which transcends such artificial divisions. And, in any case, there is an intimate link between thought and travel which predates even the Prophetic utterance about seeking knowledge even in China. In the Qur'ān (Q.18:60–82) the encounter between Moses and al-Khaḍir illustrates, as Rosenthal observes, "the need for travelling long distances in quest of knowledge".[4] This marvellous encounter between prophet and sage forms a proto-paradigm for the entire Islamic tradition of *ṭalab al-'ilm* literature, and must have inspired, *inter alia*, many a collector of *ḥadīth*. Though Moses is ultimately unsuccessful, not so much in the quest as in the test, he learns a hard lesson about the acquisition of mystical knowledge and the need for both energy in travelling, and patience in asking. Knowledge is sometimes neither won nor understood lightly.

In the first essay, in the first section of this volume, entitled *The Mysteries of Islam*, I try to show mediaeval Europe approached the 'mystery' of Islam both on a popular and a more scholarly level. With many of the scholars, their quest for knowledge about Islam and the Middle East reflected an "aspect of the Enlightenment Paradigm which considered Islam and the Middle East as an *exotic* field of study". Scholars and travellers discussed in this first essay include Edward Pococke (1604–1691), George Sale (?1697–1736), Voltaire (1694–1778) and Joseph Pitts of Exeter (c. 1663–c. 1733?).

In the second essay, *Foreign Influences and Recurring Ismā'īlī Motifs in the Rasā'il of the Brethren of Purity*, we move from the concept of knowledge as exotic to that of knowledge as esoteric. The 10th/11th century syncretic philosophers of Basra, known as the Brethren of Purity (Ikhwān al-Ṣafā'), held in their writings that all things in this world had an exoteric and an esoteric aspect. They frequently sought epistemological aspects of the latter and were highly eclectic in their knowledge and absorption of diverse bodies of knowledge which they sought with an encyclopaedic instinct. Rosenthal stresses that, for the Brethren of Purity, "the real purpose of faith is the eventual achievement of knowledge, of true esoteric knowledge . . . For the Ikhwān, as for most other Muslims, faith is inextricably connected with knowledge".[5] And it may be noted here that the Brethren's fundamental epistemological outlook is somewhat broader than, for example, Plato's. Real knowledge, in their view, *can* be gleaned in this world *and* via the senses.[6] The soul was "potentially knowledgeable" and required instruction to become so in actuality. That instruction should be through the senses, intellect and logical deduction.[7] The essay concludes that the Brethren may rightly be called "Wisdom Muslims".

The third essay, *The Neoplatonic Substrate of Suhrawardī's Philosophy of Illumination: Falsafa as Taṣawwuf*, takes as its focus the search for mystical knowledge. The philosophical quest in the great *Shaykh al-Ishrāq* (Shaykh of Illumination) Shihāb al-Dīn Abū 'l-Futūḥ Yaḥyā ibn Ḥabash ibn Amīrak al-Suhrawardī (1153–1191) becomes a spiritual and mystical quest. In his writings we find a "fundamental relationship and ultimate identification of philosophy and mysticism [which] was already prefigured in the thought of Plotinus himself".

The fourth essay, *Theophany as Paradox: Ibn al-'Arabī's Account of al-Khaḍir in His Fuṣūṣ al-Ḥikam*, stays with the concept of mystical knowledge and, as we have already noted, explores the archetypal Qur'ānic account of a search for knowledge, as it is found in Ibn al-'Arabī's *Fuṣūṣ al-Ḥikam*. Ibn al-'Arabī (1165–1240), the *Doctor Maximus* of his own and other ages, sought mystical knowledge and enlightenment which he articulated in a series of extremely complex works. The essay concludes with the idea that "for Ibn al'Arabī, concepts like divine theophany and human imagination ultimately merge as one".

The fifth and last essay of the first section of this volume, *The Breath of Felicity: Adab, Aḥwāl, Maqāmāt and Abū Najīb al-Suhrawardī*, also takes mystical knowledge as its theme but studies it through the writings of another Suhrawardī, this time 'Abd al-Qāhir Abū Najīb al-Suhrawardī (1097–1168). The latter sought to establish and codify the knowledge which was essential for the novice mystic. This he did in a work whose title has been rendered as *A Sufi Rule for Novices*. The essay identifies "a tension between the written 'frame' and the material it encapsulates" and suggests that the three concepts of instability, decline and return to "society" identified in the *Rule*, herald a "later degeneration in some of the [Sufi] Orders".

In the second section of this volume, the focus is on two of Islam's great travellers, famous through their individual *Riḥlas* or *Travelogues*, Ibn Jubayr (1145–1217) and Ibn Baṭṭūṭa (1304–1368/9 or 1377). The first travelled mainly between 1183–1185; the second between 1325 and 1354. Both sought God, Mecca and knowledge, though not necessarily, or at all times, in that order!

The first essay in this section, (the sixth in the volume), entitled *Ibn Jubayr: Penitent Pilgrim and Observant Traveller*, is a short and simple account of a Hispano–Arab traveller whose acutely sensitive conscience obliged him to undertake a pilgrimage of expiation to Mecca. In so doing "he has placed students of mediaeval Islamic art and architecture perpetually in his debt" and he is a most valuable source not just for that but for his detailed descriptions of Mecca and Medina. Ibn Jubayr sought and recorded knowledge about what he saw and where he travelled with the eagerness of a magpie.

The same is true to an even greater degree in the *Riḥla* of Ibn Baṭṭūṭa who is the subject of our seventh essay, *Myth, Miracle and Magic in the Riḥla of Ibn Baṭṭūṭa*. As I note, Ibn Baṭṭūṭa is certainly "a cataloguer and a compiler". The focus in this essay is very much on the wide-ranging interests of the traveller and his search for knowledge in the area of "anecdote, folklore, and descriptions of myths, miracles and magic, many of which derive from the author's infatuation with the Ṣūfī orders and holy men of the day".

These interests are surveyed again in the eighth essay, *Arabia and the Pilgrim Paradigm of Ibn Baṭṭūṭa: A Braudelian Approach*. Here I identify a *pilgrim paradigm* which comprises "a series of four searches: for the shrine and/or its circumambient religious geography; for knowledge; for recognition and/or power; and for the satisfaction of a basic wanderlust".

The ninth essay returns to the earlier traveller, Ibn Jubayr; it is entitled *Basic Structures and Signs of Alienation in the Riḥla of Ibn Jubayr*. It shows that Ibn Jubayr's *Riḥla* is indeed a precursor of that of Ibn Baṭṭūṭa and examines the knowledge gleaned by Ibn Jubayr on his travels in terms of alienation. He encounters, learns about and records, but is alienated by, the Christian cross, the Christian ship, Christian regal power, Christian taxation and Christian chivalry, courtesy and mores.

Finally, the tenth essay of this volume treats both these great travellers, Ibn Jubayr and Ibn Baṭṭūṭa, together. Entitled *Tourist Adab and Cairene Architecture: The Mediaeval Paradigm of Ibn Jubayr and Ibn Baṭṭūṭa*, it shows that both, consciously or unconsciously, followed a certain tourist "pattern" or "itinerary" in their thirst for new knowledge and sights, when they visited Cairo. Ibn Jubayr, and Ibn Baṭṭūṭa, furthermore, were not averse to indulging in some "travel-brochure rhetoric", or "Tourist *Adab*" as I term it, when it came to recording what they had seen. The argument of this final essay, then, is that, as a consequence of their search for knowledge of new places and people, they sometimes left behind florid descriptions in their *Riḥlas* which would not have been out of place in the modern tourist brochure of today.

There are several debts of gratitude which I must record here. My love and thanks go, once again, to my wife and family for putting up with the gestation and birth of this, my ninth book. I am grateful to Sheila Westcott, Secretary to Exeter University's Department of Arabic, for typing my manuscript with exemplary skill, speed and efficiency. Finally, the ten essays reprinted in this book first appeared in the following Journals or books. I am very grateful to the editors and/or publishers for permission to reprint them here: "The Mysteries of Islam" in G.S. Rousseau and Roy Porter (eds.), *Exoticism in the Enlightenment*, (Manchester and New York: Manchester University Press, 1990), pp. 23–45; "Foreign Influences and Recurring Ismā'īli Motifs in the *Rasā'il* of the Brethren of Purity", in *Convegno Sugli Ikhwān Aṣ-Ṣafā' (Roma, 25–26 Ottobre 1979)*, (Rome: Accademia Nazionale dei Lincei, 1981), pp. 49–67; "The Neoplatonic Substrate of Suhrawardī's Philosophy of Illumination: *Falsafa* as *Taṣawwuf*" in Leonard Lewisohn (ed.), *The Legacy of Mediaeval Persian Sufism*, (London & New York: Khaniqahi Nimatullahi Publications, 1992), pp. 247–260; "Theophany as Paradox: Ibn al-'Arabī's Account of al-Khaḍir in His *Fuṣūṣ al-Ḥikam*", *Journal of the Muhyiddin Ibn 'Arabi Society*, Vol. XI, (1992), pp. 11–22; "The Breath of Felicity: *Adab, Aḥwāl, Maqāmāt* and Abū Najīb al-Suhrawardī" in Leonard Lewisohn (ed.), *Classical Persian Sufism: From its Origins to Rumi*, (London & New York: Khaniqahi Nimatullahi Publications, 1993), pp. 457–482; "Ibn Jubayr: Penitent Pilgrim and Observant Traveller", *UR*, no. 2 (1985), pp. 14–17; "Myth, Miracle and Magic in the *Riḥla* of Ibn Baṭṭūṭa", *Journal of Semitic Studies*, vol. XXIX: 1 (Spring 1984), pp. 131–140 [printed by permission of Oxford University Press]; "Arabia and the Pilgrim Paradigm of Ibn Baṭṭūṭa: A Braudelian Approach" in Ian Richard Netton (ed.), *Arabia and the Gulf: From Traditional Society to Modern States*, (London & Sydney: Croom Helm, 1986), pp. 29–42; "Basic Structures and Signs of Alienation in the *Riḥla* of Ibn Jubayr", *Journal of Arabic Literature*, vol. XXII: 1 (March 1991), pp. 21–37 [printed by permission of E.J. Brill of Leiden]; "Tourist *Adab* and Cairene Architecture: The Mediaeval Paradigm of Ibn Jubayr and Ibn Baṭṭūṭa" in Mustansir Mir and Jarl E. Fossum (eds.), *Literary Heritage of Classical Islam: Arabic and Islamic Studies in Honor of James A. Bellamy*, (Princeton, N.J.: Darwin Press, 1993), pp. 275–284.

Although all are linked by a common theme, each essay in this volume can also be read as a self-contained unit. A minimum of changes has been made. Transliteration has been harmonised in the main but, by and large, the essays appear here as they were originally printed in article form. The opportunity has, however, been taken to correct errors and misprints: in the case of the third essay ("The Neoplatonic Substrate of Suhrawardī's Philosophy of Illumination: *Falsafa* as *Taṣawwuf*") more corrections were required than usual since the essay, as it appeared in article form in Lewisohn's *The Legacy of Mediaeval Persian Sufism*, was accidentally printed from an uncorrected proof! (A list of *Corrigenda* was issued for this latter volume in 1994 in view of the very large number of printing and other errors which had found their way into the text.)

These ten essays represent some of the fruit of fifteen years research and meditation in the two fields of Islamic Thought and Travel. It is hoped that they will provide enjoyment and stimulation both for those who have already laboured in these rich vineyards, and for those who are entering them for the first time.

September 1994
Ian Richard Netton
Professor of Arabic Studies
University of Leeds

NOTES

1 art. "'Ilm", *EI*[2], vol. 3, p. 1133.
2 Franz Rosenthal, *Knowledge Triumphant: The Concept of Knowledge in Medieval Islam*, (Leiden: E.J. Brill, 1970), p. 2.
3 For the two terms, *'ilm* and *ma'rifa*, see ibid., pp. 99 ff.
4 Ibid., p. 80.
5 Ibid., p. 108.
6 See Ian Richard Netton, *Muslim Neoplatonists: An Introduction to the Thought of the Brethren of Purity (Ikhwān al-Ṣafā')*, (London: Allen & Unwin, 1982; Islamic Surveys no. 19: Edinburgh: Edinburgh University Press, 1991), pp. 17–18.
7 Ibid.

ABBREVIATIONS

ArO	*Archiv Orientální*
BEO	*Bulletin d'Études Orientales*
D.N.B.	*The Dictionary of National Biography*
EI^2	*Encyclopaedia of Islam*, New Edition
EIS	*Shorter Encyclopaedia of Islam*
I.B. or IB, *Riḥla*	*Riḥla of Ibn Baṭṭūṭa*
I.J. or IJ, *Riḥla*	*Riḥla of Ibn Jubayr*
JRAS	*Journal of the Royal Asiatic Society*
Q.	*Qur'ān*
R.	*Rasā'il Ikhwān al-Ṣafā'*
RB	*Regula Sancti Benedicti*

TABLES

Section One

THOUGHT

1

THE MYSTERIES OF ISLAM

Introduction

'The problem is of course that the object of our enquiry is itself a mystery. The secrets of the Mysteries were fully known only to those who had been initiated into them. We have to help us no ancient text which expounds these secrets'.[1] The author here refers to the Dionysiac Mysteries portrayed in a fresco in the 'Villa of the Mysteries' near Pompeii; it must be stressed at once that no parallelism is intended between the 'Mysteries' thus displayed and the dogmas of Islam, nor between the initiatory nature of those 'Mysteries'[2] and the rituals of the Islamic faith. None the less, the above lines might neatly be borrowed and used as an epitome of the unschooled mediaeval mentality as it contemplated the Eastern religion: for the sense of mystery, suspicion and fear before the unknown and the unfamiliar which was evoked in the mind of the average Christian witness of things Islamic and Arab in the Middle East[3] must have had something in common with the feelings of the initiand in the Dionysiac Mysteries; though the 'mystery' would not have been articulated in the form of a ritual flagellation with the former as was the case with the latter![4] There *were* real differences, of course, and the analogy cannot be pressed too far: Islam *did* have an ancient text, or at least a mediaeval one, the Holy Qur'ān, which provided a solid basis for the latter development of Islamic theology and law. And the view and knowledge of Islam held by the common man in mediaeval times was not necessarily that of the scholars by any means: though misinformation abounded, perhaps sometimes as a species of 'war propaganda'[5] or as a defence of Christendom,[6] many mediaeval Christian scholars and writers showed clearly that they were only too well aware of the essential doctrines and teachings of Islam. Peter the Venerable (c. 1092–1156), for example, stated of Muḥammad, 'He was not the author, but the bearer of the divine law; not the Lord, but the messenger . . .'[7] It may be regarded as certain then that 'throughout this period every author with some pretensions to accuracy, that is, every writer who gave the matter more than a passing glance, thought that Islam stood as a third religion, as distinct from paganism as Christianity and Judaism are distinct from it, and that historically Muḥammad called the Arabs away from idolatry'.[8] Those who wilfully tried to justify ignorance can only have done so for polemical or tendentious reasons.[9]

There is clearly a radical dichotomy between the impression of Islam gained by the ignorant layman or lowly crusading soldier and that received by the learned clerk, at least the kind of clerk or scholar who revered accuracy and abhorred deception whether of the self or others. The latter species of writer was concerned more with the truth of things than deliberate propaganda on the one hand, or the false and inaccurate romanticism beloved by the courtly tradition of Europe on the other.[10] Thus, if we wish to establish here, briefly as a general introduction to this chapter, the *Mediaeval Paradigm* – or what Daniel prefers to call the *Mediaeval Canon*[11] – of the way in which the 'Mysteries of Islam' and the Middle East were viewed, we must take account of the dual perceptions of the ignorant, both wilful and otherwise, and the learned. Both perceptions may certainly be said to reflect or contain a sense of mystery before the Islamic faith but both articulated that sense of mystery in different ways: both categories of ignorant observer, as well as the polemicist, expressed it through the medium of 'fantastic legends' and 'fabulous nonsense';[12] the learned, who actually realised and appreciated the true nature of Islam, concentrated on a defence of Christianity by stressing the 'otherness' of Islam and the theological differences between the two religions: for example, the contrast between the Qur'ān and Christian scripture and especially the alien nature of the former, the lack of miracles in Muḥammad's life and the miracle-filled witness of that of Christ, and the adherence to a Trinitarian theology by Christianity and the rejection of such a theology by Islam.[13] The result was that, broadly speaking the West, as Rana Kabbani so neatly expresses it, 'had to reshape the Orient in order to comprehend it; there was a sustained effort to devise in order to rule'.[14] The sub-text of what I propose to term the *Enlightenment Paradigm*, a phrase designed to cover the reaction of scholars and travellers to the 'Mysteries of Islam' and the East during the period 1650–1800, is in part the expression of this reshaping.

The Enlightenment Paradigm (i) built upon its mediaeval predecessor and (ii) elaborated it with a variety of rationalistic, imperial and, sometimes, romantic appendages. (Indeed, the traces of all of these could be regarded as at least implicit in the first paradigm, the Crusades being a massive example of the imperial dimension.) To put the architectural image in a nutshell, mediaeval gothic became explicitly imperial baroque. Islam and the Middle East – and the two will be dealt with together in what follows as a united ideological and topographical focus[15] – were regarded variously (and sometimes together within the same author) as alien, as a threat and as an exotic temptation or field of study. The lands of the Middle East might indeed be approached overtly, and probably sincerely, out of a desire to slake an Enlightenment thirst for knowledge or to complete an education,[16] but such pure aims did not necessarily imply an absence of prejudice on the part of either the traveller or the writer. Paradoxically, however, prejudice against some facets of Islam and the Middle East could sometimes exist side by side with sympathy for others. Such sympathy or empathy may thus be said to constitute a fourth constituent element in the Enlightenment Paradigm which we have just elaborated, and it is the occasional (or even frequent) demonstration of such sympathy or intellectual appreciation on the part of the writer that perhaps sets this paradigm firmly apart from its mediaeval predecessor.

This chapter proposes to survey the way in which Islam and the Middle East were viewed over the one hundred and fifty years between 1650 and 1800 through the eyes of a selected group of scholars, writers and thinkers on the one hand, and through the eyes of a notable traveller of the age on the other. (It is, of course, recognised that such a division is somewhat arbitrary: some of those who wrote also travelled; while our representative *traveller* also wrote an account of his experiences.) Relevant quotations from the author's own works will be provided where necessary or useful and, throughout, the underlying stress will be on the Enlightenment Paradigm and its several characteristics as described above. The scholar-writers to be discussed will be (i) Edward Pococke (1604–1691), (ii) George Sale (?1697–1736), and (iii) Voltaire (1694–1778). The traveller is Joseph Pitts of Exeter (c. 1663–c. 1733?).[17]

Pococke

The interests of the seventeenth-century Dr Edward Pococke mirror that aspect of the Enlightenment Paradigm which considered Islam and the Middle East as an *exotic* field of study. And other aspects of the paradigm, as I shall show, were present in his writings as well. Firstly, however, we may note in passing that the real development of Arabic studies in Western Europe coincided with the Reformation; in England it came slightly later in the early seventeenth century;[18] there was, towards the latter part of that century, after the Restoration, some decline in the progress of such studies in England, though the decline was by no means terminal.[19] Pococke's long life, spanning as it did most of the seventeenth century, was thus a contemporary witness of, and indeed, ardent participant in, the first major flowering of Arabic studies in England. It was also clearly affected by the academic decline to which we have referred. Writing to Thomas Greaves in 1663 Pococke lamented: 'The Genius of the Times, as for these Studies, is much altered since you and I first set about them; and few will be persuaded, they are worthy taking Notice of'.[20]

Pococke was born in Oxford and educated at Thame Grammar School and Corpus Christi College, Oxford, from which he graduated as a B.A. in 1622 and M.A. in 1626. (He later added to his qualifications the degrees of B.D. in 1636 and D.D. in 1660.) In 1628 Pococke was made a probationer-fellow of Corpus Christi and he proceeded to ordination on 20 December 1629.[21]

It was his sojourn in Oxford that enabled the young scholar to start the study of Arabic: he received tuition from a German scholar, Matthias Pasor, formerly a Professor of Philosophy and Mathematics in Heidelberg, who had been constrained to flee to England on the 1622 sack of his city. These small beginnings were considerably enhanced by Pococke's posting to Aleppo as resident preacher, and during his six years there (1630–6) he took considerable pains to acquire a good knowledge of Arabic. On his return to England he accepted Archbishop Laud's offer of an Arabic Chair at Oxford University and thus became the first incumbent of the Laudian Chair of Arabic, as it became known. His academic career now began in earnest.[22]

Pococke combined this career with the incumbency of the living of Childrey, a village near Wantage, which he attended to with great care and where he did not flaunt his learning.[23] This did not, however, prevent him from visiting the East again, and in 1637 he made an important journey to Istanbul. He returned to England in 1641 to find England in ferment and Archbishop Laud in the Tower, circumstances which threatened to undermine both the scholar and his scholarship. A new patron was, however, found and Pococke continued to study and write at Childrey during the aftermath of the Civil War and the Protectorship of Oliver Cromwell.[24] With the Restoration in 1660 Pococke's fortunes revived somewhat and he was appointed Regius Professor of Hebrew and a canon of Christ Church, Oxford.[25] Holt notes that 'the history of the remaining thirty-one years of Pococke's life after the Restoration is mainly the history of his publications'.[26] So it is to these that we shall now turn to see how they mirror various aspects of what we have termed – perhaps slightly prematurely in the case of Pococke – the Enlightenment Paradigm.

Pococke's writings are certainly marked by considerable sympathy for his subject: his notes to his *Specimen Historiae Arabum* 'show the emergence of the scholarly study of Islam from the distortions of mediaeval polemic'.[27] The significance of his work in the field of Arabic history has been assessed as lying essentially 'in the fact that he, together with his predecessors Erpenius and Golius and his eighteenth-century successors, Ockley, Sale and Gibbon, helped to change the image of Islam in Christian and European minds'.[28] Yet Pococke himself was not devoid of either personal prejudice or predilection.

Although Pococke is rightly valued as a studious researcher into Islamic history,[29] it is clear from a survey of some of the major texts with which he dealt, or which he studied, that he was much fascinated by the *exotic* or esoteric in Arabic literature. He translated, for example, Ibn Ṭufayl's (died 1185) famous philosophical treatise *Ḥayy b. Yaqẓān*: its subject matter was probably the reason for Pococke's version remaining unpublished. A slightly later age had different tastes and, through Simon Ockley's first English translation in 1708, the treatise became popular in the early part of the Age of the Enlightenment: 'It is concerned with the self-improvement of man in the state of nature, a topic congenial to Western European thought in the late seventeenth and eighteenth centuries. It would appeal to those who were coming to believe in a natural religion, independent of all ecclesiastical organisations, and hence, in different ways, to Deists, Socinians and Quakers. It has also been regarded as a parent of *Robinson Crusoe* and hence of the whole subsequent literature of desert islands'.[30] Here was an exotic motif par excellence!

It is clear from Pococke's correspondence that he was also fascinated by the fabulous Neoplatonic encyclopaedia, the *Epistles of the Brethren of Purity* (*Rasā'il Ikhwān al-Ṣafā'*),[31] a copy of which Pococke had seen in Aleppo,[32] and which was sent to him by an Aleppan friend, and possibly Arabic teacher, who signed himself 'al-Darwish Ahmad'.[33] But perhaps the most interesting examples of Pococke's interest in the fabulous and the exotic are to be studied in his *Specimen Historiae Arabum.* This work, which was published in Oxford in 1650, contains a mere fifteen pages of the Arabic text of Bar Hebraeus's (Abū 'l-Faraj b. al-'Ibrī) (died 1286) *Mukhtaṣar Ta'rīkh al-Duwal* (*Historia*

Compendiosa Dynastiarum), with a Latin translation by Pococke; but these pages of text are then followed by more than three hundred pages of notes by the translator on the text. In these notes he exhibits a profound interest in some of the exotic errors about Islam which had accumulated among the scholars of Europe from mediaeval times onwards. Thus he is concerned to reject the etymology of the name Hagar from the Arabic *muhājirūn* (migrants); he pours scorn on the old Christian idea that the Prophet Muḥammad lies entombed in an iron coffin, hanging between earth and heaven; and he proves that there is no Muslim textual evidence for the dove fable in which Christians maintained that a dove had been 'trained to eat from Muḥammad's ear and was presented as a miraculous appearance of the Holy Ghost'.[34] None of these items is perhaps particularly significant alone but, taken all together, they show the considerable fascination that many of the more fabulous, exotic and esoteric elements in Arabic literature, history and folklore exercised on the mind of Edward Pococke.

This interest, however, did not preclude a certain blind prejudice which was fairly typical both of his own and preceding ages. According to this, we find that Islam, for all Pococke's sojourns in Aleppo and Istanbul, still contains an *alien* element which clearly no amount of study, literary understanding or erudition in primary sources can eradicate. It is as if, at times, a certain gut reaction in the bowels of the man takes over from the intellect and rational appreciation of the scholar. Thus, in a discussion of the Arabic word *munāfiq* (hypocrite), he writes: 'Ibn al-Athir observes that the significance of this concept [lit. theme], for a long time unknown to the Arabs, first applied under the Mohammedan religion. It is a fine thing that that great imposter introduced words too, through which his impious deeds could be expressed.'[35] The Qur'ān is referred to as 'impious sayings of Mohammed'.[36] For Pococke, as for other luminaries in the field before and after him like Bedwell, Pasor, Castell and Hyde, Arabic had a particular value in providing a greater understanding of the Bible.[37] In Pococke we sometimes find a devout Christian missionary impulse lurking just below the surface: in 1660, for example, he translated Hugo Grotius's piece of missionary propaganda entitled *De veritate religionis Christianae* into Arabic.[38] Twells described the purpose of this Arabic translation thus:

> In no Tongue could it be thought more useful, than in the *Arabick*, being a Language understood, not only in the *Ottoman* Empire, but in *Persia*, *Tartary*, and all those parts of *India* and *Africa*, where *Mahometism* has prevailed. Among the Professors of that Superstition, doubtless there are some well-meaning People, who

> would entertain favourable Thoughts of Christianity, were they sufficiently made acquainted with the Reasonableness and Excellency of it. *The Conversion of such, Dr Pocock had in view, when he first resolved upon this work . . .*[39]

With such sentiments vying for place in Pococke's teeming mind, it is hardly surprising that he should sometimes have regarded Islam 'as the religion of the false prophet'.[40] He was, after all, by trade not only a Professor of Arabic but also a seventeenth-century Anglican clergyman.[41]

In sum, Edward Pococke exhibits in his academic career and writings at least three of the four major features of the Enlightenment Paradigm which was adumbrated above: Islam, Arabic and the Middle East as deserving of intellectual sympathy and respect; as intrinsically exotic fields for antiquarian research and sometimes Biblical support; and as alien antagonists of the Christian faith.

Sale

George Sale, whose life just, but neatly, embraces the seventeenth and eighteenth centuries, has the interesting distinction of being the first major English Arabist who was not ordained: he was, in fact, a lawyer.[42] His father was a merchant in London but Sale's early education is obscure.[43] Although he became a student of the Inner Temple in 1720, it was as a solicitor rather than a barrister that he subsequently pursued a professional career.[44] Not long afterwards he began to study Arabic and was employed by the S.P.C.K. to work on their Arabic New Testament.[45] It is likely that he continued his legal work while engaged in his Arabic studies,[46] and the major fruit of the latter, by which Sale is best remembered, was the publication in November 1734 of his translation of the Qur'ān.[47] The full title of the first edition of this work was *The Koran, commonly called the Alcoran of Mohammed, translated into English immediately from the original Arabic; with explanatory notes, taken from the most approved commentators. To which is prefixed a Preliminary discourse.*[48] The work was both a major effort to correct current errors about Islam[49] and 'indicative of the trend towards popularization'.[50] One of its most important features, particularly from the point of view of the Enlightenment Paradigm, was the *Preliminary Discourse*, and we shall be returning to this as a major source of Sale's own attitudes and sympathies with regard to Islam and the Prophet Muḥammad.

Sale gradually grew apart from the S.P.C.K. after his great translation of the Qur'ān was published. The latter may have caused the Society to suspect his genuine commitment to Christianity in view of what was, for his age, a much more objective and sympathetic attitude towards an alien religion than was usual.[51] Indeed, this attitude has been commented upon and admired by several modern scholars.[52] Khairallah sees it as his major contribution that, 'although necessarily retaining a few traditional ideas on Islam, he reduced the element of bias without substituting new prejudices for the old'.[53] Thus, it is clear from Sale's dwindling relationship with the S.P.C.K. that, whereas his predecessor Edward Pococke was able to combine with reasonable harmony the careers of Professor of Arabic and Anglican clergyman and occasional Christian missionary propagandist without undue upset either to himself or others, Sale's much stronger sympathies for Islam and abhorrence of wilful error progressively may have alienated him from some of the conservative elements in the Anglican Church. Indeed, Edward Gibbon called Sale 'half a Musulman'.[54] But this was too strong. Sale never in any respect contemplated relinquishing his Christian faith.[55]

The general framework of sympathy for his subject within which Sale worked is evident in a variety of his statements. We see it, for example, strongly expressed in the preface to his translation of the Qur'ān, entitled 'To the Reader', where he writes:

> I have thought myself obliged to treat both with common decency, and even to approve such particulars as seemed to me to deserve approbation: for how criminal soever Mohammed may have been in imposing a false religion on mankind, the praises due to his real virtues ought not to be denied him; nor can I do otherwise than applaud the candour of the pious and learned Spanhemius, who, though he owned him to have been a wicked imposter, yet acknowledged him to have been richly furnished with natural endowments, beautiful in his person, of a subtle wit, agreeable behaviour, shewing liberality to the poor, courtesy to everyone, fortitude against his enemies, and, above all, a high reverence for the name of God; severe against the perjured, adulterers, murderers, slanderers, prodigals, covetous, false witnesses etc., a great preacher of patience, charity, mercy, beneficence, gratitude, honouring of parents and superiors, and a frequent celebrator of the divine praises.[56]

Elsewhere, in the famous *Preliminary Discourse*, Sale defends Muḥammad and Islam against the charge of idolatry: 'It was from this gross idolatry, or the worship of inferior deities, or companions of God, as the Arabs continue to call them, that Mohammed reclaimed his country-men, establishing the sole worship of the true God among them; so that, how much soever the Mohammedans are to blame in other points, they are far from being idolaters, as some ignorant writers have pretended.'[57]

Indeed, Sale shows himself willing to blame Muḥammad more for ignorance than for malice, in so far as Islam may have damaged Christendom:

> The terrible destruction of the eastern churches, once so glorious and flourishing, by the sudden spreading of Mohammedism, and the great successes of its professors against the Christians, necessarily inspire a horror of that religion in those to whom it has been so fatal; and no wonder if they endeavour to set the character of its founder, and its doctrines, in the most infamous light. *But the damage done by Mohammed to Christianity seems to have been rather owing to his ignorance than malice*; for his great misfortune was his not having a competent knowledge of the real and pure doctrines of the Christian religion, which was in his time so abominably corrupted, that it is not surprising if he went too far, and resolved to abolish what he might think incapable of reformation.[58]

The three quotations which we have just cited from Sale's translation of the Qur'ān are significant for two reasons. They demonstrate clearly the framework of sympathy within which Sale worked and which, as we have already noted, was perhaps more developed than that of some of his contemporaries. But they also exhibit very clearly the limits of that sympathy, and show the alien aspect of the Enlightenment Paradigm at work even within the mind of one of the eighteenth century's most perspicacious and least prejudiced scholars and commentators on Islam. In other words, and this is hardly surprising, we find even in Sale traces of the old mediaeval polemic.[59] Thus, in the quotations, Muḥammad is characterised as 'criminal' for his imposition of 'a false religion on mankind'; Sale applauds Spanhemius' description where Muḥammad is described, among other epithets, as 'a wicked imposter'; it is agreed that Muslims may, indeed, be worthy of blame on points other than idolatry; and Islam is seen to have the capacity to inspire horror in the minds of those Christians who have been directly affected by it. There is a clear sub-text to all Sale's writing on Islam and it is that it stands in the shade of the invincible truth of Christianity. Islam, for all the Christian Englishman's sympathy and respect for it, remains an *alien* growth which has had the unfortunate capacity over the centuries to supplant, in some areas, a true one.

We may summarise here by saying that there are two discourses about Islam fighting for supremacy in Sale's mind – a rational, sympathetic articulation of that religion striving for objectivity and hostile to all the errors and misrepresentations which have been spread and perpetrated about it over the centuries on the one hand; and a conditioned antipathy or distaste born of the Christian prejudices of those centuries and a sense of 'otherness', on the other. But there is a third and that is the exotic discourse. Like Pococke before him, Sale is fascinated by the strange, fantastic and unfamiliar aspects of Islam and the Middle East.

The fascination is apparent, most obviously, in the work entitled *The Lives and Memorable Actions of many Illustrious Persons of the Eastern Nations* which was planned and started by Sale, and published posthumously by Hamerton in London in 1739. The tales contained in the volume, translated by Sale and, after his death, by an anonymous scholar who had lived in Turkey for nearly twenty years, deal with fifty-two lives of eminent Arabs, Persians and Turks.[60] On this work, Khairallah comments: 'The *Lives and Memorable Actions* was another attempt at popularization, taking into account the public taste for the exotic, while providing a moral'.[61] And while, in Sale's translation of the Qur'ān and the *Preliminary Discourse* which precedes it, there are clearly elements which his own age would have regarded as exotic (like Muḥammad's Ascension into Heaven which Sale holds was a story made up by Muḥammad, and the popular belief that Muslim women had no souls which Sale refutes),[62] it is in the *Lives and Memorable Actions* that Sale's real fascination with the exotic is to be found, with its tales of 'Jamshid, king of Persia', 'Bahaloul, Haroun al-Rashid's jester' and 'the strange adventure of a dervish'.[63]

Finally, the latent, and sometimes overt, threat which Islam represented, not only to formerly Christian lands in the East but to Europe as well – one thinks in particular of the Ottoman sieges of Vienna in 1529 and 1683[64] – is clearly visible sometimes in Sale's mind. Islam has had the success which it has enjoyed *because of the power of the sword*. And for Sale 'It is certainly one of the most convincing proofs that Mohammedism was no other than a human invention, that it owed its progress and establishment almost entirely to the sword . . .'[65]

Voltaire

By profound contrast with Sale, Voltaire in his writings exhibits a hostile attitude towards Islam and Muḥammad 'compounded of the worst aspects of mediaeval obscurantism, even in small matters'. As is well known, Voltaire also used his attack on Islam as a cover for attacking all revealed religions including Christianity.[66] The sympathetic framework within which Sale wrote is frequently replaced by one of crude and scurrilous invention,[67] and Voltaire thus presents, in the main, the first three aspects of the Enlightenment Paradigm – distaste for the alien, fear of the threat and fascination with the exotic – infrequently mixed with any genuine sympathy for his subject. Voltaire's attitudes, indeed, may usefully be compared here briefly with those very similar ones of his French compatriot and contemporary Montesquieu (1689–1755). The views of the latter were similarly coloured by the prevailing (hostile) wisdom about Islam in the seventeenth- and eighteenth-century European milieu. Montesquieu, too, resorted to outright invention, pleading an author's licence, rather in the style of Voltaire and his notorious play *Mahomet.* Montesquieu certainly disliked Islam but, like Voltaire, was fascinated by its alleged 'fantastic and sensual elements'. In sum, Montesquieu 'saw in Islam only what he was trying to find or what he had himself substituted'.[68]

Voltaire's life has been surveyed and examined in a multiplicity of easily accessible works, English and French,[69] and it will not, therefore, be reviewed again in this essay. We may move, instead, immediately to his concept of Islam and the East and an examination of the Enlightenment Paradigm as it appears in his work. It should perhaps be noted, right at the beginning however, that his views did not always betray *totally* unrelieved disdain and contempt, despite the usual emphasis, which we stressed above, on the first three aspects of the paradigm. Thus, for example, at one point, he admits Muḥammad's good faith though his comments are underpinned by a stress on deceit: 'It is to be supposed that Muhammad, like all fanatics, violently struck by his ideas, preached them initially in good faith, reinforced them with delusions, deceived himself at the same time as others, and finally, using whatever treachery was necessary to validate it, promoted a doctrine which he believed to be right'.[70] Elsewhere, in his early part *Zaïre* (1732), it has been pointed out that the play 'presents a comparison of Christian and Moslem customs from which the Moslems emerge with credit' and that 'it is the Moslem who achieves the great Christian act of redemption and forgiveness'.[71]

Voltaire's more derogatory opinions, however, generally outweigh any good comments. The historical approach adopted in his *Essai sur les moeurs* (1756) is indeed in stark contrast to the mediaeval polemic and outright invention in his play *Le Fanatisme, ou Mahomet le prophète* (1741).[72] We shall have occasion to refer to both in due course, but it is worth noting here that while the scurrilous nature of the latter is more readily apparent than that of the former, Voltaire's *Essai sur les moeurs* also contains its fair share of invective and disparaging comments. So it is to this that we may first turn for some examples of Voltaire's distaste for the *alien*.

Here the Arabian Desert is 'this wretched country' inhabited by Arabs who are 'itinerant thieves'.[73] Muḥammad at his death is regarded 'as a great man by those who knew him as an imposter, and revered as a prophet by others'.[74] Voltaire admits the primacy over Europe which the Arabs achieved in the sciences and arts but then adds, 'in spite of their faith which seems to be the enemy of the arts'.[75] The Qur'ān is full of 'incoherent declamations', and 'contradictions, absurdities, anachronisms'.[76]

The same themes are reiterated in the longer version of Voltaire's famous *Dictionnaire Philosophique.* Under the rubric 'Arabes' the philosopher writes: 'all it took was a charlatan, a rogue, a false prophet preaching his delusions, to make Mecca a sacred place and a meeting point for neighbouring nations'.[77] It is clear from the context, even though it is not specifically stated, that Voltaire has in mind here Muḥammad on the one hand and the annual pilgrimage to Mecca by Muslims on the other. Under another rubric, 'Alcoran, ou plutot le Koran', the author proclaims that 'this Qur'an of which we speak is a collection of ridiculous revelations and of vague and incoherent predictions'.[78] It is, furthermore, 'a rhapsody without union, order or art'.[79] Confucius is preferable to the 'sublime and brazen charlatan' Muḥammad, for the former has received no revelation and uses only his reason.[80]

There is a further element in Voltaire's alienation, a more general one, and that is that the East *(l'Orient)*, in oriental tales like *Zadig* (1747) for example, becomes at times (though by no means always) a symbol of absurdity, bad taste and even derangement of the imagination.[81] That which is alien is nonsensical: in what is perhaps Voltaire's most famous tale, *Candide*, we find that the Muslims are shown to have no qualms in combining massacre and the prayer ritual prescribed five times a day.[82] Thus Voltaire demonstrates with particular venom what he holds to be the foolishness of the rules of organised religion. The Goddess of Reason, revered by the Enlightenment, is clearly to the fore here with the East, Muḥammad and Islam all representing the forces of Unreason. In the last analysis, the tales of the Arabs are 'tales which are without reason, and which signify nothing'.[83] This is why Voltaire uses such plays and stories like *Zaïre* and *Zadig* to represent the antithesis of Reason.

That which is alien often represents a threat and this brings us to a second major aspect of the Enlightenment Paradigm which may be briefly surveyed here. Muḥammad is described as killing his former compatriots without mercy.[84] The first Muslim conquerors were imbued with a spirit of rapine and religion.[85] The Muslim is the equivalent of a demon in *Zaïre* and to be hated as such.[86] There is then here, the age-old European fear of a religion which was perceived to have begun in struggle and violence, extended itself by means of the conquests and *jihād*, clashed with Christendom in the bloody wars of the Crusades, and finally threatened Europe itself at the 1683 siege of Vienna, just eleven years before the birth of Voltaire himself. All the above themes then, and perceptions of Islam as that which was alien and constituted a threat, may be seen as parts of a general canvas of fear, drawn by a Europe which still blanched at the prospect of Islam militant.

Yet there was another gentler aspect of all this, present in the writings of Voltaire as in those of his predecessors. It is the third part of the Enlightenment Paradigm, the fascination with the exotic. Voltaire's obsession with the exotic is evident in diverse sections of his corpus: we will confine our illustration here to his two oriental plays, *Zaïre* and *Le Fanatisme, ou Mahomet le prophète*, and the tale *Zadig*, all of which have already been mentioned. The first two plays are set in Jerusalem at the time of the Crusades, and Mecca respectively. *Zadig* is set in Babylon and other areas of the Middle East, including Egypt. While it may be true that '*Mahomet*. . . is even less *preoccupied* with exoticism than *Zaïre*',[87] it is also none the less true that both, like *Zadig*, function as vehicles of the idea that the Middle East is essentially an exotic space 'of mystery and magic'. The Babylon of *Zadig* may well be Paris[88] but the real point is that it is Paris 'exoticised'. Yet the exotic colouring is never overdone. *Zaïre*, for example, does not suffer from a surfeit of 'moeurs turques' and Voltaire's own interests are exhibited here by endowing the play with 'a superficial oriental flavour just sufficiently strong to interest the ordinary eighteenth-century theatre-goer without in any way distressing or even disconcerting him'.[89] This play at least then, despite its superficial oriental flavour, is an example of the exotic as captive of the pragmatic. Its oriental counterpart, *Mahomet*, is perhaps another example with a similar discernible attempt by Voltaire 'to include a number, if limited, of words of exotic flavour: *chameaux*(1), *déserts*(4), *olive*(1), *olivier*(1), *orient*(1), *prophète*(17), *sables*(1), *shérif*(1)'.[90] We may compare these with the 'few linguistic props of an oriental nature' like 'sérail, *esclave*, *calife*, *soudan*' which occur in *Zaïre*,[91] and perhaps conclude from all this that, for Voltaire, it was the *milieu* in which he set his plays and stories which constituted his major attempt at portraying and transmitting the feel of the genuinely exotic, rather than the *language* which he employed in those works.

To summarise, Voltaire's treatment of Muḥammad and Islam, on the one hand, wallowed in the tradition of mediaeval Christian polemic.[92] He was happy to paint Muḥammad as an imposter and fanatic and, in a play like *Mahomet*, totally distort the historical, or at least received, Islamic portrait.[93] Indeed, Voltaire did not seem to care if history were falsified provided this were done in the interests of dramatic art.[94] But there are two other sides to this treatment: firstly, as we have noted, the attack on Islam provides an excellent disguise by which other religions like Christianity and Judaism might be attacked and reviled;[95] ironically, Muḥammad is often lauded at the expense of Moses, whom Voltaire clearly detests.[96] This brings us to the final aspect: an undoubted element of grudging admiration which, almost despite himself, surfaces in the author's writings. Badir puts it in a nutshell: Voltaire's 'false prophet [in *Mahomet*] is still an incarnation of evil, but, as distinct from authors from the Middle Ages and Prideaux, he endows his character with talent and genius'.[97] Voltaire recognises that Muḥammad was the promoter of a massive religious, political and social transformation and his religion was 'one of humanity's most significant phenomena'.[98]

The historian in Voltaire thus accords a species of respect to the Prophet while the dramatist revels in the portrait of an imposter. It is indeed a paradoxical combination.[99]

Pitts

We move now from the intellectuals to a representative traveller who will be reviewed more briefly. Of course, as was noted before, some of the intellectuals travelled too. It is true that Sale, contrary to Voltaire's statements, never left England.[100] But Pococke, as we have seen, lived in both Aleppo and Istanbul; and Voltaire, although he did not go to the Middle East, travelled in Europe and even visited England.[101]

Perhaps one of the most articulate and honest witnesses of the period, yet one of the least expected in view of his rudimentary education which did not really progress beyond the elementary level,[102] was Joseph Pitts of Exeter. Born into a Nonconformist family, he went to sea at an early age, only to be captured at about fifteen years old by an Algerian corsair and sold into slavery in Algiers with the rest of his ship's crew. He was forcibly converted to Islam, and later made the pilgrimage to Mecca in the company of one of his masters. He proved to be careful observer of what he saw there and 'gives us the first detailed account through Western eyes of the observances of Mecca'.[103] After many vicissitudes Pitts finally reached his native England again[104] and recorded for posterity what he had endured and witnessed in his book entitled, long-windedly but explicitly, *A True and Faithful Account of the Religion and Manners of the Mohammetans. In which is a particular Relation of their Pilgrimage to Mecca, the Place of Mohammet's Birth; and a Description of Medina, and of his Tomb there. As likewise of Algier, and the Country adjacent: and of Alexandria, Grand-Cairo, etc. With an Account of the Author's being taken Captive, the Turks' Cruelty to him, and of his Escape. In which are many things never Publish'd by any Historian before.* It was published in Exeter in 1704 by Philip Bishop and Edward Score of the High Street.[105] The volume is a goldmine for Pitts's attitudes and, accordingly, it is to this work that we must now turn.

There was much that Pitts found to be *alien* both in Islam and the Near and Middle East.[106] He clearly hated the new religion to which he had been forced to convert[107] and he characterised Muḥammad at one point, in true mediaeval fashion, as 'that bloody imposter'.[108] Elsewhere, he railed against 'the skulking, thievish Arabs'[109] and deplored the tendency to sodomy which he observed among those whom he calls the Turks, noting with regret that 'this horrible sin of sodomy is so far from being punish'd amongst them, that it is part of their ordinary Discourse to boast and brag of their detestable Actions of that kind'.[110]

Not only was the milieux in which Pitts moved alien to him, but it also represented a threat and was a source of real fear to him. The extremely brutal circumstances of his forced conversion to Islam are clear evidence of this,[111] not to mention his seizure by corsairs at a very early age and being sold into slavery. It is hardly surprising then that, having learned to equate Islam with fear, he should have found little that was exotic in the Middle East.[112] Not for him the forced or even false romanticism of a later generation! It is true that he mentions and abhors the whores of Egypt,[113] and betrays *some* fascination at the table manners he encounters in the East.[114] But, unlike other visitors to Mecca and Medina before and after him, he remained profoundly unimpressed by those cities.[115] None of this indifference, however, prevented his being a superb observer and recorder of all that he saw. In this sense, he is like a latter-day Ibn Jubayr but stripped of that Spanish Arab traveller's sense of religious devotion.[116]

In sum, what in another traveller might have been described as 'a sense of the exotic' was replaced in Pitts by what can only be characterised as 'a sense of the mundane'! There are perhaps few better examples of this than Pitts's extraordinary comparison between the Meccan Mosque and the Royal Exchange in London: '*Secondly*, I shall next give you some Account of the *Temple* of *Mecca*. It hath about forty-two Doors to enter into it, not so much, I think, for Necessity, as Figure; for in some places they are close by one another. The Form of it is much resembling that of the *Royal Exchange* in *London*, but I believe it's near ten times bigger'.[117]

It might be asked by way of conclusion whether Joseph Pitts felt any sympathy at all for the religion he had been forced to adopt so unwillingly as his own? He *did* admire the devotion and piety of the average Muslim pilgrim to Mecca when he encountered it.[118] And, strangely in the light of his real views about Islam, he appears to make a connection between his recent visit to Mecca and his later recovery from the plague:

> Such a Signal Mercy I hope I shall never forget; a mercy so circumstantiated, considering everything, that my Soul shall thankfully call to mind as long as I have any Being. *For I was just returned from Mecca when this Mercy was dispenc'd to me*, I do observe the divine providence plainly in it; and hope ever to make the best use of it.[119]

Looked at *in toto*, Joseph Pitts of Exeter's attitudes towards Islam and the Near and Middle East are perhaps best encapsulated in the following summary assessment of Robin Bidwell: 'His tale is that of an honest Englishman, full of prejudices and distrust of foreigners but is accurate and truthful'.[120]

Conclusion

Early orientalism, including that of the period 1650–1800, produced a mixed legacy. It certainly led to a greater knowledge of its subject but horizons were sometimes narrowed rather than broadened. Orientalism 'served to distance and objectify non-European cultures, lumping their very different characteristics into a general category of 'Oriental' merely because they [were] not European. These [were] seen as 'exotic', and viewed as inert or passive in the face of European dynamism'.[121] And it was the nineteenth century, as far as Western perceptions of the Middle East were concerned, which was the *real* age of the exotic. The attitudes of this century lie outside the scope of our essay but the following concluding remarks may serve to illuminate the way in which one model was replaced by another. The Enlightenment Paradigm, which has served as the principal focus or reference throughout the course of this essay, had, as we have seen, four principal elements: a dislike of the alien, a fear of the threat, a fascination with the exotic and an occasional slight sympathy towards its subject. This was now displaced by a nineteenth-century Romantic Paradigm. The change from the one to the other was, of course, a gradual process and did not take place overnight. But the motors which produced this change are easily discernible. In the first place, what might be termed 'the imperial circle', whereby religious knowledge had been garnered for imperial ends by the West from the East and technical knowledge had been collected for similar ends by the East from the West, had often benefited Europe but not always the Ottomans. The Middle East as a disparate and discordant group of political entities was no longer powerful and so, no longer to be feared: its once mightiest unit, the Ottoman Empire, was in decline; Napoleon had decisively beaten the Mamluks at the Battle of the Pyramids in 1798.[122] Furthermore, enough was now known of the Middle East and Islam by the diverse means of trade, travel and war for both to be perceived as far less alien than in any preceding period. The elements of alienation, fear and threat of the Enlightenment Paradigm were thus dead, or at least moribund. More importantly, however, what survived and triumphed over all these into the nineteenth century was the exotic element. The West's fascination – indeed obsession – with the exotic East in this age may be characterised as both the last progeny of the Enlightenment Paradigm and the first element in its successor, the Romantic.[123]

NOTES

1 R.A.S. Seaford, 'The Mysteries of Dionysos at Pompeii' in H.W. Stubbs (ed.), *Pegasus: Classical Essays from the University of Exeter*, (Exeter, 1981), p. 59.

2 Ibid., esp. pp. 52–8.

3 E.g. see Norman Daniel, *Islam and the West: The Making of an Image*, (Edinburgh, 1960), p. 265, where he notes the suspicions of the French prisoners held by the Ayyūbid ruler Tūrān-Shāh (ruled 1249–50) and his amirs as described in Joinville's account.

4 Seaford, 'Mysteries of Dionysos', p. 60.

5 Daniel, *Islam and the West*, pp. 309–13; the best and most scholarly history of the Crusades, using both Western and Eastern sources, is Kenneth M. Setton (general editor), *A History of the Crusades*, 6 vols., (Madison, Milwaukee & London, 1969–85). For a summary account of the age, see P.M. Holt, *The Age of the Crusades: The Near East from the Eleventh Century to 1517*, (London & New York, 1986).

6 Daniel, *Islam and the West*, p. 244.
7 Ibid., pp. 17–18.
8 Ibid., p. 313; see also p. 45.
9 See ibid., p. 266.
10 See ibid., p. 313. The intellectuals' comprehension of Islam contrasted vividly with that of the more popular writers: 'The most popular life of Muhammad referred to a "concealed divinity" in him which Khadījah [his wife] was supposed to have recognised', (Daniel, *Islam and the West*, p. 19).
11 Ibid., pp. 271–94.
12 Ibid., p. 241; see also pp. 27–8, 32, 83–4.
13 Ibid., pp. 47–67, 73–7, 175–84, 276. See also Rana Kabbani, *Europe's Myths of Orient: Devise and Rule*, (London, 1986), pp. 5–6.
14 Kabbani, *Europe's Myths of Orient*, p. 138.
15 This is not to say that either Islam or the Middle East *actually* was (or is) a unity, ideological or otherwise: they were simply frequently perceived in such monolithic terms by Western mediaeval and post-mediaeval observers and commentators.
16 See Peter Brent, *Far Arabia: Explorers of the Myth*, (London, 1977), p. 51; Anita Damiani, *Enlightened Observers: British Travellers to the Near East 1715–1850*, (Beirut, 1979), p. 2.
17 Zahra Freeth and H.V.F. Winstone, (*Explorers of Arabia from the Renaissance to the End of the Victorian Era*, (London, 1978), p. 295) note that 'Pitts was living in Exeter in May 1731, aged 68. Place and date of death are not known'. Robin Bidwell (*Travellers in Arabia*, (London, 1976), p. 26), states that Pitts 'reached home in 1693 . . . He then seems to have lived quietly in Exeter for another forty years'.
18 See P.M. Holt, 'The study of Arabic historians in seventeenth-century England: The background and the work of Edward Pococke' in P.M. Holt, *Studies in the History of the Near East*, (London, 1973), pp. 28–9.
19 See P.M. Holt, 'An Oxford Arabist: Edward Pococke (1604–91)' in P.M. Holt, *Studies in the History of the Near East*, p. 19; see also Shereen Nagib Khairallah, 'Arabic studies in England in the late seventeenth and early eighteenth centuries', unpublished PhD thesis, University of London, 1972, esp. pp. 61 ff.
20 Holt, 'An Oxford Arabist', p. 19.
21 Ibid., pp. 3, 5, 15. Pococke's whole career may best be studied in the whole of this article by Holt and also, more briefly, in Leslie Stephen & Sidney Lee (eds.), *The Dictionary of National Biography* (hereafter referred to as D.N.B.), (Oxford, 1959–60), vol. XVI, pp. 7–12.
22 Holt, 'An Oxford Arabist', pp. 3–5.
23 Ibid., p. 9.
24 Ibid., pp. 8, 12.
25 Ibid., p. 15.
26 Ibid., p. 16.
27 Ibid., p. 11.
28 Holt, 'Arabic historians in seventeenth-century England', p. 36.
29 See ibid., p. 27.
30 Holt, 'An Oxford Arabist', p. 14; see also A.J. Arberry, *Oriental Essays*, (London, 1960), pp. 18–23. For the Arabic text of Ḥayy b. Yaqẓān, see

Aḥmad Amīn (ed.), *Ḥayy b. Yaqẓān li-Ibn Sīnā wa Ibn Ṭufayl wa 'l-Suhrawardī*, Dhakhā'ir al-'Arab, 8, (Cairo, 1952), pp. 57–131; see also Sami S. Hawi, *Islamic Naturalism and Mysticism: A Philosophic Study of Ibn Ṭufayl's Ḥayy Bin Yaqẓān*, (Leiden, 1974). See also Byron Porter Smith, *Islam in English Literature*, 2nd edn. (Delmar, New York, 1977, (repr. of 1939 edn.)), pp. 67–8: 'This tale is supposed to have had some influence on Defoe's *Robinson Crusoe* through its description of the methods used by Hayy to obtain food, clothing and shelter. By its implied criticism of primitive concepts in religion, it may be classed as an early example of that type of literature which employs a foreign observer to criticize the sins and follies of a given social group. It also links up with the idea of the 'noble savage' which Rousseau was to make his own'. As noted, Simon Ockley's translation into English of the *Ḥayy b. Yaqẓān* was first published in 1708; the first part of Defoe's *Robinson Crusoe* was published in 1719. (See A.M. Goichon, 'Ḥayy B. Yakẓān', *Encyclopaedia of Islam*, new edn., vol. III, p. 333.)

31 See I.R. Netton, *Muslim Neoplatonists: An Introduction to the Thought of the Brethren of Purity (Ikhwān al-Ṣafā')*, (London, 1982).

32 Ms. Poc. 432, f. 7, Bodleian Library, Oxford, cited in Holt, 'Arabic historians in seventeenth-century England', p. 43.

33 Ms. Poc. 432, ff. 6, 7, 8, cited in ibid., pp. 42–4.

34 Holt, 'Arabic historians in seventeenth-century England', p. 35.

35 Cited in Latin in P.M. Holt, 'Arabic studies in seventeenth-century England with special reference to the life and work of Edward Pococke', B.Litt. thesis, University of Oxford, 1951–2, p. 66. I am grateful to Dr S.H. Braund, University of Bristol, for translating these lines of Latin for me.

36 Translated from Holt, B.Litt. thesis, p. 80.

37 Holt, 'Arabic historians in seventeenth-century England', p. 29; see also idem, 'An Oxford Arabist', p. 12.

38 Holt, 'Arabic historians in seventeenth-century England', p. 29.

39 (My italics). Holt, 'An Oxford Arabist', p. 21; idem, B.Litt. thesis, p. 89.

40 Holt, B.Litt. thesis, p. 66; idem, 'An Oxford Arabist', p. 18.

41 See Holt, B.Litt. thesis, p. 80.

42 Holt, 'The treatment of Arab history by Prideaux, Ockley and Sale', in Holt, *Studies in the History of the Near East*, p. 57.

43 See D.N.B. (Oxford, 1963–64), vol. XVII, p. 668.

44 Ibid.; Holt, 'The treatment of Arab history by Prideaux, Ockley and Sale', p. 57.

45 Ibid.

46 D.N.B., vol. XVII, p. 668.

47 Ibid.; Holt, 'The treatment of Arab history by Prideaux, Ockley and Sale', p. 57; see also David A. Pailin, *Attitudes to Other Religions: Comparative Religion in Seventeenth- and Eighteenth-Century Britain*, (Manchester, 1984), p. 83.

48 The volume was published in London by J. Wilcox (printed by C. Ackers).

49 See Pailin, *Attitudes to Other Religions*, p. 83; Khairallah, 'Arabic studies in England', p. 242.

50 Khairallah, 'Arabic studies in England', p. 251.

51 D.N.B., vol. XVII, p. 669; Holt, 'The treatment of Arab history by Prideaux, Ockley and Sale', p. 57.

52 E.g. see Daniel, *Islam and the West*, pp. 299–300; Holt, 'The treatment of Arab history by Prideaux, Ockley and Sale', p. 60; Pailin, *Attitudes to Other Religions*, pp. 83, 92–3.
53 Khairallah, 'Arabic studies in England', p. 263.
54 Edward Gibbon, *The History of the Decline and Fall of the Roman Empire*, vol. V, (London, 1898), p. 333n. [68], cited in Pailin, *Attitudes to Other Religions*, pp. 83, 309n.24; see also *D.N.B.*, vol. XVII, p. 668.
55 See Pailin, *Attitudes to Other Religions*, p. 83.
56 George Sale, *The Koran, Commonly Called the Alcoran of Mohammed, Translated from the Original Arabic; with Explanatory Notes, taken from the most Approved Commentators. To which is prefixed, A Preliminary Discourse*, (Bath: printed by S. Hazard for J. Johnson *et al.* of London, 1795), vol. I, p. VI. (Further references in the notes are to this edition.) The Spanhemius mentioned by Sale is Friedrich Spanheim (1632–1701).
57 *The Preliminary Discourse* in ibid., p. 21; see also Khairallah, 'Arabic studies in England', p. 254; Pailin, *Attitudes to Other Religions*, p. 84.
58 (My italics) *Preliminary Discourse* in *The Koran* . . . 1795 edn., p. 52.
59 See Daniel, *Islam and the West*, p. 300; Khairallah, 'Arabic studies in England', p. 240.
60 *D.N.B.*, vol. XVII, p. 670; Khairallah, 'Arabic studies in England', pp. 238–9.
61 Khairallah, ibid., p. 238.
62 *Preliminary Discourse* in *The Koran* . . . 1795 edn., pp. 61, 136.
63 Khairallah, 'Arabic studies in England', pp. 239–40.
64 See Stanford Shaw, *History of the Ottoman Empire and Modern Turkey: Volume I: Empire of the Gazis: The Rise and Decline of the Ottoman Empire, 1280–1808*, (Cambridge, 1976), pp. 93, 214. Samuel C. Chew (*The Crescent and the Rose: Islam and England during the Renaissance*, (New York, 1974 (first pub. 1937), pp. 100–1) puts it thus: 'In the fourteenth century a cloud arose in the East and from the fifteenth till far into the seventeenth the Ottoman peril hung over Europe.'
65 *Preliminary Discourse* in *The Koran* . . . 1795 edn., p. 65; Pailin, *Attitudes to other Religions*, p. 103.
66 Daniel, *Islam and the West*, pp. 289–91; see also Haydn Mason, *Voltaire* (London, 1975), pp. 24–7; and Magdy Gabriel Badir, *Voltaire et l'Islam*, Studies on Voltaire and the Eighteenth Century, vol. CXXV, (Banbury, 1974), p. 141.
67 See Daniel, *Islam and the West*, pp. 289–91; Mason, *Voltaire*, pp. 24–7.
68 Ahmad Gunny, 'Montesquieu's view of Islam in the *Lettres persanes*', in Haydn Mason (ed.), *Studies on Voltaire and the Eighteenth Century*, vol. CLXXIV (Oxford, 1978), pp. 151–66, esp. pp. 151, 160–1, 163–6. See also Montesquieu, *Lettres persanes*, ed. Paul Vernière, Classiques Garnier (Paris, 1960).
69 E.g., see Theodore Besterman, *Voltaire*, 3rd rev. and enlarged edn., (Oxford, 1976); Jean Orieux, *Voltaire ou la royauté de l'esprit*, (Paris, 1966). I would like to express my deep gratitude here to my former colleague Professor Malcolm Cook of the Department of French, University of Exeter, for guiding me through the labyrinth of works by and about Voltaire.

70 *Essai sur les moeurs et l'esprit des nations*, ed. René Pomeau, (Paris, 1963), vol. I, p. 257; Besterman (*Voltaire*, pp. 424–5), translates this passage as follows: 'We must suppose that Mohammed, like all enthusiasts, violently impressed by his own ideas, retailed them in good faith, fortified them with fancies, deceived himself in deceiving others, and finally sustained with deceit a doctrine he believed to be good.'

71 Mason, *Voltaire*, pp. 21–2; the French text of the play *Zaïre* may be studied in *Zaïre*, ed. by Eva Jacobs, (London, 1975).

72 Aziz Al-Azmeh, *Islamic Studies and the European Imagination*, Inaugural Lecture, University of Exeter, 17 March 1986, (Exeter, 1986), p. 2; Daniel, *Islam and the West*, p. 289. The French text of *Le Fanatisme* may be studied in *Mahomet ou le fanatisme*, Collection L'Immortel, (Nantes, 1979). For an analysis of the structure of this play, see Badir, *Voltaire et l'Islam*, pp. 99–125.

73 *Essai sur les moeurs*, vol. I, p. 53.

74 Ibid., p. 259.

75 Ibid., p. 261; see also pp. 267–8, 477.

76 Ibid., p. 271; see Badir, *Voltaire et l'Islam*, p. 165.

77 S.v. 'Arabes', *Dictionnaire Philosophique*, vol. I in *Oeuvres complètes de Voltaire*, vol. 17, nouv. éd., (Paris, 1878), p. 340.

78 S.V. 'Alcoran, ou plutot le Koran' in ibid., p. 101.

79 Ibid., p. 103.

80 Ibid., pp. 103, 105.

81 *Zadig*, ed. by C. & P. Blum, (Paris, n.d.), p. 158.

82 *Candide, ou l'Optimisme*, ed. Lester G. Crocker, (London, 1970), p. 48; Mason, *Voltaire*, pp. 58–9.

83 Cited in Mason, *Voltaire*, p. 57.

84 *Essai sur les moeurs*, vol. I, p. 275.

85 S.v. 'Alcoran, ou plutot le Koran' in *Dictionnaire Philosophique*, vol. I, p. 106.

86 Mason, *Voltaire*, p. 22; see *Zaïre*, p. 114.

87 Mason, *Voltaire*, p. 24 (my italics).

88 See ibid., p. 56.

89 Eva Jacobs, 'Introduction' to Voltaire, *Zaïre*, p. 48; see also pp. 46–7.

90 Keith Cameron, 'Aspects of Voltaire's style in *Mahomet*', in Theodore Besterman (ed.), *Studies on Voltaire and the Eighteenth Century*, vol. CXXIX, (Banbury, 1975), p. 12.

91 Eva Jacobs, 'Introduction' to Voltaire, *Zaïre*, p. 47.

92 See Badir, *Voltaire et l'Islam*, pp. 73, 146.

93 Ibid., pp. 131, 135, 165.

94 Ibid., pp. 78, 216.

95 Ibid., pp. 141, 167, 178–82, 217.

96 Ibid. and pp. 199–214.

97 Ibid., pp. 11, 216.

98 Ibid., pp. 11–12, 215.

99 Ibid., p. 15.

100 See *D.N.B.*, vol. XVII, p. 668; Voltaire erroneously claims that Sale 'vécut vingt-cinq ans parmi les Arabes' (s.v. 'Alcoran, ou plutot le Koran' in *Dictionnaire Philosophique*, vol. I, p. 100).

101 See his *Lettres Philosophiques* (either in the édition critique by Gustave Lanson and André-M. Rousseau, 2 vols. (Paris, 1964) *or* the René Pomeau edition (Paris, 1964)) which, despite the title, reflects Voltaire's sojourn in England. The work has been translated into English under the title *Letters on England* by Leonard Tancock, (Harmondsworth, 1980). See also Dennis Fletcher, *Voltaire: Lettres Philosophiques*, Critical Guides to French Texts, (London, 1986).

102 See Freeth and Winstone, *Explorers of Arabia*, p. 54; and Sir William Foster's 'Introduction' to his edition of *The Red Sea and Adjacent Countries at the Close of the Seventeenth Century as Described by Joseph Pitts, William Daniel and Charles Jacques Poncet*, Hakluyt Series II, vol. C, (London, 1949), p. ix.

103 Freeth and Winstone, *Explorers of Arabia*, p. 50.

104 Joseph Pitts's life may be briefly studied in Bidwell, *Travellers in Arabia*, pp. 23–7; Freeth and Winstone, *Explorers of Arabia*, pp. 43–60; and the 'Introduction' to Foster (ed.), *The Red Sea*, pp. ix–xiii.

105 The third edition of 1731, published in London by Osborn, Longman and Hett, is the definitive edition. (See 'Introduction' to Foster (ed.), *The Red Sea*, p. xiii; Freeth and Winstone, *Explorers of Arabia*, p. 295.) The title of the third edition commences *A Faithful Account of the Religion and Manners of the Mahometans* . . .

106 See Bidwell, *Travellers in Arabia*, p. 24; Freeth and Winstone, *Explorers of Arabia*, p. 44; see also Aziz Al-Azmeh, *Islamic Studies and the European Imagination*, pp. 1–2.

107 Pitts, *Religion and Manners*, pp. 137–42 (1704 edn.), pp. 192–9 (1731 edn.); ibid. in Pailin, *Attitudes to Other Religions*, pp. 210–12; see also Bidwell, *Travellers in Arabia*, p. 24; Freeth and Winstone, *Explorers of Arabia*, pp. 45–7.

108 *Religion and Manners*, p. 110 (1704 edn.), p. 156 (1731 edn.); ibid. in Foster (ed.), *The Red Sea*, p. 46; see also Freeth and Winstone, *Explorers of Arabia*, p. 57.

109 *Religion and Manners*, p. 109 (1704 edn.), p. 154 (1731 edn.); ibid. in Foster (ed.), *The Red Sea*, p. 45; see also Brent, *Far Arabia*, p. 47 and Freeth and Winstone, *Explorers of Arabia*, p. 56.

110 *Religion and Manners*, p. 18 (1704 edn.), p. 26 (1731 edn.); see also Freeth and Winstone, *Explorers of Arabia*, p. 48.

111 *Religion and Manners*, pp. 137–42 (1704 edn.), pp. 192–9 (1731 edn.); ibid. in Pailin, *Attitudes to Other Religions*, pp. 210–12; see also Bidwell, *Travellers in Arabia*, p. 24 and Freeth and Winstone, *Explorers of Arabia*, pp. 45–7.

112 See Brent, *Far Arabia*, pp. 44–5.

113 *Religion and Manners*, p. 67 (1704 edn.), pp. 98–9 (1731 edn.); ibid. in Foster (ed.), *The Red Sea*, p. 11.

114 *Religion and Manners*, p. 16 (1704 edn.), pp. 21–2 (1731 edn.); see also Freeth and Winstone, *Explorers of Arabia*, p. 48.

115 *Religion and Manners*, pp. 84–5, 110 (1704 edn.), pp. 121–3, 155 (1731 edn.); see also Bidwell, *Travellers in Arabia*, pp. 25–6; Brent, *Far Arabia*, pp. 46–7; and Freeth and Winstone, *Explorers of Arabia*, p. 51.

116 Ibn Jubayr (1145–1217) visited Mecca and Medina for the first time in the

period 1183–1185. His journey is recounted in his *Riḥla*, (Beirut, 1964), trans. by R.J.C. Broadhurst, *The Travels of Ibn Jubayr*, (London, 1952). See also my essay 'Ibn Jubayr: Penitent Pilgrim and Observant Traveller', in this volume.

117 *Religion and Manners*, p. 86 (1704 edn.), p. 124 (1731 edn.); ibid. in Foster (ed.), *The Red Sea*, p. 27. (The passage cited here is taken from the 1731 edn.)

118 *Religion and Manners*, pp. 81–2, 97 (1704 edn.), pp. 118, 138 (1731 edn.); ibid. in Foster (ed.), *The Red Sea*, pp. 23, 35–6; see also Bidwell, *Travellers in Arabia*, p. 25; Brent, *Far Arabia*, p. 46; Freeth and Winstone, *Explorers of Arabia*, pp. 49, 54; Pailin, *Attitudes to Other Religions*, pp. 15, 209.

119 (My italics) *Religion and Manners*, p. 114 (1704 edn.), pp. 162–3 (1731 edn.); ibid. in Foster (ed.), *The Red Sea*, p. 49.

120 *Travellers of Arabia*, p. 27.

121 Martin Bernal, *Black Athena: The Afroasiatic Roots of Classical Civilization: Volume I: The Fabrication of Ancient Greece 1785–1985*, (London, 1987), p. 236.

122 See P.M. Holt, *Egypt and the Fertile Crescent 1516–1922: A Political History*, (London, 1966), p. 156; for the decline of the Ottoman Empire see Shaw, *History of the Ottoman Empire*, vol. I, esp. pp. 169–301.

123 See Mary Anne Stevens (ed.), *The Orientalists: Delacroix to Matisse. European Painters in North Africa and the Near East*, (London, 1984). See also C.E. Bosworth, 'The influence of Arabic literature on English literature', *Azure*, no. 5 (Spring 1980), pp. 14–19; Raymond Schwab, *The Oriental Renaissance: Europe's Rediscovery of India and the East, 1680–1880*, trans. by Gene Patterson-Black and Victor Reinking, (New York, 1984); and Zeinab A.M.A. Shirazi, 'Eastern themes in the fiction of D.H. Lawrence', unpublished PhD thesis, University of Exeter, 1987 (see esp. Chapter Two entitled 'The place of the exotic in the nineteenth century: a cultural reconstruction with special reference to the Middle East' on pp. 57–111).

2

FOREIGN INFLUENCES AND RECURRING ISMĀ'ĪLĪ MOTIFS IN THE *RASĀ'IL* OF THE BRETHREN OF PURITY

In one of the many didactic stories which appear in the *Rasā'il Ikhwān al-Ṣafā'*, two men from India, one blind and the other crippled, enter a garden: the owner has pity on them and allows them to take their fill. However, they become greedy and plunder the garden in the owner's absence, the cripple mounted on the shoulders of the blind man. They are discovered, forgiven once by the supervisor of the garden but, on doing the same thing again, they are expelled from the garden and cast into the desert, in the Ikhwān's words, 'as was done with Adam and Eve, peace be upon them, when they tasted the tree'. An elaborate exegesis of this heavily symbolic tale is provided by the Ikhwān: the body is the blind man and the soul is the cripple. The body is led where the soul wishes. The garden is the world whose owner is God while the garden's fruits are the good things of this world. The supervisor or warden (*al-Nāṭūr*) of the garden is the Intellect (*al-'Aql*).[1]

This parable is a typical example of the syncretic nature of the thought of the Ikhwān al-Ṣafā' and, indeed, it is no exaggeration to say that syncretism is a keynote of the *Rasā'il*. The parable is set in India but the symbolism of the body and the soul in the *tafsīr* could be labelled Platonic in inspiration. The ethics of the parable are also Judaeo-Christian in their emphasis on charity, forgiveness and final damnation. The whole is given a further Neoplatonic dimension by the introduction of the Intellect as the warden in that garden.[2] Finally, the parable is not unique to the *Rasā'il*: it is to be found in the Talmud where two watchmen, one blind and one lame, combine to raid the figs of the king's orchard. They are therefore jointly judged as one by the owner.[3]

However, perhaps one of the most significant aspects of the above parable is the way in which its meaning is clearly spelled out by the Ikhwān. They are not content that it should be received at face value, or given what we might term a *ẓāhir* interpretation. The whole story, which is a didactic tour de force, has a deeper, *bāṭin*, meaning which the Ikhwān intend that even the most junior, and least knowledgeable of their brothers should glean. But such clarity is not always to be found in the *Rasā'il* and consequently, the real significance of some of the doctrine contained in these epistles has sometimes been insufficiently stressed.

This essay begins with a survey of some of the Ismā'īlī terminology in the *Rasā'il*, which I have termed motifs, and attempts to show that, paradoxically, these Ismā'īlī terms are linked to evidence suggesting that the Ikhwān were not themselves *Ismā'īlīs*. It continues by applying the Ikhwān's statement that everything in this world has an exoteric (*ẓāhir*) and an esoteric (*bāṭin*) aspect[4] to the *Rasā'il* themselves and asks: what are the *bāṭin* elements in the *Rasā'il*? Finally, this essay asks whether the Ikhwān should in fact be considered as being within or without the pale of Islam *because of* these *bāṭin* elements. Much ink has been spilled in trying to assess whether the Ikhwān were Ismā'īlīs; less, I think, has been expended on the broader topic – surely a worthy one for our discussion – of whether the Ikhwān al-Ṣafā' should even be considered to be Muslims.

* * *

In another article[5] I have argued that the Ikhwān al-Ṣafā' should not be regarded as Ismā'īlīs because of the inferior role which they allocated to the *doctrine* of the *imāmate*. I concluded that the Ismā'īlī elements in the Epistles should be considered as influences only, rather than as indigenous factors in the Ikhwān's doctrine. Now, in this essay, I am not concerned with the occasional eschatological Ismā'īlī phrases, such as those cited by Hamdānī (e.g. *Ṣāḥib al-Nāmūs al-Akbar*)[6] but rather with Ismā'īlī motifs which have a widespread application in the *Rasā'il*. Paramount among these are the number seven, and, more importantly, the joint concepts of *ẓāhir* and *bāṭin*.

The number seven held a position of paramount importance in the thought of the Ismā'īlīs[7] and its popularity seems to have been transmitted to the Ikhwān. They devote considerable attention to it throughout the *Rasā'il*, and it may be said to run a close second in numerical prestige to the number four. It is considered, for example, to be the first 'Perfect [or Complete] Number' (*'adad kāmil*) in their mathematics.[8] They identify seven kinds of triangle,[9] seven moving planets,[10] seven major regions or divisions of the earth (*aqālīm*),[11] and seven kinds of natural science.[12] Of the fifteen ranks of soul, there are seven above and seven below the human soul.[13] There are seven kinds of bodies (*al-ajsām*) beneath the sphere of the moon comprising the

Empedoclean elements of fire, air, water and earth together with the three divisions of animal, plant and mineral.[14] The Sphere (*al-Falak*) was likened to the number seven and it ranked as number seven in the Ikhwān's Hierarchy of Being after the Absolute Body (*al-Jism al-Muṭlaq*).[15] The *ḥakīm* is defined as the man in whom is found seven specified praiseworthy qualities,[16] while in the famous simile in which the body is compared to a city, the workmen (*al-ṣunnāʿ*) are sevenfold, comprising such bodily functions as digestion and growth.[17] In view of the previous examples it is therefore significant that the *Sūra* entitled 'The Heights' (*al-Aʿrāf*), which seems to have been a favourite of the Ikhwān to judge by the amount of reference to, and quotation from, it in the *Rasāʾil*,[18] ranks as *Sūra* Seven in the Qur'ān.

However, despite their manifest affection for this number, the Ikhwān clearly had considerable reservations about those thinkers who founded much of their theology upon it – like the Ismāʿīlīs. The Ikhwān have been called Ismāʿīlīs themselves; yet how can we accept this when we find, as A.L. Tibawi points out, that the *Rasāʾil* completely discredit 'the significance of "number seven" and those who believe in it as contrary to the Ikhwān's creed'?[19] This is forcibly brought out in the disparaging tone and vocabulary of the following quotation which reveals a genuine distaste on the part of the Ikhwān for some of the excesses of partisans of the number seven:

> The Seveners (*al-Mussabiʿa*) immerse themselves in revealing things consisting of seven parts, and finding amazing things therefrom. They are infatuated with them and mention them excessively. They ignore anything not counted in sevens.[20]

The allied concepts of *ẓāhir* and *bāṭin* played a key role in the system and theology of the Ismāʿīlīs. The Ismāʿīlī Qāḍī al-Nuʿmān (d.974) was moved to observe, for example: 'Islam is like the *ẓāhir* and faith (*al-īmān*) is like the *bāṭin*, and there is no *ẓāhir* without *bāṭin* nor *bāṭin* without *ẓāhir*'.[21] Elsewhere, the science of the *ẓāhir* was likened to food, and that of the *bāṭin* to drink.[22] The Ikhwān al-Ṣafāʾ shared this belief in the omnipresent reality and applicability of the two terms and insisted in their turn: 'Then know, oh brother, that everything found in this world has an exoteric and an esoteric aspect (*ẓāhir*^{an} *wa bāṭin*^{an}). The external senses of things (*ẓawāhir al-umūr*) are skin and bone while their internal senses (*bawāṭinuhā*) are core and marrow'.[23]

They cited, as a prime example, the divine law (*al-nāmūs*): it consisted of clearly expressed regulations and ordinances known to both the ordinary man and the specialist who followed the *Sharīʿa*. But these regulations and ordinances also had secrets and esoteric meanings known only by the specialists (*al-khawāṣṣ*) and those deeply versed in such knowledge.[24] Elsewhere, in a section dealing with the divine wisdom behind the difference in the various characteristics of the stars, the Ikhwān noted that the Creator made some things manifest (*ẓāhir*) and some hidden (*bāṭin*) so that they could not be perceived by the senses. They placed in the first category the substances, accidents and states of bodies, as well as temporal affairs, and in the latter the substances of the soul and the affairs of the hereafter. God made the things which were manifest as a token of, or pointer to, those which were hidden. Thus the sun was a token of things eternal because of its qualities of completeness, perfection, light and radiance. The planets too, served as reminders of both temporal and eternal affairs.[25]

Though they are not in the habit of citing both *bāṭin* and ẓāhir interpretations beside the many Qur'ānic verses which appear in the *Rasā'il*, the Ikhwān *do* quote the following apocryphal *ḥadīth*, attributed to the Prophet, in which he observes:

> The Ḳur'ān has been revealed according to seven *aḥruf*, each effective, sufficient. Every verse has both an exoteric (*ẓāhir*) and an esoteric (*bāṭin*) aspect.[26]

The first part of this constitutes, in varying forms, a common *ḥadīth*[27] but the second, Ismā'īlī-sounding part is much rarer.[28]

The faith itself (*al-dīn*) is described as having the two aspects of *ẓāhir* and *bāṭin*[29] and this theme is developed in an important passage:

> Then know, may God help you, that the knowledge of the faith and its culture and what pertains to it, is of two kinds: one kind is exoteric and clear (*ẓāhir jalī*) and one kind is esoteric and hidden (*bāṭin khafī*). There is (also) a kind which is in-between. The most suitable aspects of religious regime and culture for the common people (*al-'āmma*) fall into the category of what is exoteric, clear and open. Examples include knowledge about prayer, fasting, obligatory and voluntary almsgiving, reciting the Qur'ān, glorifying God and acclaiming His oneness and knowledge about acts of devotion as well as information, tales and stories and the like pertaining to instruction, resignation to God's will and faith.
>
> The most suitable kind of religious knowledge for those in between the specialists (*al-khāṣṣa*) and the common people comprises legal study, study of the life of the Prophet Muḥammad and examination of the meanings of words like *tafsīr*, *tanzīl*, and

> *ta'wīl*,[30] the examination of the unambiguous and the obscure passages in the Qur'ān, and the searching for evidence and proof. (The man belonging to this in-between category) should not be content with blind convention (*taqlīd*[an]) in (his) faith if he possessed the capacity for individual judgement (*al-ijtihād*) and (the quality of) perspicacity.
>
> (Finally) the aspects of theology suitable for study, and worthy of examination and investigation by the specialists (*al-khawāṣṣ*) who are steeped in wisdom and deeply rooted in the sciences, comprise the examination of the secrets of the faith, the hidden esoteric aspects of matters, and their concealed secrets which no-one may have anything to do with except those who are purified from the filth of the appetites and the dirt of pride and hypocrisy . . .

The passage goes on to note and explain that the subjects of study for this class of experts will also include the symbolism of 'the Masters of the Divine Laws' (*Aṣḥāb al-Nawāmīs*) and the significance of some of the content of such texts as the Torah, Gospels, and Psalms, as well as the Qur'ān and prophetic books.[31]

Three interesting points emerge from all this. Firstly, the study of foreign scripture is confined, here at least, to the third and highest class of student, which embraces the specialists or experts who have distinguished themselves by their knowledge. Of all men, perhaps these are the least likely to be led astray by reading foreign scriptures, since they are so firmly grounded themselves in their faith.

Secondly, the Ikhwān's division of mankind into the three classes of common person, specialist or expert, and the man who is between the two (and who might be described as the intelligent layman) is an intellectual and not a class division. Each man is capable of, and fitted to, a certain kind of knowledge about his religion according to his intellectual capacities. Thus the passages states that 'the common people' (*al-'āmma*) are fitted only for the exoteric (*ẓāhir*) aspects of their faith, but the Ikhwān do not look down upon them because they are peasants, but because they lack knowledge. As we see from other parts of the *Rasā'il*, the term 'common people' is to be equated more with 'the ignorant' than with the peasantry in this sort of discussion.[32]

Thirdly, and most importantly, the idea that the Ikhwān were Ismā'īlīs takes a further jolt with the Brethren's astonishing declaration above that the man whom I have termed 'the intelligent layman' may employ individual judgement (*ijtihād*), a legal term which is given a theological application here. They do not even bother to confine this faculty to the third class of men, the experts. This is confirmed in another part of the *Rasā'il* where the brother is urged not to be content with *taqlīd* if he has a medium amount of knowledge – here is our intelligent layman once again! The *Ikhwān* then go on to press him to attend their *majlis* where they extend the promise of learning their secrets. One may surely understand from all this that *ijtihād* rather than *taqlīd* would have been a dominant characteristic of such a *majlis*.[33]

The whole concept of *ijtihād*, that ability to exercise independent and individual judgement on legal questions, roused much controversy in Sunnī Islam, and after the tenth century A.D. 'the door of ijtihād' was deemed to be closed by the Sunnīs.[34] But for the Ismā'īlīs and Ithnā 'Asharī Shī'ites, with their doctrine of an infallible *Imām*, the door was never opened in the first place. Only the *Imām* was entitled to exercise full judgement in legal and theological matters, or the mujtahids who acted as spokesmen for him when he was in concealment.[35] The idea that the Ikhwān put forward therefore, that someone between an ignoramus and a man of academic distinction might exercise *ijtihād* would surely have been anathema to a true Ismā'īlī; yet the Ikhwān al-Ṣafā' are called Ismā'īlīs! The Qāḍī al-Nu'mān indeed, devoted the last chapter of one of his works to a refutation of the whole concept of *ijtihād*.[36]

The Ikhwān, of course, realised that different capacities for *ijtihād* resulted in different interpretations of the Qur'ān, even among the professional exegetes. Each man's *ijtihād* varied according to 'the power of his soul and the purity of his substance (*ṣafā' jawharihi*)'.[37] What the Ikhwān themselves frowned upon was the wilful abuse of *ijtihād* by men such as those who joined the aspirants to leadership from among the common people (*al-'awāmm*). They deluded the people that they were cornerstones of the faith and the holy law and that by their personal opinion (*ra'y*), reasoning by analogy (*qiyās*) and individual judgement (*ijtihād*) they could make the crooked straight and elucidate the obscure. The Ikhwān prayed to be preserved from inclining towards, or joining, such men.[38] The use of the term *ijtihād* here with other legal terms indicates that the Ikhwān were well aware of its full legal implications.

Not all the references to *ẓāhir* and *bāṭin* in the *Rasā'il* give rise to such a dramatic conclusion as the passage in R. III, pp. 511–512 with which we have dealt, which goes a long way towards undermining the idea that the Ikhwān were true Ismā'īlīs. However, some of these references are well worth including and surveying here briefly, since they underline the diversity of use to which the Ikhwān put these two Ismā'īlī terms and incorporated them into their own intellectual system. They applied them, for example, to skills (or crafts) and the concept of belief, as well as to such things as the 'diagnosis' of illness and the celebration of feasts. Thus the Ikhwān noted that the external aspects (*ẓawāhir*) of all skills (or crafts) (*ṣanā'i'*) were devised for the good of the body, and their internal aspects (*bawāṭin*) for the good of the soul.[39] True belief (*al-īmān*) was divided into two kinds: *ẓāhir* belief and *bāṭin* belief. The first consisted in affirming five things with the tongue, an idea which may be said to parallel, on a theological level, the Sunnī doctrine of the five pillars of Islam. These affirmations were (1) of a single, unique creator, (2) of the existence of angels, (3) of the role of prophets, (4) of the importance of revelation and (5) of the ineluctable truth of the final Resurrection when all men will be judged, and rewarded or punished according to how they have behaved in this world. *Bāṭin* belief, on the other hand, consisted, in L. Gardet's words, of 'the innermost thoughts of the heart brought to bear, with experienced certainty, upon the truths professed by the tongue'. This is described as the essence or reality of belief (*ḥaqīqat al-īmān*) by the Ikhwān.[40] It is interesting how the outlines of this system parallel that described by al-Nu'mān: the Ismā'īlī Qāḍī divided belief (*al-īmān*) into three parts:

1 profession by the tongue (*qawl bi'l-lisān*);
2 belief or confirmation in the heart (*taṣdīq bi'l-janān*) and
3 action which accords with the seven Ismā'īlī pillars (*'amal bi'l-arkān*).[41]

By contrast, the terms *ẓāhir* and *bāṭin* also form part of a medical 'diagnosis' in the Ikhwān's narrative about one of the kings of Persia. The king falls victim to an illness which spoils his life, emaciates his body and deprives him of his former pleasures. The *wazīr* who seeks to help him is told by a wise old man that the king's illness is 'known from an external point of view (*bi-ẓāhirihā*) but hidden from the internal point of view (*bi-bāṭinihā*)'. In other words, the external symptoms are readily discernible but the internal cause is a mystery.[42]

However, perhaps the most dramatic contrast of the ideas of manifestation and concealment which lie behind the concepts of *ẓāhir* and *bāṭin* occurs in the description of the Ikhwān's feasts which they derived from the Sabaeans.[43] These feasts were held when the sun entered the signs of Aries, Cancer and Libra and were Spring, Summer and Autumn feasts respectively. They were three events full of joy, openness and happiness but they were followed by a fourth day in which the advent of winter was linked to a withdrawal into the cave of Dissimulation of Religion (*taqiyya*) and a general sadness, desolation and concealment. The Ikhwān likened their philosophical feast days to notable ones in the orthodox Sunnī and Shī'ite calendars: to the feasts of *'Īd al-Fiṭr*, *'Īd al-Aḍḥā*, 'Alī's designation as successor of the Prophet Muḥammad at Ghadīr Khumm and the commemoration of Muḥammad's death. This last was linked to their fourth day which was, above all, a day of concealment and *taqiyya*. It contrasted vividly with the Spring feast which was a day of manifestation (*al-ẓuhūr*).[44] In this manner the themes of manifestation and concealment were linked to the seasons and the whole became an allegory for the open revelation or careful dissimulation and concealment of religion itself.

Such concealment was, of course, particularly important where the more unorthodox elements of their faith were concerned, and the Ikhwān's reference to *taqiyya* brings us to the second theme of this essay. The element of *taqiyya* in the *Rasā'il* was nicely emphasised recently by A. Hamdānī when he wrote, at the conclusion to one of his articles, about these *Rasā'il*: 'Its ambiguities, allusions, insinuations and even contradictions were calculated to evade 'Abbāsid censorship and attack . . .'[45] (Such indeed, is the material from which one attempts to construct an accurate picture of what the Ikhwān really believed!) Now, it has already been noted that the Ikhwān endowed earthly phenomena with both an exoteric and an esoteric aspect.[46] If this statement is upheld, then it may be inferred that the *Rasā'il* themselves are infused with this dual element of *ẓāhir* and *bāṭin*. So, for the remainder of this essay, I want to examine some of what may be called the *bāṭin* aspects of the Epistles of the Brethren of Purity.

The Epistles speak with two voices on a number of topics: one may be termed an 'orthodox Qur'ānic' voice and the other an 'unorthodox foreign' voice. I have given this term to the latter because several of the unorthodox elements in the *Rasā'il* are the result of foreign influences. The clash between these two voices gives rise to a number of unresolved contradictions and it is these which I would identify as the *bāṭin* elements of the *Rasā'il*.

The foreign elements which the eclectic Ikhwān felt obliged to incorporate in their encyclopaedic writings, for the sake of completeness or as evidence to back up a particular doctrine, sometimes contradicted the views of orthodox Islam and indeed, the Ikhwān's own, more orthodox statements elsewhere in the *Rasā'il*. Such elements were not heavily disguised but then, neither were the full implications of what they stated specifically underlined. Discussion of such foreign elements may have been work for a closed session of the *majlis*[47] and it would be interesting to know how aware the Ikhwān were of the contradictions into which their syncretic thought sometimes led them. Two notable arenas in which such contradictions may be seen to arise are their view of God and their view of Jesus Christ.

The God of the *Rasā'il* is sometimes presented very much as the God of the Neoplatonic stream of Islamic thought. He is at the top of a complex hierarchy of emanation which goes considerably beyond the simplicity of the Plotinian triad of One, Intellect and Soul, and comprises nine tiers of being which include Prime Matter (*al-Hayūlā 'l-Ūlā*), the Sphere (*al-Falak*) and the four elements (*al-Arkān*).[48] The Unknowableness of the Plotinian One is translated in Islamic terms in the *Rasā'il* into the concept of *tanzīh*, incomparability, whereby God is not to be considered in anthropomorphic terms;[49] this was, of course, a facet of the doctrine of the *Mu'tazila* as well. It is from this foreign Neoplatonic view of God that difficulties immediately arise: for the God of the *Rasā'il* is also portrayed in a traditional fashion guiding and helping His people.[50] The Ikhwān end many of their *Rasā'il* with the fervent hope that God will make them successful in acting correctly and show them the path of righteousness which they should follow.[51] Furthermore, nearly all the *Rasā'il* begin with the traditional *Basmala*, 'In the name of God, the Merciful, the Compassionate'. So, on the one hand, the *Rasā'il* portray an almost unapproachable, Plotinian-type God; on the other, they describe the traditional deity of orthodox Islam who is a God of both guidance and mercy, if not of love in the sense which leads the Christian to address his deity boldly with the words 'Our Father'. Nonetheless, He is still a God who can inspire love and longing (*shawq*) for Himself[52] and create an unquenchable desire in man to vacate the prison of his earthly life and body for the joys of a Paradise which is sometimes conceived, Qur'ānically, in very physical terms.[53] This then, is an example of the Ikhwān speaking with two voices – 'orthodox Qur'ānic' and 'unorthodox foreign' – about the same theme. In the last analysis the two are, of course, irreconcilable and the Ikhwān do not try to reconcile them.

The picture of God which they present is further confused by the question of God's power and man's will, and the extent to which God may be said to be portrayed in the *Rasā'il* as being totally in control of events. Does He exercise the plenitude of powers possessed by the Islamic God of the Qur'ān, or 'delegate', albeit voluntarily, to the emanations, like a Neoplatonic deity? The answer is that He does both. As far as Islamic eschatology is concerned, it is clearly the orthodox God of Islam who will reward the souls of the good and the just with the Kingdom of Heaven after their deaths and who will equally ensure that the wicked suffer in torment.[54] But elsewhere, power is exercised

Neoplatonically by or through the Universal Soul (*al-Nafs al-Kulliyya*) and it is strange that the exercise of such extraordinary power has not been regarded as being in any way an infringement of the Islamic deity's basic omnipotence, even if it is with His permission and authority. Thus the Universal Soul is a divine instrument in the production of the material world[55] and one of its responsibilities is the movement of that world,[56] onto which it pours those qualities which it derives from the Universal Intellect (*al-'Aql al-Kullī*).[57] It is clear too, from the *Rasā'il*, that there is an astrological delegation of powers to the stars which are permitted to have a profound affect on the course of man's life.[58] It has been well pointed out by M. Fakhry that this idea of the ruling influence of the stars directly contradicts the concept of man's free will embraced by the Ikhwān from the *Mu'tazila*.[59]

If we turn to the Jesus of the *Rasā'il* we find that He is portrayed, in one place at least, as being much closer to the Jesus of Christianity than to the Prophet Jesus of the Qur'ān. There can be no doubt about the availability in Arabic translation of the New Testament since the Ikhwān advise their brother to read the Gospels (*al-Injīl*);[60] they themselves display a considerable familiarity with Christ's life and death, providing an account which is quite unlike that in the Qur'ān and which is, in Islamic doctrinal terms, thoroughly heretical.[61] Yet their justification seems to be that, like Socrates, Jesus is firstly, a hero, and secondly, a prime example of one who is convinced of his own future immortality and the sublime joys of eternal life.[62] We are told little about His early life – in this the Epistles resemble the canonical Gospels – but later we find that His followers are recruited from a group of bleachers (*qaṣṣārūn*) rather than fishermen. He is shown touring Palestine curing the bodily and spiritual ills of the people to whom He has been sent. Finally Herod, unnamed in the *Rasā'il*, seeks to catch Him and Jesus gathers His disciples together for what is known as the Last Supper in Christian terms; however, the *Rasā'il* again make no mention of such a meal nor of the institution of the Eucharist during it. The focal point of the whole meeting is the missionary covenant made between Jesus and His followers. Jesus the hero is later crucified and the description by the Ikhwān of the manner of His death, with their references to His being given vinegar to drink and being pierced by a lance, bears many resemblances to the accounts in the canonical Gospels.[63] The story is completed with Christ's resurrection from the dead, appearance to His disciples and the first missionary journeys which these disciples undertake, unblessed by the Paraclete. There can be no doubt about the meaning of the Arabic text here: as Fakhry puts it, 'the crucifixion and resurrection of Christ, which the Koran declared to be an allusion, are alluded to in clearly affirmative terms'.[64]

Now it is true that elsewhere in the *Rasā'il* the Ikhwān are less inclined towards Christianity and appear to go back upon some of what has been stated in *R*.IV pp. 28–32.[65] Yet the fact remains that, in these passages at least, we find a group of Neoplatonic philosophers accepting as fact the Christian doctrines of the crucifixion of Christ and His resurrection from the dead, with no reference at all to the Qur'ānic account which states that Christ was neither slain nor crucified but *shubbiha lahum*.[66] The life, passion, death and resurrection of Jesus Christ are stated here in the *Rasā'il* simply and starkly in clear, uncompromising and unambiguously Christian terms.

It is obvious that, just as there can be no reconciliation between the Christian and Islamic views of the crucifixion and resurrection, so there can be no total reconciliation between the account of Christ's life summarised above and much of the rest of the *Rasā'il*. The links are the factors of heroism and the belief in eternal life. The contradictions arise when the full implications of the account are examined. For example, since the Ikhwān believed that Christ was crucified and rose from the dead, did they, in any way, also believe in His divinity? After all, Christ is quoted several times in the *Rasā'il* as saying that He will return to a father who, from the context, is certainly not of this world.[67] So we see that, once again, one of the puzzles of the *Rasā'il* is produced by foreign influence – in this case Christian – which threatens to undermine the fabric of the Epistles which is cemented by so much Qur'ānic quotation.

It is surely clear from all this that the Ikhwān cannot be regarded as orthodox Muslims by any stretch of the imagination – neither, of course, can the Ismā'īlīs. But in view of the accounts which they provide of the God whom they worship, and of Jesus Christ, should they be considered to be Muslims at all? It is tempting to give a dogmatically negative answer to this but to do so would be to neglect a large amount of other evidence in favour of their Islamic affiliation. Perhaps the most important aspect of this is the enormous Qur'ānic substrate which underlies their Epistles. The Ikhwān certainly regarded themselves as Muslims, part of the great *millat Ibrāhīm*,[68] and it was to the Qur'ān, more than any other body of scripture, foreign or Islamic, that they had recourse in seeking verses to justify the elements of their teaching. The prophetology of the *Rasā'il*, whose pages are imbued with such major Qur'ānic figures as Adam, Abraham, Moses and Solomon, is, for the most part, Qur'ānic, and the Ikhwān's devotion to the person of Muḥammad, even if tempered by some Shī'ite sympathies,[69] is beyond question.

So perhaps the question which should be asked instead, by way of conclusion, is: what *kind* of Muslims were the Ikhwān al-Ṣafā'? One appropriate way of summing them up is to describe them as 'Wisdom Muslims'. The key to this term lies in their veneration of knowledge and wisdom (*ḥikma*), epitomised in their ready acceptance of the knowledge and wisdom inherent in every science, book and way of thought.[70] It was the intellect which the Ikhwān revered, not the body, and a majestically Platonic contempt for the body runs like an ascetic threat through the whole complex fabric of the Epistles. Though the Ikhwān did not accept the dualist theology of the Mānichees, they had considerable admiration for the contempt in which some of them held their bodies.[71] Furthermore, the title 'Wisdom Muslims' is appropriate since it provides a neat link between the 'orthodox Qur'ānic' element and the 'unorthodox foreign' element in the writings of the Ikhwān: wisdom (*ḥikma*) is common to, and sought from, both. The sage Luqmān, who may be said to represent the 'orthodox Qur'ānic' side (he has a whole *sūra* called after him in the Qur'ān, *Sūra* 31), and who was one to whom wisdom (*al-ḥikma*) had been given,[72] has been identified with both the Greek Aesop and the Biblical Balaam.[73] One of Luqmān's Qur'ānic sayings to his son is quoted by the Ikhwān,[74] together with a further series of counsels which, thought not found in the Qur'ān, emulate the style of exhortation in the *Sūra* of Luqmān:[75] Luqmān urges his son to beware of arguing with the scholars for the wisdom (*al-ḥikma*) which comes down from Heaven is pure.[76] God revives dead hearts with the light of knowledge just as the dead earth lives again with a heavy downpour of rain. Here, typically, the stress is on two major themes of the *Rasā'il*, purity and wisdom.

Jesus, who represents, in terms of the *Rasā'il*, the 'unorthodox foreign' side, also gives some advice to His followers: He urges them not to waste 'the wisdom' (*al-ḥikma*) by bestowing it on people who do not merit it, and not to hurt those who truly merit it by withholding such wisdom from them.[77] He is thus a true representative of a foreign *madhhab* which the Ikhwān cannot afford to neglect if their devotion to wisdom and the cultivation of the intellect is to be as eclectic as they evidently desire it to be.[78] It is in the light of all this that I believe that the Ikhwān may justly be termed 'Wisdom Muslims'.

NOTES

1 *Rasā'il Ikhwān al-Ṣafā'*, (hereafter referred to as *R.*), (Beirut: Dār Ṣādir, 1957), vol. III, pp. 156–160.

2 Provided that by *al-'Aql* we understand the Universal Intellect. The word could also be rendered here simply as 'the human mind'.

3 Sanhedrin 91 a-b, *Hebrew-English Edition of the Babylonian Talmud*, ed. by I. Epstein, (London: Soncino Press, 1969).

4 *R.* I, p. 328.

5 'Brotherhood versus Imāmate: Ikhwān al-Ṣafā' and the Ismā'īlīs', *Jerusalem Studies in Arabic and Islam*, vol. 2 (1980), pp. 253–62.

6 Ḥusain F. al-Hamdānī, 'Rasā'il Ikhwān aṣ-Ṣafā' in the literature of the Ismā'īlī Ṭaiyibī Da'wat', *Der Islam*, 20 (1932), p. 286; see *R.* IV, p. 18.

7 See W. Madelung, 'Ismā'īliyya', *Encyclopaedia of Islam*, new edn. (hereafter referred to as *EI*[2]), (Leiden: E.J. Brill/London: Luzac, 1960–), vol. 4, pp. 198–206; W. Ivanow, 'Ismā'īlīya', *Shorter Encyclopaedia of Islam* (hereafter referred to as *EIS*), (Leiden: E.J. Brill/London: Luzac, 1961), pp. 179–183; R. Strothmann, 'Sab'īya', *EIS*, pp. 478–480.

8 *R.* I, p. 57. The Ikhwān later explain that seven is the first 'Perfect [or Complete] Number' because it unites all the *ma'ānī* of number, e.g. if the first odd number, 3, is added to the second even one, 4, or the first even number, 2, is added to the second odd number, 5, the answer is 7. (*R*, I, pp. 58–59.)

9 *R.* I, pp. 105–6.

10 Ibid., p. 115.

11 Ibid., p. 165.

12 Ibid., pp. 270–2.

13 Ibid., p. 311.

14 *R.* II, pp. 52–3.

15 Ibid., p. 462, *R.* III, pp. 181, 203.

16 *R.* III, p. 384.

17 *R.* II, p. 382.

18 See, for example, *R.* III, pp. 65, 314, *R.* IV, pp. 246, 290. (Many of the Qur'ānic quotations from this *Sūra* in the *Rasā'il* are not, of course, identified as belonging to it, unlike these examples.)

19 A.L. Tibawi, 'Ikhwān aṣ-Ṣafā and their Rasā'il: a Critical Review of a Century and a Half of Research', *Islamic Quarterly*, vol. 2, no. 1 (1955), p. 34.

20 *R.* III, p. 180; see also ibid., p. 206.

21 *Ta'wīl al-Da'ā'im*, ed. by Muḥammad Ḥasan al-A'ẓamī, (Cairo: Dār al-Ma'ārif, 1967), vol. 1, pp. 53–4.

22 *Gnosis-Texte der Ismailiten*, ed. by R. Strothmann, (Göttingen: Vandenhoeck & Ruprecht, 1943), p. 58 (Arabic text).

23 *R.* I, p. 328.

24 Ibid.

25 *R.* I, pp. 141–2.

26 *R.* III, p. 488. The translation of the first part of the *ḥadīth* (up to '. . . sufficient') is by H. Fleisch ('Ḥarf', *EI*[2], vol. 3, p. 205), who shows that the translation of *aḥruf* here has roused considerable speculation.

27 E.g. al-Bukhārī, *Ṣaḥīḥ*: Faḍā'il al-Qur'ān, (Cairo: al-Ḥalabī, 1926), Pt. 6, pp. 227–8; al-Tirmidhī, *al-Jāmi' al-Ṣaḥīh wa-huwa Sunan al-Tirmidhī*: Kitāb al-Qirā'āt, ed. by Ibrāhīm 'Aṭwah 'Awaḍ, (Cairo: al-Ḥalabī, 1965), Pt. 5, pp. 193–4.

28 A similar *ḥadīth* to this second part (using the words *baṭn* and *ẓahr* instead of *bāṭin* and *ẓāhir*) transmitted on the authority of Ibn Mas'ūd, is to be found in al-Tabrīzī, *Mishkāt al-Maṣābīḥ*: Kitāb al-'Ilm, ed. by Muḥammad Nāṣir al-Dīn al-Albānī (Damascus: al-Maktab al-Islāmī, 1961), Pt. 1, p. 80. I have not been able to find the words *ẓāhir* and *bāṭin*, as part of this *ḥadīth*, in any of the major *ḥadīth* collections.

29 *R*. III, p. 492.

30 *Ta'wil*, with the Ismā'īlīs, meant 'the educing of the *bāṭin* from the ẓāhir text'. See M.G.S. Hodgson, 'Bāṭiniyya', *EI*², vol. 1, p. 1099.

31 *R*. III, pp. 511–2.

32 See *R*. III, p. 515; see also p. 511. See M.G. S. Hodgson, *loc. cit*, who stresses that, in the *Bāṭinī* system, (which influenced the Ikhwān) man was 'divided into *khāṣṣ*, the elite who know the *bāṭin* and '*āmm*, the ignorant generality'.

33 *R*. IV, p. 66.

34 See A.A.A. Fyzee, *Outlines of Muhammadan Law*, 3rd edn., (London: Oxford University Press, 1964), p. 35; J. Schacht, *An Introduction to Islamic Law*, (Oxford: Clarendon Press, 1964), pp. 69–73.

35 Fyzee, *op. cit*, pp. 45–6.

36 *Ikhtilāf Uṣūl al-Madhāhib*, ed. by Muṣṭafā Ghālib (Beirut: Dār al-Andalus, 1973). pp. 203–28.

37 *R*. III, pp. 488–9.

38 Ibid., pp. 155–6.

39 *R*. IV, p. 395.

40 Ibid., pp. 67–8; L. Gardet, 'Īmān', *EI*², vol. 3, p. 1171.

41 *Da'ā'im al-Islām*, ed. by A.A.A. Fyzee, (Cairo: Dār al-Ma'ārif, 1963), vol. 1, p. 3 (Arabic text).

42 *R*. IV, p. 316.

43 Yves Marquet, 'Sabéens et Iḥwān al-Ṣafā'', (*suite et fin*), *Studia Islamica*, 25 (1966), pp. 96–101.

44 *R*. IV, pp. 265–70; See H. Corbin, 'Rituel Sabéen et Exégèse Ismaélienne du Rituel', *Eranos Jahrbuch*, 19 (1950), pp. 210–16.

45 'An early Fāṭimid source on the time and authorship of the *Rasā'il Iḥwān al-Ṣafā", Arabica, Tome XXVI: Fasc. I (1979), p. 73.*

46 *R*. I, p. 328.

47 See *R*. III, p. 512.

48 Ibid., p. 56.

49 E.g. *R*. III, p. 403, *R*. IV, p. 387.

50 E.g. see *R*. IV, pp. 62–3.

51 E.g. Ibid., p. 40.

52 See *R*. III, p. 286.

53 E.g. *R*. IV, p. 30.

54 *R*. III, p. 290.

55 Ibid., p. 352.

56 Ibid., p. 328.

57 Ibid., p. 185.

58 See, e.g. *R*. I, p. 142.

59 M. Fakhry, *A History of Islamic Philosophy*, (New York & London: Columbia University Press, 1970), p. 204.

60 *R.* IV, p. 245.
61 Ibid., pp. 28–32.
62 See ibid., pp. 58, 73–4.
63 See, in particular, *John* 19 and *Matthew* 27.
64 M. Fakhry, *op. cit*, p. 203.
65 E.g. *R.* II, p. 284, *R.* III, pp. 72, 523.
66 *Qur'ān* IV: 156. (I have adopted Flügel's numbering of verses.)
67 *R.* IV, pp. 31, 58, 175.
68 Ibid., p. 126; see the citation of *Qur'ān* II: 124 in *R.* I, p. 76.
69 E.g. *R.* IV, p. 33.
70 E.g. see ibid., pp. 41–2.
71 *R.* II, p. 369; see Geo. Widengren, *Mani and Manichaeism*, (London: Weidenfeld & Nicolson, 1965), pp. 25–6, 96–8.
72 *Qur'ān* XXXI: 11.
73 T. Fahd, *La Divination Arabe*, (Leiden: E.J. Brill, 1966), pp. 88–9.
74 *R.* I, p. 374: *Qur'ān* XXXI: 15.
75 *R.* I, p. 348.
76 Compare *Epistle of Saint James* 3: 17.
77 *R.* IV, pp. 122, 166.
78 See *supra*, footnote 70.

3

THE NEOPLATONIC SUBSTRATE OF SUHRAWARDĪ'S PHILOSOPHY OF ILLUMINATION

Falsafa as *Taṣawwuf*

As in the case of so many philosophers and thinkers who were mystics, it is clear that the life of Shihāb al-Dīn Abū'l-Futūḥ Yaḥyā ibn Ḥabash ibn Amīrak al-Suhrawardī (548/1153–587/1191), the great *Shaykh al-Ishrāq*, has become enveloped in mystery and myth. This is particularly true of Suhrawardī's strange end. Of this Corbin observed: 'Notre jeune shaykh mourut de *façon mystérieuse* dans la citadelle d'Alep'.[1] S.H. Nasr noted that 'he was either suffocated to death or died of starvation'.[2] The mysterious end of the man reflects, emphasizes and, in a very real sense, re-creates the mystery of love which is at the heart of the man's thought. (This point will be elaborated later.) Of course, we frequently use the word 'myth' in a loose sense to convey an aura of vagueness or mystery or legend.

Yet there is a more scholarly and useful sense of the word 'myth' which might be employed here in any discussion of Suhrawardī. It is true that it is both complex and multivalent: Ruthven cites St Augustine on the topic of time: 'I know very well what it is, provided that nobody asks me; but if I am asked to try to explain, I am baffled'; and Ruthven suggests that Augustine here anticipates 'the predicament of anybody who is pressed for a brief and comprehensive definition of myth'.[3] He goes on to note that 'it was Voltaire's opinion that the study of myths is an occupation for blockheads';[4] and that, furthermore, 'we have no direct experience of myth as such, but only of particular myths: and these, we discover, are obscure in origin, protean in form and ambiguous in meaning'.[5] However, it is the contention of the author of this essay that 'myth', properly and specifically defined, and 'myths', properly and specifically analysed, may illuminate rather than obscure whatever subject is viewed through the window, or in the context, of its own 'mythic' substrate, and the manifold, multivalent and multi-layered structures of that subject's 'mythic' baggage. As Claude Lévi-Strauss puts it: 'From a logical point of view we can understand why images borrowed from experience can be put to use. This is the originality of mythical thinking – to play the part of conceptual thinking'.[6] Lévi-Strauss goes on to note: 'The really important point is that in all American mythology, and I could say in mythology the world over, we have deities and supernaturals, who play the roles of intermediaries between the powers above and humanity below'.[7] This is of vital importance in any analysis of the content of myth; it is also of importance if we choose to define myth, from the point of view of *usage*, as 'a narrative vehicle for a primal event, or series of events, which may function as essential dogma, paradigm or key referent in the future development of any culture, religion or philosophy'.[8] Or, as Schneidau observes: 'Myth either is simply a story, or in Lévi-Strauss's even more reductive view, the story is merely a vehicle through which the repeated themes make themselves heard'.[9] Such definitions, of course, imply no value judgement whatsoever as to the objective truth, or otherwise, of the myth: and it is in the light of such definitions that we shall here examine the life and thought of al-Suhrawardī.

The Islamic faith clearly has its 'myth' of martyrdom (and here it must be stressed again that the term does not in any way imply a lack of reality or truth): the myth stretches from the age of the great martyr of Karbalā', Ḥusayn, through Ḥallāj (executed 309/922) and (perhaps) al-Fārābī[10] up to our own subject Suhrawardī – and, of course, beyond into the present. It is an ineluctable reality that the tragic ends of each of these figures enhance, if only unconsciously, the message which they bore during their lifetimes, in the mind of the reader.

Late antiquity, and indeed Islamic philosophy, also had their 'myth' – in the sense of a vehicle for the framing and conveyance of a message – the myth of Neoplatonism, deliberately designed by its doctrine of emanation to provide a link – however tenous – between the corporeal known and the Unknowable Divine.[11] Here if anywhere was a mythology, with deities and supernaturals metamorphosed into intellects which played 'the roles of intermediaries between the powers above and humanity below'.[12]

Finally mysticism, whether of the Plotinian kind or Islamic *taṣawwuf*, constitutes the mythic frame within which man generally declined to articulate, *intellectually*, his love of the Divine, and frequently chose instead to *feel*: mysticism was thus more a vehicle of pure feeling than pure intellection though this is not by any means to suggest that *taṣawwuf*, for example, was totally devoid of intellectual content and was never described in manual or philosophical treatises. Far from it.

Mysticism, and the rituals of mysticism, may be described as the 'myth' – indeed, the 'sacrament' – of and for God's divine love. And the essence of the hierarchy of Neoplatonism is itself mystical in impulse: with Plotinus the 'ladder' of emanation becomes a 'ladder' of feeling. 'The emanation process itself was compared by Plotinus to the way in which sunlight was continually generated by the sun . . . each hypostasis was moved or filled by a deep yearning for the principle immediately above it'.[13] In such a wise does the 'myth' of Neoplatonism metamorphose the philosophical mechanics of emanation into a mode of love itself. And Islamic Neoplatonism, even of the Ishrāqī model espoused by al-Suhrawardī, *as we shall show*, was no different, with that key motif of philosophical Neoplatonism, *fayḍ* (emanation), becoming a light-filled channel for the movement of *'ishq*, passionate love of and for the Divine.

Firstly, though, to place the above proposition in perspective, we can highlight the basic dynamics of martyrdom at the end of Suhrawardī's life, since these contributed to the *myth* of Suhrawardī, then examine briefly the semiotics of the Qur'ān and, finally, elaborate a few of the many definitions of *falsafa* and *taṣawwuf*. I have noted elsewhere that 'al-Suhrawardī is also called "The Executed" (*al-Maqtūl*) by his detractors and "The Martyr" (*al-Shahīd*) by his friends' and that 'in the second of these designations, which is as common as that of *Shaykh al-Ishrāq*, there may lie an early attempt to endow the mystic with an almost Ḥallājian charisma'.[14] Certainly, the two titles, regardless of who applied them, were specifically designed to situate and establish Suhrawardī within a particular context or *myth*, and not simply to differentiate him from two other notable figures who bore the same surname: 'Abd al-Qāhir Abū Najīb al-Suhrawardī (d. 564/1168) and the latter's nephew and pupil Shihāb al-Dīn Abū Ḥafs 'Umar al-Suhrawardī (540/1145–632/1234).[15] Seyyed Hossein Nasr has neatly summarised the grounds of the myth:

> His outspoken manner, his lack of prudence in exposing esoteric doctrines before all kinds of audiences, the keen intelligence which enabled him to overcome all opponents in debate, his mastery in both discursive philosophy and Sufism – all these factors combined to make many enemies for him, especially among some of the doctors of the law (*ulamā'*). Finally, they asked for his execution on the grounds of propagating doctrines against the tenets of the faith, and when Malik Ẓāhir [the son of Ṣalāḥ al-Dīn] refused they petitioned Ṣalāḥ al-Dīn directly. At a time when Syria

> had just been recaptured from the Crusaders and the support of the doctors of the law was essential to maintain his authority. Ṣalāḥ al-Dīn had no choice but to yield to their demand. Pressure was therefore put on Malik Ẓāhir to carry out the wish of the group of religious authorities who opposed the young sage. Suhrawardī was therefore imprisoned and in the year 587/1191 he died, the immediate cause of his death unknown. And so, at the young age of 38, the Master of Illumination met with the same fate as his illustrious Ṣūfī predecessor Ḥallāj, to whom he had been so much attracted throughout his youth and whose sayings he quotes so often in his works.[16]

The elementary dynamics of the myth are immediately clear from this succinct account by Professor Nasr: jealousy, and fear of another's trespass on one's own intellectual power combine with religious and political motives in the minds of the custodians of orthodox knowledge and, therefore, religious power, the *'ulamā'*, the latter package such fears in a suitable fashion and confront the holders of secular power and authority with them to ensure that they, the *'ulamā'*, engineer the downfall of one whom they perceive as a profound threat. (The circumstances of Ḥallāj's own overthrow were a similar combination of religion and politics, and that latter's execution was by no means solely the product of that ill-advised and notorious declamation, which has become the most famous of all the *shaṭḥiyāt: Anā 'l-Ḥaqq.*)

Semiotics has gained a reputation, sometimes, for being rather more arcane than it actually is. It is true that it should be considered more a methodology than a 'science'. And it is also true that some of its most famous guardians, and practitioners, for example the well-known Italian scholar Umberto Eco, have developed that methodology of semiotics in a highly complex way.[17] But they have also used that same methodology to illustrate the daily phenomena of life in a way which clarifies rather than mystifies. We note, for example, Eco's essay 'A Theory of Expositions' which tries to answer its opening sentence: 'What does Expo' 67 – that unsurpassed, quintessential, classic World's fair – mean in today's world?'[18] But it is not just major expositions to which one might attach theories of semiotics. 'Everything signifies'.[19] and this is as true of fundamental 'meaning-infused' texts like the Qur'ān as it is of mystico-philosophical works like the *Ḥikmat al-Ishrāq (Philosophy of Illumination)* of al-Suhrawardi. Indeed the Qur'an may be said to precipitate or actively seek its own semiotic analysis. Not only do we note the dichotomous sense of the Arabic word *āya* (verse of the Qur'ān *and* sign) but it is clear from the most cursory reading that the entire text is 'riddled with references to the signs of God'.[20] As one *Sūra* puts it:

> We shall show them Our signs in the horizons and in themselves. (*Sa-nurīhim āyātinā fī 'l-āfāq wa fī anfusihim.*)[21]

But this Islamic text par excellence is by no means the only one to lend itself readily to semiotic analysis. What, we may ask, are the 'signs' of *falsafa* and *taṣawwuf* in Suhrawardī's magnum opus, the famous *Ḥikmat al-Ishrāq*?[22] Before an identification is made of these, it might be useful to examine briefly what is meant by such words as *falsafa* and *taṣawwuf*. How have such words been defined?

Many definitions exist. *Inter alia*, *falsafa* has been described as follows:

> The origins of *falsafa* are purely Greek; the activity of the *falāsifa* . . . begins with Arabic translations of the Greek philosophical texts (whether direct or through a Syriac intermediary). Thus *falsafa* appears first as the continuation of *philosophia* in Muslim surroundings . . . [But] thought *falsafa* may be called a continuation of Greek thought there is no perfect continuity.[23]

The warning in the last line is timely and has been stressed in a different form elsewhere by the author of this essay: it does a grave disservice to Islamic philosophy to see it simply as Greek philosophy in Islamic guise, though, of course, no one would, or should, deny the impact of Greek thought.[24] 'Islamic philosophy and theology, like every other, grew to some degree according to the intellectual and cultural milieu of which they were a part, or as a considered reaction to that *milieu*'.[25] And part of the Islamic *milieu* was – or became – the cities of Alexandria, Gondēshāpūr, and Ḥarrān.[26] We may, then, in the light of these remarks, loosely define *falsafa* here, for our present purposes, as a mode of intellectual inquiry in Islamic thought which at various times placed a primary on reason, which drew on both the Western (i.e. Plato, Aristotle, Plotinus) and the Eastern traditions for its vocabulary and, often, content, but which was much more than a mere syncretism composed of the aforementioned influences. Of course, such a definition is open to argument, elaboration or, indeed, contradiction but what cannot be denied is that one of the 'signs' or basic characteristics of *falsafa* in Islam is the stress on *reason*.

Annemarie Schimmel has provided one of the best introductions to, and definitions of, *taṣawwuf*. While admitting that 'to write about Sufism, or Islamic mysticism, is an almost impossible task',[27] she notes:

> To approach its [Islamic Mysticism's] partial meaning we have to ask ourselves first, what *mysticism* means. That *mysticism* contains something mysterious, not to be reached by ordinary means or by ordinary effort, is understood from the root common to the words *mystic* and *mystery*, the Greek *myein*, 'to close the eyes'. Mysticism has been called 'the great spiritual current which goes through all religions'. In its widest sense it may be defined as the consciousness of the One Reality – be it called Wisdom, Light, Love, or Nothing.[28]

Two of Professor Schimmel's words here are of particular significance as motifs or 'signs' for our discussion of *taṣawwuf* in a Suhrawardian context: Light and Love. The first will be dealt with later. The latter may be stressed here as an, albeit, well-known, indeed clichéd, 'sign' of *taṣawwuf*. As Rābi'a al-'Adawiyya famously articulated it:

> Oh my Lord,if I worship Thee from fear of Hell, burn me in Hell, and if I worship Thee in hope of Paradise, exclude me thence, but if I worship Thee for Thine own sake, then withhold not from me Thine Eternal Beauty.[29]

Any semiotic analysis of *taṣawwuf* must, therefore, be infused by the vocabulary of human and divine love. If the stress on reason, to put it succinctly if somewhat simplistically, is a sign or basic characteristic of *falsafa*, then a stress on love is a sign or basic characteristic of *taṣawwuf*. And, just as it may be argued, with some justification, that the basic source and origin in Islam of knowledge, all intellectual inquiry, the use of reason and, by extension, *falsafa* itself, lies in the Qur'ān,[30] so too it may equally well be argued that the primary motors of *taṣawwuf* are Qur'ānic: '"God was well-pleased with them, and they were well-pleased with God":[31] so God describes the blessed saints in Paradise; for "He loveth them, and they love Him".[32] This last text is of great significance as supporting the Sufi doctrine of love (*maḥabba*) and as providing the ultimate authority for the idea of a trinity of Lover, Loved and Love. The conception of a remote, indifferent Potentate of the Universe is wholly overthrown by this picture of the Merciful Allāh ever taking the first step towards man, the elect of His creation, to draw him unto Him by the powerful cords of love.'[33] This is not to say that the 'remote Potentate' paradigm was absent from Islamic philosophical thought, especially of the Neoplatonic kind. What Arberry stresses here, however, is the motif of *maḥabba*, and this is the one which we shall examine as a key sign of *taṣawwuf* in the *Ḥikmat al-Ishrāq*.

What has been isolated, then, for the sake of simplicity, are two distinct motifs in our argument: the sign of *reason* in *falsafa* and the sign of *love* in *taṣawwuf*. They confronted each other in mediaeval Islam, almost in the manner of the well-known confrontation of revelation and reason,[34] and like the latter the confrontation was not always or necessarily a confrontation of mutual hostility. Certainly, this was not the case with Suhrawardī in whose philosophy, it may be demonstrated, the key technical philosophical terminology of reason acts as a *vehicle* for the 'signs' of *taṣawwuf*.

Suhrawardī's philosophy in his *Ḥikmat al-Ishrāq* and elsewhere fits neatly though partially into the classical paradigm, articulated and outlined above by Arnaldez, of *falsafa* as *philosophia*.[35] As such it has a number of readily-identifiable recurring strands: Pythagorean, Platonic, Aristotelian and Neoplatonic; to these may be added *inter alia* the Islamic, Zoroastrian, Ishrāqī and Hermetic.[36] And if we are to seek the intention of *Ḥikmat al-Ihsrāq*, we could do worse than examine the author's statement on this work – it is significant not only for what it tells us about the motivations of its author but for its reiteration of several of the above-mentioned strands:

> This book of ours is intended for [both] students of mysticism (*al-ta'alluh*)[37] and academic research (*al-baḥth*). It is not for the scholar who has no mystical orientation or ambition. We only propose to discuss this book and its symbols with those who are seriously engaged in the mystic effort or quest. At the very least the reader of this book is expected to have reached the stage at which the Divine Light (*al-Bāriq al-Ilāhī*) has come to him and rooted itself within him . . . So whoever just wants academic research can follow the path of the peripatetics which is all well and good for academic research on its own. Our talk and discourse about the groundrules of illuminationism (*al-qawā'id al-ishrāqiyya*) cannot be with such a person. Indeed, the basic concern of the illuminationists remains disorganised without [the help of God-given] luminous insights (*sawāniḥ nūriyya*).[38]

There are several points of interest for our discussions in this passage: the very first line forges an immediate link between academic and intuitive knowledge, between *falsafa qua falsafa* in its purely Greek (here Aristotelian) sense (= *al-baḥth*) and the lights of insight associated with *taṣawwuf* (= *al-ta'alluh*). The mystical *Ishrāqī* element is clearly elevated above – though ideally linked to – the peripatetic products of contemporary academic research. Suhrawardī does not here denigrate the academic researcher; what he does is establish and exhibit an order of priorities in intellectual thought. The ideal paradigm is perhaps akin to Abū Ḥāmid al-Ghazālī whose life mirrors, in a frequently idealised way, the combination of the academic and the mystic. This passage which we have examined then, constitutes a vehicle of two key motifs in Suhrawardian thought: that of reason and that of light, the latter being associated with a more intuitive kind of reason or intellection.

Ziai believes that the *Ḥikmat al-Ishrāq* constitutes Suhrawardian thought in its ultimate form.[39] If we accept this to be the case, then there is an added merit in identifying the particular signs of *falsafa* and *taṣawwuf* in this text since, identified in their final state, they may be used as useful analytical tools for the examination of any earlier work. If we now isolate within *falsafa* some of its '*purely Greek*' elements, and recognise the doctrine of emanation as the key development in later Greek (Plotinian) philosophy, then there are three major semiotic triggers or key words which may be discussed here, as being of vital importance in the *Ḥikmat al-Isrāq: fayḍ, fayyāḍ*, and *ṣudūr* (emanation, emanative and procession). And since it is emanation, one of the key technical terms of later Greek philosophy, which becomes the vehicle of Sufism, and, in particular, the *love* implicit and explicit within that term, we may also examine here some of the key words associated with *taṣawwuf* which appear in the *Ḥikmat*; the most notable are *'ishq*, *'āshiq*, *'ushshāq*, *ma'shūq*, and *maḥabba* (*love*, *lover*, *lovers*, *beloved* and *loving-kindness*). It was noted earlier that emanation was a Plotinian device designed to provide a *reasonable, reasoned* – if not wholly, or always completely reasoned or easily comprehensible – link between the Divine and the Human, the pure incorporeal and the sullied corporeal.

Emanation is a bridge between these two seemingly antipathetical realities. And it is an intellectual device which becomes, as we shall show, a bridge or vehicle of love: in other words, the technical intellectual terminology of philosophy – *fayḍ*, etc – becomes associated with – indeed, may be said in one real sense to become – the vocabulary of *taṣawwuf*, whether the words employed are *maḥabba* or *'ishq*. And, of course, the key Suhrawardian development in all this is that not only do we have a bridge of love, but also a bridge of light, or rather many lights, between the diluted reality of earth and the sublime reality of the 'Light-of-Lights' (*Nūr al-Anwār*), God Himself. Suhrawardian emanation, in other words, is inevitably part of a larger theology of light and love. It is in that light-infused and light-enriched philosophy of emanated love that we find the true uniqueness of al-Suhrawardī, and his *Ishrāqī* philosophy.

Such key words as we have just itemised constitute some of the most easily identifiable 'signs' of the substrate of Neoplatonic doctrine which underlies Suhrawardī's text. Here it is proposed to examine some of the usages or contexts of the words in isolation, then note how they often form certain recurring groups or phrases, centred on the motif or theme of love, and finally survey what I will term Suhrawardī's 'Ladder of Yearning': this is the mythic vehicle in which emanation and love merge and the vocabulary of *falsafa* becomes identical with that of *taṣawwuf.* Let us turn firstly to the technical *philosophical* vocabulary of Neoplatonism: here the key 'sign' or keyword is 'emanation' and it informs and underpins in one form or another the whole of Suhrawardī's text. Its various associated forms in Arabic, whether they be *fayḍ, fayyāḍ* or *ṣudūr*, are scattered throughout the *Ḥikmat al-Ishrāq* and appear in a variety of different contexts. Thus we are told that emanation (*al-fayḍ*) is eternal,[40] has many different features[41] and is a characteristic of the Suhrawardian lights in their different kinds.[42] The substrate of emanation is emphasized in such phrases as *al-Nūr fayyāḍ li-dhātihi* and similar which also, of course, reinforce the all-important Suhrawardian link between light and emanation.[43] All things derive ultimately by emanation (*ṣudūr*) from the Light of Lights (*Nūr al-Anwār*)[44] but the manner of the emanation (*ṣudūr*) of multiplicity from God who is the Light-of-Lights and the One[45] clearly requires some explanation and this is attempted by Suhrawardī.[46]

The other register of Plotinian Neoplatonism which also underpins the *Ḥikmat al-Ishrāq* is also highly visible in the vocabulary of love.[47] In the *Ḥikmat* the principal signs of this are such Arabic words as *'ishq* (passionate love, *éros*), *'āshiq* (and its plural *'ushshāq), ma'shūq* and the less intensive synonym for *'ishq,* which is *maḥabba* (a form which, incidentally, seems to be preferred by Suhrawardī to *ḥubb*). The word *'ishq* is much associated with the Suhrawardian lights in their various forms and often appears in conjunction with another popular word from the vocabulary of Sufism: *shawq* (longing, yearning),[48] which is clearly intended as a virtual synonym of *'ishq*. The Light-of-Lights is a solitary and self-centred Lover (*'āshiq*), but at the same time is much-loved (*ma'shūq*) by others as well.[49] It is a key motif – almost paradox – of the text that this much-loved Light-of-Lights is wrapped in eternal, 'selfish' contemplation of itself, in an almost Aristotelian[50] isolation; and Suhrawardī's universe of light is filled with loyal lovers (*'ushshāq*)[51] who love and yearn perpetually for the light. All these examples, it will be noted, which we have just cited, employ variations on the root *'ashiqa*; however, the text's synonym for *'ishq,* which is *maḥabba*, is even more common, as can be seen below.

The juxtaposition or association of the words *'ishq* and shawq has already been noted. If we now examine more closely the *structure* of the text of Shurawardī's *Ḥikmat al-Ishrāq* it is possible to detect three important themes or intellectual configurations in his thought, in each of which love is a prime component. It is through the articulation of these that we may reach most easily what I propose to call Suhrawardī's 'Ladder of Yearning' paradigm[52] where the vocabulary of emanation becomes the vehicle – indeed, is – the vocabulary of love. *Falsafa* (*fayḍ*) metamorphoses into *taṣawwuf* (*'ishq, maḥabba*). The three configurations suggested as important here, from a structural point of view, in forming a primary and constant substrate of the *Ḥikmat* are those of (i) *Love and Light*, (ii) *Love and Emanation*, and (iii) *Love and Dominion or Subjugation* (*qahr*). Let us examine each briefly in turn as they appear in a single key statement of Suhrawardī's:

(i) Light (*al-nūr*) (as we have already noted), is characterized as *fayyāḍ li-dhātihi*, ('emanative in essence') and it has 'in its substance' (*fī jawharihi*) love (*maḥabba*) for its origin and dominion (*qahr*) over what is beneath it.[53] Love and light appear in equal measure in such citations.
(ii) The previous statement also stresses the *Emanationist* essence and character of that *Light*.
(iii) Finally this same statement also neatly links the concepts of Love and Dominion, a linkage which reappears on many other pages of the *Ḥikmat al-Ishrāq*,[54] and constitutes a basic duality which underpins the entire text.

The present author has pointed out elsewhere – in an Avicennan context, but the statement is equally true of Suhrawardī's thought – that 'in one sense emanation (*fayḍ*) and love (*'ishq*) may be viewed as two sides of the same channel of cosmic movement: all things come from God by a process of necessary emanation and all things desire to return to God by a process of innate or necessary love.'[55] It is this basic concept which informs what I propose to call here the fundamental Suhrawardian paradigm of the *Ḥikmat al-Ishrāq*, the 'Ladder of Yearning'. Indeed, if we accept with Ziai that the *Ḥikmat* is the ultimate expression of Suhrawardian thought, we can legitimately hold that this 'Ladder of Yearning' at the heart of the *Ḥikmat* must also mirror in some way the essence of much else that Suhrawardī thought and wrote.

Paul Henry has neatly outlined the basic Plotinian paradigm which prefigures what is found in *Ḥikmat al-Ishrāq*, noting that 'in Plotinus . . . every being is constituted by means of a two-way dynamism which is dialectically simultaneous, the departure from the principle immediately prior and superior and the return to that same principle. As a result any being, whether the universal intellect or the individual soul, while it is not actually identical with its principle – this would be excluded by the law of diminishing causality – nevertheless exists in its self-identity only in the measure in which it is an immediate relationship of union with and dependence upon its principle. In consequence "the being which knows itself will know also that from which it comes" (Enneads) vi.9.7.'[56]

In Suhrawardī's *Ḥikmat al-Ishrāq* we find a domination of lower lights by the higher, with the former exhibiting a profound longing for the latter. This constitutes the underlying pattern for the whole order of existence. God is the only One who loves only Himself and has no yearning for anyone or anything else.[57] 'The paradigm which is established whereby each inferior light (*nūr sāfil*) loves the higher light (*al-nūr al-'ālī*) to a degree that transcends its own self-love or self-interest extends right up to the top of al-Suhrawardī's ontological hierarchy of lights'.[58]

It is in this fashion that philosophy merges into mysticism, *falsafa* becomes *taṣawwuf* and the fundamental technical terms of both such as *fayḍ/ṣudūr* (emanation) and *'ishq/maḥabba* (love) assume a breadth of meaning in which the one may be said to encapsulate or incorporate the other. And, as we have already hinted above,[59] this fundamental relationship and ultimate identification of philosophy and mysticism was already prefigured in the thought of Plotinus himself.[60] It is thus clear that the Suhrawardian paradigm of the 'Ladder of Yearning' upon which the philosopher-mystic has based his text, or rather with which he has infused it, reflects a more ancient *Plotinian* paradigm. Any attempt therefore, such as that made in this essay, to claim that in Suhrawardian thought *falsafa* and *taṣawwuf* ultimately merge, must acknowledge at least here a Greek antecedent or model. What makes Suhrawardī's thought unique, however, is the way in which he builds upon Plotinus' 'simple' threefold hierarchy and establishes a much larger emanating hierarchy of lights with Plotinus' One or Good now metamorphosed into the Light-of-Lights (*Nūr al-Anwār*), and a complex baroque series of angelic orders of lights beneath that Supreme Light. What he also emphasizes in his thought is the duality of love and dominion inherent in the structure of his emanationist scheme. Emanation *qua* emanation was clearly known to, and used by, many of his philosophical predecessors such as al-Fārābī and Ibn Sīnā, for example. But in the metaphysics of the first it is difficult to detect much mysticism whether in vocabulary or content; while in that of the second, in whose later thought we can indeed detect a mystical strain, the *stress* in emanationist theory at least, seems to be more on such themes as 'awareness', 'contemplation', 'knowledge' and 'intellection'[61] than 'love' and 'yearning', though this is not to deny the existence of such latter themes altogether. It is a question of *emphasis* and Suhrawardī, in a particularly vivid way chooses to *emphasize* what we have termed above the 'Ladder of Yearning', with its 'batteries' of emanated lights.

A final question remains to be answered briefly: to what extent is the philosophical vocabulary of Suhrawardī in the *Ḥikmat al-Isrāq*, such as we have just surveyed, solely a vehicle for that author's mysticism which is known popularly as 'illuminationism'? There is no doubt that much in the development of Islamic philosophy has changed with Suhrawardī's advent: 'the old terminology of *al-'Aql al-Kullī* and *al-Nafs al-Kulliyya* has been supplanted by that of *anwār* in all their complex manifestations and interdependent relationships. Aristotelian concepts of substance have also given way before his light cosmology'.[62] Whereas with the thought of his great intellectual predecessor Ibn Sīnā, it is possible to attempt an assessment in terms of two distinct – if not equal – registers, the Aristotelian and the Neoplatonic, the same approach is much more difficult with Suhrawardian thought; this is because the intimate link which has been demonstrated between some of the technical vocabulary of philosophy, and that of mysticism, 'absorbs' and indeed dominates many of the older vocabularies and schools of thought.[63] There is no doubt in all this where Suhrawardī's own inclinations lie. In a highly significant comment in *Ḥikmat al-Ishrāq* he plays down the role of in-depth study by Peripatetics which he believes is by no means indispensable: one can do without much of what they have discussed at length.[64] Anthony K. Tuft summarizes the situation thus: 'Suhrawardī . . . devotes the entire first half of his *Ḥikmat al-Ishrāq* to a sceptical review of logical definition, concluding that it is unable to provide a clear picture of reality . . . Suhrawardī's purpose in this attack on Aristotelian logic is the destruction or revision of the doctrines of physics or metaphysics which, among most contemporary Islamic thinkers, depend directly on this system of logic for their consistency . . . [Suhrawardī] opens the second section of the *Ḥikmat al-Ishrāq* by noting that light is the one reality so clearly manifest that no definition is needed to clarify it'.[65]

Bylebyl, neatly, proposes that Suhrawardī 'found himself in the presence of a new set of determining coordinates'.[66] I would suggest here that, foremost among such coordinates, is Suhrawardī's own emanationist 'Ladder of Yearning' which is the vehicle, the primal, Suhrawardian narrative or myth, whereby light and darkness, God and man, encounter each other and under the impetus of which *falsafa* dissolves almost imperceptibly into *taṣawwuf*. And if voluntary or even involuntary martyrdom, or execution, for one's beliefs may be said to betoken in some way a 'sign' of love for those beliefs (and the Deity within them), then we may say that the 'myth' of Suhrawardī's life and death conforms to a very similar paradigm to that of his thought. The 'myth' of Suhrawardī's almost Ḥallājian disregard for – and ultimate 'abdication' of – his own life (voluntarily or involuntarily) constitutes as much 'a bridge of love or yearning', as well as a literary motif, as the intellectual emanationist paradigm of the 'Ladder of Yearning', which is equally a 'Ladder of Love', adumbrated above. There is only this major distinction: Suhrawardī's death brings together the Divine and the human *at a moment in time*; Suhrawardian emanation eternally bridges the two worlds of Supreme Light and corporeal darkness.

NOTES

[A version of this essay, under the title 'The Neoplatonic Substrate of Sohrawardī's Philosophy of Illumination', first appeared in *Sufi: A Journal of Sufism*, No. 8 (Winter 1990–91), pp. 7–13. It was later printed under the present title, *in an uncorrected form*, in Leonard Lewisohn (ed.), *The Legacy of Mediaeval Persian Sufism*, (London & New York: Khaniqahi Nimatullahi Publications, 1992), pp. 247–60. (See list of *Corrigenda* issued in 1994.) The essay was also translated into Persian by Alireza Nurbakhsh in *Sufi* (Persian edn.), no. 21 (1994), pp. 7–15.]

1 (my italics) Henry Corbin, *Histoire de la Philosophie Islamique*, (Paris: Gallimard, 1964), vol. 1, p. 285.
2 S.H. Nasr, 'Shihāb al-Dīn Suhrawardī Maqtūl' in M.M. Sharif (ed.), *History of Muslim Philosophy*, (Wiesbaden: Otto Harrassowitz, 1963), vol. 1, p. 373.
3 K.K. Ruthven, *Myth, The Critical Idiom*, no. 31 (London: Methuen, 1976), p. 1.
4 Ibid., p. 3.
5 Ibid., p. 1.
6 Claude Lévi-Strauss, *Myth and Meaning*, (London: Routledge & Kegan Paul, 1978), p. 22.
7 Ibid., p. 32.
8 See my *Allāh Transcendent: Studies in the Structure and Semiotics of Islamic Philosophy, Theology and Cosmology*, (London: Routledge, 1989), p. 234.
9 Herbert N. Schneidau, *Sacred Discontent: The Bible and Western Tradition*, (Baton Rouge: Louisiana State University Press, 1976), pp. 272–3.

10 See Netton, *Allāh Transcendent*, p. 101.
11 See Netton, *Allāh Transcendent*, pp. 115–17.
12 Claude Lévi-Strauss, *Myth and Meaning*, p. 32.
13 See Netton, *Allāh Transcendent*, p. 62; Plotinus, *Enneads*, V.1.6; III.8.8; III.8.11.
14 Netton, *Allāh Transcendent*, p. 257.
15 See ibid.
16 Seyyed Hossein Nasr, *Three Muslim Sages: Avicenna, Suhrawardī, Ibn 'Arabī*, (New York: Caravan Books, 1976, repr. of Harvard University Press edn. of 1969), pp. 57–8.
17 See, for example, Eco's *A Theory of Semiotics, Advances in Semiotics*, (Bloomington & London: Indiana University Press, 1976).
18 Umberto Eco, *Travels in Hyperreality*, (London: Pan Picador, 1987), pp. 291–307.
19 The phrase is Roland Barthes': see Jonathan Culler, *Barthes*, (London: Fontana Paperbacks, 1983), p. 111; see also *Allāh Transcendent*, pp. 77ff.
20 *Allāh Transcendent*, p. 321.
21 Qur'ān XL1:53; trans. A.J. Arberry, *The Koran Interpreted*, 2 vols., (London: Allen & Unwin/New York: Macmillan, 1971), vol. 2, p. 191.
22 For the Arabic text, see *Kitāb Ḥikmat al-Ishrāq* in *al-Suhrawardī, Oeuvres Philosophiques et Mystiques*, vol. 2, ed. Henry Corbin, Académie Impériale Iranienne de Philosophie, Publication no. 13, Bibliothèque Iranienne, N.S. (Tehran: Académie Impériale Iranienne de Philosophie/Paris: Librairie Adrien-Maisonneuve, 1977), pp. 2–260 [referred to hereafter simply as *Ḥikmat al-Ishrāq*].
23 R. Arnaldez, art. 'Falsafa', *EI*[2], vol. II, p. 769.
24 *Allāh Transcendent*, esp. pp. 20–1, 128, 264.
25 Ibid., pp. 20–1.
26 Ibid., pp. 7–16.
27 *Mystical Dimensions of Islam*, (Chapel Hill: University of North Carolina Press, 1975), p. xvii.
28 Ibid., pp. 3–4.
29 Trans. by Margaret Smith, *Studies in Early Mysticism in the Near and Middle East*, (Amsterdam: Philo Press, 1973; repr. from the London: Sheldon Press edn. of 1931), p. 224, from Farīd al-Dīn 'Aṭṭār, *Tadhkirat al-Awliyā'* ed. R.A. Nicholson, (London: Luzac/Leiden: E.J. Brill, 1905), vol. 1, p. 73.
30 See Wan Mohd Nor Wan Daud, *The Concept of Knowledge in Islam and its Implications for Education in a Developing Country*, (London: Mansell, 1989), esp. pp. 36–8.
31 Qur'ān V: 122.
32 Qur'ān V: 57.
33 A.J. Arberry, *Sufism: An Account of the Mystics of Islam*, (London: Allen & Unwin, 1950), p. 21.
34 For an introduction to this, see A.J. Arberry, *Revelation and Reason in Islam*, (London: Allen & Unwin, 1957).
35 Hossein Ziai, 'Suhrawardī's Philosophy of Illumination' (PhD thesis, University of Harvard, 1976), p. ix.
36 See Nasr, *Three Muslim Sages*, p. 59.

37 Lit. 'self-deification': see Soheil M. Afnan, *A Philosophical Lexicon in Persian and Arabic*, (Beirut: Dār al-Mashriq, 1969), p. 10.
38 *Ḥikmat al-Ishrāq*, pp. 12–13 (my trans.).
39 *Shurawardī's Philosophy of Illumination*, p. 21.
40 *Ḥikmat al-Ishrāq*, p. 181, see also p. 236.
41 Ibid., p. 178.
42 E.g. see ibid., pp. 141, 218, 236. For further information about the different types of Suhrawardian lights, see Netton, *Allāh Transcendent*, pp. 256–320.
43 See e.g. *Ḥikmat al-Ihsrāq*, pp. 117, 134, 150, 195, 204.
44 See e.g. ibid., pp. 131–2.
45 See e.g. ibid., pp. 131, 138.
46 See ibid., pp. 131–5, 138–48.
47 See Plotinus, *Enneads* III 8.7–III 8.8; V.1.6.
48 See e.g. *Ḥikmat al-Ishrāq*, pp. 136, 242; see also pp. 134, 185, 223, 224.
49 See ibid., p. 136; see also p. 177.
50 See Aristotle, *Metaphysics*, Bk. 12, 7, 1072b.
51 See e.g. *Ḥikmat al-Ishrāq*, p. 227.
52 The term is preferred to Parviz Morewedge's 'Platonic "Ladder of eros"': see his 'Sufism, Neoplatonism, and Zaehner's Theistic Theory of Mysticism' in Parviz Morewedge (ed.), *Islamic Philosophy and Mysticism, Studies in Islamic Philosophy and Science*, (New York: Caravan Books, 1981), p. 231. The terminology of the 'Ladder of Yearning' is consciously modelled here by me on the story of Jacob's ladder in Genesis 28:10–19 where the ladder, like the classical doctrine of emanation, forms a bridge between earth and heaven. Just as the angels of God ascend and descend Jacob's ladder, so with the doctrine of emanation there is an outpouring from higher to lower, and a yearning from lower to higher. The motif of love in Suhrawardian emanation 'replaces', as it were – or better, *supplements or clothes* – the angel figure of Jacob's ladder. For in this context, it is interesting to note the identification in Suhrawardī's thought of 'angel' and emanated 'light'. For more on this identification of 'angel' and 'light', see especially Netton, *Allāh Transcendent*, pp. 256–68.
53 (my italics) *Ḥikmat al-Ishrāq*, p. 204, see also p. 225.
54 E.g., see pp. 143, 147–8, 160, 196, 225, 227–8.
55 Netton, *Allāh Transcendent*, p. 176.
56 Paul Henry, 'Introduction: Plotinus' Place in the History of Thought' in Plotinus, *The Enneads*, trans. by Stephen MacKenna, 2nd rev. edn. (London: Faber & Faber, 1956), p. XLVII; Netton, *Allāh Transcendent*, pp. 261–2.
57 See *Ḥikmat al-Ishrāq*, pp. 135–37; Netton, *Allah Transcendent*, p. 262.
58 Netton, *Allāh Transcendent*, p. 262.
59 See above, nn. 47, 55, 56.
60 See Netton, *Allāh Transcendent*, p. 261.
61 See ibid., pp. 114–17, 163–5.
62 See ibid. p. 268.
63 Ibid.
64 *Ḥikmat al-Ishrāq*, p. 31. See also, M. Y. Hairi, 'Suhrawardī's *An Episode and a Trance*. A Philosophical Dialogue in a Mystical Stage', in Morewedge (ed.), *Islamic Philosophy and Mysticism*, pp. 177–89, especially the citation of Aristotle's words on p. 187.

65 Anthony K. Tuft, 'Symbolism and Speculation in Suhrawardī's "The Song of Gabriel's Wing"' in Morewedge (ed.), *Islamic Philosophy and Mysticism*, pp. 209–10.

66 Michael Edward Bylebyl, 'The Wisdom of Illumination: A Study of the Prose Stories of Suhrawardī' (PhD thesis, University of Chicago, 1976), p. 226.

4

THEOPHANY AS PARADOX

Ibn al-ʿArabī's Account of al-Khaḍir in His *Fuṣūṣ al-Ḥikam*

Dedicated to the memory of Dom Sylvester Houédard OSB
who died on 15 January 1992, and with whom
I discussed this topic briefly

The Qur'ān and al-Khaḍir

The story of Moses and his encounter with God's Servant (*ʿabd* in Arabic) in *Sūrat al-Kahf (The Sūra of the Cave)* is very well-known, and it constitutes perhaps one of the most mystically beautiful of all the passages in the entire Qur'ān.[1] The mysterious Servant, sage or *pīr* is not named by the sacred text but he is usually identified as al-Khaḍir or al-Khiḍr. The *structure, symbolism* and *paradox* of the Qur'ānic narrative will briefly be adumbrated in what follows; this will constitute the backcloth, as it were, against which I will then examine Ibn al-ʿArabī's own account with particular reference to the latter's *Fuṣūṣ al-Ḥikam*.

The Qur'ānic narrative adopts what might be described here as a 'triple-test' *structure* where the hero is set a finite number of hurdles which he must overcome in order to be judged successful. In Moses' case, in the Qur'ān, the hurdle is that of a quiescent silence in the face of *imagined* wrong. The testing and refining of the hero is, of course, a commonplace in world literature: one thinks immediately of the labours of Hercules, Christ's three temptations in the desert, or the quest of Jason for the Golden Fleece. The latter includes the motif of 'the search' as, indeed, does the quest for the Holy Grail in the Arthurian legend. In the Qur'ānic account, of course, the search itself acts structurally as a kind of prelude to the triple testing: Moses and his companion have been seeking the meeting place of the two seas (*majmaʿ al-baḥrayn*). Arriving at that mysterious place, whose identification need not delay us here, they forget about their strange fish which has clearly been with them on their journey. Yusuf Ali provides the following commentary on their initial progress:

> Moses was to go and find a servant of God, who would instruct him in such knowledge as he had not already got. He was to take a fish with him. The place where he was to meet his mysterious teacher would be indicated by the fact that the fish would disappear when he got to that place. *The fish is the emblem of the fruit of secular knowledge*, which merges itself in divine knowledge at the point where human intelligence is ready for the junction of the two. But the mere merger of secular knowledge does not in itself produce divine knowledge. The latter has to be sought patiently.[2]

The fish, therefore, as the embodiment of secular learning, contrasts powerfully with the gnostic sage, 'the Servant', whom Moses encounters and who is the custodian of *Divine* knowledge.

The Qur'ānic story unfolds as follows: Moses and his companion, after the departure of the fish, encounter one of God's servants [al-Khaḍir] who has significantly already been blessed with God's mercy (eternal salvation) and taught by God Divine knowledge (eternal prescience). Already then, in this Qur'ānic text, we have the glimmerings of a theophany as al-Khaḍir stands, as it were, wearing the cloak of God Himself, endowed or enrobed (almost) with *Divine* attributes. Moses begs to be allowed to follow the Master and learn from him. But the infusion of Divine Knowledge requires time and patience, and al-Khaḍir, supernaturally aware of Moses' deficiencies, points this out. He tells Moses that he will not be able to bear patiently that of which he has no experience or cognition. Moses persists and al-Khaḍir yields, but tells Moses that he is not to question anything which follows until al-Khaḍir himself raises the subject.

So the testing, the Divine Testing, begins. And the tests focus respectively on a Ship, a Youth and a Wall. Moses and the Sage set off in a ship which the Sage then promptly holes. Moses, forgetting his previous agreement, cannot restrain himself from commenting adversely on what has just happened. But when al-Khaḍir tells him, in effect, that he knew Moses would not be able to be quiet, Moses repents. They then meet a youth whom al-Khaḍir kills, precipitating an anguished objection from Moses and a similar response to the last from the Sage. Moses again repents, telling the Sage that if he questions the Sage's actions once more, then the latter should part company with Moses. But the inevitable happens: having been inhospitably treated by the people of a certain town to which they have come, al-Khaḍir sets up a wall which is about to collapse, provoking the mercenary comment from Moses that if the Sage had wished, he could have charged for his labours. The implication is clearly that in this way they might have revenged themselves on the ungenerous townsfolk.

But Moses has questioned the actions of al-Khaḍir once too often and according to Moses' own previous injunction, they must now part company. The Sage confirms the necessity of this parting but firstly explains the rationale behind his three strange actions: the *ship* was rendered unusable because it belonged to a group of poverty-stricken people behind whom lurked the spectre of a rapacious king who was forcibly seizing each ship. A tyrant was thus deprived of his spoils. The *youth* was the unbelieving son of believing parents who al-Khaḍir hopes will be replaced by God with a more filial and righteous one. Finally, the *wall* belonged to two orphans in the city. Underneath the wall a treasure had been buried as a legacy for them from their father at the proper time. By rebuilding the wall al-Khaḍir prevented the premature exposure of the treasure and its probable theft by others in the town. Before his departure, al-Khaḍir concludes significantly, stressing and revealing the theophany that lurks even behind the Qur'ānic account: "I did not do this of my own accord" (*wa mā fa'altuhu 'an amrī*).[3]

Such, in brief, is the threefold structure of the story of Moses and al-Khaḍir in the Qur'ān. Moses' voice is that of the common man, of *ordinary* knowledge, simply outraged by what he cannot understand, impotent in the face of what seems to him to be gross violations of *human* law. His 'literalist' *imagination* is that of Everyman as he, Moses, is confronted with the indirect theophany unfolding in the person of the Sage, one endowed with *supernatural* knowledge, as we saw earlier. Moses has failed the tests but, the Qur'ān seems to teach, so does – and will – Everyman.

The stress is on the gulf – unbridgeable gulf – between God's knowledge and man's. It is clear that each of the actions undertaken by the Sage has a dual aspect, and herein, perhaps, lies the principal *symbolism* of the narrative: it is not simply or only, as Yusuf Ali suggests, that the fish represents secular knowledge and the *pīr* or Sage divine knowledge. The matter, in its symbolism, is profounder than that, though we may easily accept Yusuf Ali's comments by way of an introduction to the symbolism of the Qur'ānic account. The essential symbolism lies in the fact that each of the actions undertaken by al-Khaḍir has a *salvific* aspect, known only to God and His Sage and revealed, *theophanically*, by the latter at the end to Moses; and a *damnatory* aspect, *imagined* by Moses at the time of living through each event. The essential contrast, then, is between salvation and *union* with God/His Sage, born of *theophanic* Divine Knowledge on the one hand; and absence, parting, *separation* (in effect, damnation) from that God and Sage, born of the common human *imagination* on the other. To summarise, the symbolism comprises a triple set of contrasts: Salvation and Damnation, Union and Separation, Theophany and Imagination. And since damnation, in Divine terms, means eternal separation from the Divine, we may formulate the following Qur'ānic paradigm: man's weak *imagination* in the person of Moses, confronted by the partial *theophany* of God's omniscience in the person of al-Khaḍir, produces separation. It is a powerful and vivid lesson which the Qur'ān is teaching its readers. The question which we shall now go on to examine, in a moment, is this: does the thought of Ibn al-'Arabī, as we find it expressed in his famous *Fuṣūṣ al-Ḥikam*, conform to the above Qur'ānic paradigm or even develop it?

Before we go on to consider this, however, we should briefly examine one final aspect of the Qur'ānic account in *Sūrat al-Kahf* of al-Khaḍir and Moses. We have already surveyed its *structure* and underlined what I believe to be its principal *symbolism*; what, we might ask, is the *real* nature of the *paradox* implicit in the entire narrative?

Among the definitions provided by *The Concise Oxford Dictionary*, 'paradox' is defined as a 'seemingly absurd though perhaps actually well-founded statement' and also as a 'person or thing conflicting with preconceived notions of what is reasonable or possible'.[4] Yusuf Ali, succinctly commenting on the whole Qur'ānic account of al-Khaḍir, notes: 'There are paradoxes in life: apparent loss may be real gain; apparent cruelty may be real mercy; returning good for evil may really be justice and not generosity . . . *God's wisdom transcends all human calculation*'.[5]

Each action undertaken by the Sage, al-Khaḍir, is clearly a mini-paradox, resulting in a mini-theophany, that theophany being here in the Qur'ān, more precisely, the manifestation of God's overriding omniscience in response to man's ignorance and weak imagination. Taken together, the whole Qur'ānic narrative may be said to yield or encapsulate a simple, *indirect* theophany and a simple paradox whose essence is: 'God's Ways are not your ways'. We have an *indirect theophany* in that, here in the Qur'ān, God acts through and via His Sage. We have a mystical and *paradoxical theodicy* where God acts in a way contrary to man's expectation and *imagination*. And the paradox thus outlined underlines and links to the symbolism emphasised above: the real fruit of theophany, properly realised and appreciated, is company and union.

The fruit of a theophany, misunderstood, weakly imagined, is a parting of company, separation, damnation. The Sage, al-Khaḍir, will no longer walk with Moses and keep him company. And, thus the Qur'ān teaches, God will no longer walk within the soul of that man whose *imagination* misunderstands, or, worse, rebels against, or questions, the *theophany* when it is manifested even partially.

Ibn al-'Arabī's *Fuṣūṣ al-Ḥikam* and al-Khaḍir

We turn now to an examination of the views of the 'Greatest Shaykh' (*al-Shaykh al-Akbar*), Ibn al-'Arabī, on the subject of al-Khaḍir, as expressed in the *Fuṣūṣ al-Ḥikam*. As I mentioned above, I want to explore the extent to which our *Doctor Maximus* conforms to the Qur'ānic paradigm of al-Khaḍir and Moses which I have outlined earlier. I will do so, once again, by surveying the material under the three headings of *structure, symbolism* and *paradox*.

Structurally, as is well-known, the *Fuṣūṣ al-Ḥikam* is formulated round twenty-seven prophets. As Dr Ralph Austin puts it:

> As the title suggests, the intention of the work is to present particular aspects of the divine wisdom within the context of the lives and persons of twenty-seven prophets. Although the first of the twenty-seven chapters is concerned with Adam, the first of the prophets according to Islam, and the last with Muhammad, the prophets in between are not arranged in any chronological order. Indeed, they do not seem to be arranged according to any particular pattern.[6]

Austin goes on to note that in the case of some of the chapters 'there would seem to be very little relationship between the prophet whose name appears in the chapter heading and the topics discussed in the chapter itself'.[7] All this is of considerable interest in any survey of the general structure of the *Fuṣūṣ*.

There is *no* individual chapter called after al-Khaḍir but that is hardly surprising since the twenty-seven chapters of Ibn al-'Arabī's *Fuṣūṣ al-Ḥikam* use the names of *prophets*, mainly Qur'ānic, at least as a starting point. (And al-Khaḍir, great Servant of God though he is, as well as gnostic *pīr* endowed with many supernatural attributes, never bears *in the Qur'an* the titles of *rasūl* (Messenger) or *nabī* (Prophet) however *popular belief* might regard him. Though al-Khaḍir has sometimes been confused with that great Old Testament prophet of Mount Carmel, Elias also called Elijah,[8] (that is, the Qur'ānic Ilyās[9]), this is *not* the case with

Ibn al-'Arabī. The latter in his *Fuṣūṣ al-Ḥikam* not only consecrates an entire chapter to Elias (Ilyās), whose title Dr Austin has rendered in English as 'The Wisdom of Intimacy in the Word of Elias',[10] but specifically states right at the beginning of his chapter: 'Elias is the same as *Idrīs*, who was a prophet before Noah whom God had raised to a high rank'.[11] It is thus to another chapter altogether that we must go in the *Fuṣūṣ al-Ḥikam* if we seek Ibn al-'Arabī's brief views here on *al-Khaḍir*. That chapter is the twenty-fifth in the Master's text and, unsurprisingly, it is called Moses,[12] the other great protagonist of the Qur'ānic account. We shall deal with this chapter in greater detail in a moment.

Firstly, however, we might note that, while the Qur'ānic al-Khaḍir lacks such titles as *rasūl* and *nabī*, Moses in the Qur'ān *is* characterised both as a *rasūl* and a *nabī*.[13] As we have already seen, al-Khaḍir's principal Qur'ānic title by contrast is 'Servant' (*'abd*), or more precisely, 'one of Our Servants' (*'abdan min 'ibādinā*).[14] A significant question therefore arises. What is the *real* relative rank of Moses, Messenger and Prophet, in relation to al-Khaḍir, Servant of God? The Qur'ānic account in *Sūrat al-Kahf* shows itself unaware of any possible problem or conflict of rank, portraying Moses by and large as an *inferior* pupil in the presence of a vastly *superior* gnostic master. As we shall see, however, Ibn al-'Arabī's account portrays al-Khaḍir as very much aware of Moses' true rank and standing with God. This subtly alters the perspective to be derived both from the basic Qur'ānic data and the Qur'ānic paradigm adumbrated above. Furthermore, since it is a text by Ibn al-'Arabī with which we are now dealing, there may now be derived from the combined data of Qur'ān and *Fuṣūṣ* the interesting presence of what we might term a 'double-paradox', the inevitable product of his basic doctrine of 'the unity of existence [or being]' (*waḥdat al-wujūd*).[15]

Alteration, or even apparent contradiction of the Qur'ānic data, need not surprise us in any text by Ibn al-'Arabī. As Dr Austin usefully reminds us in the 'Introduction' to his excellent translation of the *Fuṣūṣ al-Ḥikam*:

> Indeed, it is mystical exegesis, sometimes of a startling and unusual kind, that is the dominant feature of this work, since throughout it Ibn al-'Arabī draws heavily on Qur'ānic material to illustrate his points. In common with many other Sufi writers, he approaches the Qur'ānic text in a way different from that of the more familiar exoteric commentators. That is to say, he deals with the texts on the premise that every verse of the Qur'ān has many

more meanings than the one that might be obvious to the ordinary believer, who sees merely the surface of things . . . Thus the mystic exegete claims to see in the sacred texts meanings that are not apparent to ordinary mortals.[16]

And Dr Austin goes on to point out that in the chapter on Noah, Ibn al-ʻArabī 'goes one step further and actually interprets verses from the last part of *Sūrah Nūḥ* as meaning the very opposite of what the words appear to mean'.[17] In the light of all this it is perhaps not surprising that, in Ibn al-ʻArabī's own account of, and brief references to, the story of al-Khaḍir and Moses in the *Fuṣūṣ al-Ḥikam*, the relationship which we identified above between *theophany* and *imagination* in the Qur'ānic narrative is now subtly altered. Indeed, it would perhaps be truer to say that our Qur'ānic paradigm is almost destroyed. (I say 'almost' because 'separation' is *still* the end product in Ibn al-ʻArabī's text, as in the Qur'ān, of the whole mini-cosmic drama enacted on the mystic stage.)

Let us now turn to a rather fuller survey of the *structure* and content of Ibn al-ʻArabī's account of al-Khaḍir in the *Fuṣūṣ*. As we have already noted, this appears in the twenty-fifth chapter, called after Moses. Its full title in Arabic is *Faṣṣ ḥikma ʻalawiyya fī kalima Mūsiyya*[18] which Dr Austin translates as 'The Wisdom of Eminence in the Word of Moses'.[19] The stress on *ḥikma ʻalawiyya* ('Wisdom of Eminence') is hardly accidental and must be of considerable significance in any assessment of Moses' *rank* in Ibn al-ʻArabī's account. Furthermore, unlike some of the chapters of the *Fuṣūṣ*, this is one whose content *does* reflect its title.[20]

The references to al-Khaḍir and Moses are structured, basically, in two parts around (1) Moses' three tests (the Youth, the Ship and the Wall) and (2) the final parting between al-Khaḍir and Moses. The tests are generally spoken of in a comparative context: reference is made to Moses' disapproval of the killing of the youth by al-Khaḍir, but Moses has apparently forgotten that he himself killed an Egyptian. Al-Khaḍir's sinking of the ship – an action whose outward sense appeared to be wanton destruction but which, beneath the surface, was really the ultimate salvation of that ship from a rapacious king – has its analogy in the way that Moses was cast adrift in a basket on the water by his mother (and later saved). In each case, apparent destruction is followed, *in one sense or another*, by actual salvation.[21] Finally, reference is made to Moses' disquiet at al-Khaḍir's generous rebuilding of the wall, but Moses himself has previously obtained water for two women's flocks without asking payment for his actions.[22]

Lastly, we come to Ibn al-ʻArabī's account of the final parting between al-Khaḍir and Moses. It takes the form, almost, of a kind of stately cosmic game. *For al-Khaḍir is aware that Moses holds the exalted rank of Messenger (rasūl),*[23] *which he, al-Khaḍir, does not.*[24] Yet it is al-Khaḍir, a *Servant* of God, who has tested Moses, a *Messenger* of God. Al-Khaḍir also acknowledges that each of them has some divine gnostic knowledge not possessed by the other.[25] Indeed, Ibn al-'Arabī describes both men as having 'perfection . . . in knowledge' (*kamāl . . . fi'l-'ilm*).[26] And *because* al-Khaḍir is aware that Moses is a Messenger, and *despite* the fact that he is obliged to test him, (and *despite* also, Moses' own ignorance or unawareness of aspects of al-Khaḍir's position), al-Khaḍir is careful not to embarrass Moses.[27] Thus, the final parting and separation is not so much the sad result of Moses' *failure* in the three tests – the Qur'ānic scenario – as a Qur'ānically interpreted *mutual agreement* between two figures of almost supernatural stature that it is time to part and that they will not pursue the matter further, an agreement based on the spirit of obedience and on *mutual* respect.[28] *There is no Master/Pupil relationship here* in Ibn al-'Arabī's text in which al-Khaḍir is the Supreme Master.

Here then, in Ibn al-'Arabī's narrative, the overwhelming emphasis appears to be on *rank* and *knowledge*. The three actual tests are mentioned for comparative purposes but little else. Both figures, as the text stresses, possess some divine knowledge not possessed by the other.[29] Are they, indeed, to be considered gnostic equals in the eyes of God? Or is Moses to be considered, even, as the *superior* of the two in rank because he is a *rasūl*? At times, al-Khaḍir appears to indicate that this might indeed be the right approach.[30] Whatever the case, and whether al-Khaḍir and Moses are to be considered here as inferior and superior respectively, or merely equals, it is clear that the Qur'ānic perspective (together with the Qur'ānic paradigm established above whereby al-Khaḍir is canonised as by far the superior of the two figures), is turned inside out in Ibn al-'Arabī's *Fuṣūṣ al-Ḥikam*.

Let us move now, briefly, to the *symbolism* implicit in Ibn al-'Arabī's account. In the Qur'ānic account, it was stressed that the prime symbolism lay within or comprised a triple set of contrasts: salvation and damnation, union and separation, theophany and imagination. These contrasts derived from the three tests administered by al-Khaḍir to the Qur'ānic Moses. But in the *Fuṣūṣ al-Ḥikam* the tests are simply and mainly pegs on which to hang the concept of a failure on the part of Moses' imagination to remember past analogues in his, Moses', life to what al-Khaḍir has done. The latter Sage is justified already in Ibn al-'Arabī's text by the previous actions of Moses and there is thus no need, before the parting, for formal explanations by al-Khaḍir. No, the facts outlined by Ibn al-ʻArabī denote, or symbolise, at first sight much more the interaction between two cosmic giants in a divine hierarchy where the figure of the *rasūl*, the bringer of a new revelation or religion, ranks highly indeed.

We turn finally to examine the *paradox*, or paradoxes, implicit in the Greatest Shaykh's account. Elsewhere in his *Fuṣūṣ al-Ḥikam* Ibn al-ʻArabī states: 'The truth is that the Reality [*al-Ḥaqq*] is manifest in every created being and in every concept . . .'[31] I have argued elsewhere:

> It is therefore possible to formulate a thumbnail sketch of semiosis in Ibn al-ʻArabī's thought according to a paradigm that has only two parts: all verbs in the philosopher's lexicon ultimately mean 'to manifest' (by or of God), while all nouns are simply signs of God Himself. This might sound like a *reductio ad absurdum* but it is a logical consequence of the profoundly complex doctrine of *waḥdat al-wujūd*.[32]

Thus it can be argued that, for Ibn al-ʻArabī, the appearance of al-Khaḍir in *Sūrat al-Kahf* is a *direct* theophany, rather than an *indirect*, or kind of, theophany as in any 'orthodox' or 'traditional' interpretation of the Qur'ānic data. For Ibn al-ʻArabī, al-Khaḍir is not simply an agent of God's Divine Will; he *is* that Will.

The *Fuṣūṣ al-Ḥikam* and the Qur'ān thus suggest or yield a 'double-theophany' and a 'double paradox':

> (i) There is the single partial theophany of God acting *indirectly* in the Qur'ān, via His great mystic Sage al-Khaḍir, enlarged or doubled by the implicit perception from Ibn al-ʻArabi's doctrines that what we really have is a *direct* theophany.
>
> (ii) There is the single Qur'ānic paradox of the triple 'wrong' set of actions perpetrated by al-Khaḍir, enlarged or doubled by a perception via Ibn al-ʻArabī of *who* is the real Doer[33] and the consequent establishment from al-Khaḍir's actions of a 'correct' theodicy.

But that is by no means all. We can multiply both theophanies and paradoxes and obtain a third, different perspective which, paradoxically, builds upon but also dissolves the above two. If, according to Ibn al-ʻArabī's doctrines, the Qur'ānic al-Khaḍir must logically and ultimately be viewed as a direct manifestation of the Deity, then what, we might ask, of the figure of *Moses*? Let us repeat the phrase I quoted earlier from the *Fuṣūṣ*: 'The truth is that the Reality is manifest in every created being . . .'[34]

For Ibn al-'Arabī, concepts like divine theophany and human imagination ultimately merge as one. Moses' prophethood and al-Khaḍir's knowledge confront each other as aspects of the One Reality. Moses, indeed, must be a theophany too. And there can logically and finally be no *real* tension between the relative ranks of al-Khaḍir and Moses, between the Servant of God and the Messenger of God if all are manifestations of the Divine. The greatest paradox implicit in any text produced by our Shaykh is neither the actual power of *Theophany* nor the relative weakness of man's *Imagination*: it is Ibn al-'Arabī's perennial doctrine of the Oneness of Being.

[This essay was first presented as a paper to the ninth annual symposium of the Muhyiddin Ibn 'Arabī Society on *Theophany and Imagination* held at Wadham College, Oxford, between 20–22 March 1992.]

NOTES

1 *Qur'ān* 18:60–82.
2 Abdullah Yusuf Ali, *The Holy Qur'ān: Text, Translation and Commentary*, (Kuwait: Dhāt al-Salāsil, 1984), p. 747, n. 2408 (my italics).
3 *Qur'ān* 18:82.
4 J.B. Sykes (ed.), *The Concise Oxford Dictionary of Current English*, 6th edn., (Oxford: Clarendon Press, 1976), p. 798, s.v. 'paradox'.
5 (My italics) Ali, *Holy Qur'ān*, p. 747, n. 2404.
6 Ibn al-'Arabī, *The Bezels of Wisdom*, trans. and introd. by R.W.J. Austin, The Classics of Western Spirituality, (New York: Paulist Press, 1980), [hereafter referred to as Austin, *Bezels*], p. 18.
7 Ibid.
8 See especially III Kings 18; A.J. Wensinck-G. Vajda, art. 'Ilyās', *Encyclopaedia of Islam, New Edition*, 6 vols to date, (Leiden: E.J. Brill, 1960–), vol. III, p. 1156; see also A.J. Wensinck, art. 'al-Khaḍir (al-Khiḍr)', *Encyclopaedia of Islam, New Edition*, vol. IV, p. 903; Cyril Glassé, *The Concise Encyclopaedia of Islam*, (London: Stacey International, 1989), s.v. 'al-Khiḍr', pp. 224–5; W.M. Watt, *Companion to the Qur'ān*, (London: Allen & Unwin, 1967), p. 141; A.J. Wensinck, art. 'Ilyās', in H.A.R. Gibb and J.H. Kramers, *Shorter Encyclopaedia of Islam*, (Leiden: E.J. Brill/ London: Luzac, 1961), pp. 164–5.
9 See *Qur'ān* 6:85; 37:123–32 and the articles on Ilyās cited above in n. 8. In Q.37:123 Ilyās is described as 'one of those who have been sent' (*min al-mursalīn*) [i.e. by God]; in Q.37:132 he is called 'one of Our Servants' [*min 'ibādinā*]. It is intriguing that al-Khaḍir in Q.18:65 is called also 'one of Our Servants' (*'abd*^{an} *min 'ibādinā*). This kind of Qur'ānic nomenclature must surely have contributed to the links which some have identified between the names of al-Khaḍir and Ilyās.

10 Austin, *Bezels*, p. 229.
11 Ibid. (my italics); for the original Arabic see Ibn al-'Arabī, *Fuṣūṣ al-Ḥikam*, ed. A.A. 'Afīfī, (Beirut: Dār al-Kitāb al-'Arabī, n.d. [reprinted from the al-Ḥalabī, Cairo edn. of 1946]), Pt. 1, p. 181 [referred to hereafter simply as *Fuṣūṣ*; all references are to Pt. 1]. For Idrīs, often identified with the Old Testament Enoch, see D. Eustache, art. 'Idrīs, *Encyclopaedia of Islam, New Edition*, vol. III, p. 1030.
12 See *Fuṣūṣ*, pp. 197–213; Austin, *Bezels*, pp. 249–66.
13 See *Qur'ān* 19:51.
14 *Qur'ān* 18:65. See above n. 9.
15 For more on this doctrine, see Ian Richard Netton, *Allāh Transcendent: Studies in the Structure and Semiotics of Islamic Philosophy, Theology and Cosmology*, (London: Routledge, 1989), pp. 272–4.
16 Austin, *Bezels*, 'Introduction', pp. 18–19.
17 Ibid., p. 19.
18 See *Fuṣūṣ*, pp. 197–213.
19 See Austin, *Bezels*, pp. 249–66.
20 Ibid., pp. 18, 249.
21 See *Fuṣūṣ*, pp. 202–3; Austin, *Bezels*, pp. 256–7.
22 See *Fuṣūṣ*, p. 205; Austin, *Bezels*, p. 259.
23 *Fuṣūṣ*, p. 206; Austin, *Bezels*, pp. 259, 260.
24 *Fuṣūṣ*, p. 206; Austin, *Bezels*, p. 260.
25 *Fuṣūṣ*, p. 206; Austin, *Bezels*, p. 260.
26 *Fuṣūṣ*, p. 206; Austin, *Bezels*, p. 260.
27 *Fuṣūṣ*, p. 206; Austin, *Bezels*, pp. 259–60.
28 *Fuṣūṣ*, p. 206; Austin, *Bezels*, pp. 259–60.
29 See above, n. 25.
30 See above, n. 24.
31 Austin, *Bezels*, p. 73; see *Fuṣūṣ*, p. 68.
32 Netton, *Allāh Transcendent*, p. 304.
33 Some support for these ideas may be found in the great *magnum opus* of Ibn al-'Arabī, the *Futūḥāt al-Makkiyya*. See William C. Chittick's brilliant commentary and selection of translations: *Ibn al-'Arabī's Metaphysics of Imagination: The Sufi Path of Knowledge*, (Albany: State University of New York Press, 1989), pp. 209–10.
34 See n. 31.

5

THE BREATH OF FELICITY

Adab, Aḥwāl, Maqāmāt and Abū Najīb al-Suhrawardī

Like the more famous Abū Ḥāmid al-Ghazālī (450/1058–505/1111), the Persian mystic 'Abd al-Qāhir Abū Najīb al-Suhrawardī (490/1097–563/1168) had a career which embraced both the academic and the mystical. Like Abū Ḥāmid, too, he later taught for some time at the Niẓāmiyya College in Baghdad. Earlier, Abū Najīb had studied *fiqh* at this college but he had left his academic work there 'in order to associate with Shaykh Aḥmad al-Ghazālī [i.e. Abū Ḥāmid's brother] who wafted upon him *the breath of felicity*[1] [*nasīm al-sa'āda*] and guided him along the Sufi Path. He cut himself off from ordinary society in order to lead a life of seclusion and retreat. *Murīds* came to put themselves under him and the fame of his *baraka* spread widely'.[2] But it is also clear that he did not totally turn his back on the life of academe. Indeed, again like Abū Ḥāmid al-Ghazālī, Abū Najīb al-Suhrawardī made a return to academic life when he assumed a Chair of *fiqh* in the Niẓāmiyya.[3] And these two aspects of his life, the academic and the mystical, merge most neatly in his famous manual of instruction, the *Kitāb Ādāb al-Murīdīn*.[4] This title has loosely but accurately been rendered into English by Milson as *A Sufi Rule for Novices*.[5] However, other renditions of the Arabic could produce *The Book of the Manners of the Novices* or even *The Book of the Courtesies of the Novices*; and one of the themes of this essay will be that of Ṣūfī correct behaviour, manners or courtesy (*adab*, plural: *ādāb*),[6] as exemplified in Abū Najīb's famous text: two secondary themes will be his treatment here of *aḥwāl* and *maqāmāt*. The *Kitāb Ādāb al-Murīdīn* will be the basic framework within which these three themes are explored.

However one chooses to translate *adab*, there is no doubt that the word has a special role throughout Abū Najīb's book. As Milson puts it: '*Kitāb Ādāb al-Murīdīn* is unique among Sufi compositions known today in that Sufism in its entirety is viewed here from the standpoint of *ādāb* (rules of conduct).'[7] Milson contrasts the prominence of the theme of *adab* in the work with the relatively low profile of such typical Ṣūfī themes as *aḥwāl* and *maqāmāt*:

> A full exposition of Sufi mystical theory is not included in it. One reason for this omission may lie in the fact that the system of stations and states (*maqāmāt* and *aḥwāl*) had already been explained by famous Sufi authors in the two centuries preceding Abū Najīb. A more important reason is that the mystical theory and, in particular, the matter of mystical states (*aḥwāl*) constituted the inner aspect of Sufism, whereas novices, for whom the book was primarily intended, were expected to become versed in the external aspect as a first step. This is presumably why, except for a brief summary on the stations and states, Abū al-Najīb deals with the stations *only insofar as the matter was required for novices*.[8]

In the light of this, it is intended here to (1) survey the *structure* of the *Kitāb Ādāb al-Murīdīn*, (2) assess the major role played by *adab* with its real meaning and significance for Suhrawardī, together with the more minor roles within that *adab* taken by *aḥwāl* and *maqāmāt*, and finally (3) attempt an answer to two questions: how *successful* was Suhrawardī in incorporating, or 'institutionalizing', within the framework of a Rule (a code of Ṣūfī *adab* or 'earthly manners') such spiritual states as the *aḥwāl*, the *maqāmāt* and other aspects of Ṣūfī spirituality? What is the true significance of his *Kitāb*?

Before examining the structure however, it is worth trying to identify the exact nature of the clientele for whom the Manual was intended. From its title, it is clear that they are novices (*murīdīn*) within a Ṣūfī order. But what *kind* of novices? Were they permanent or temporary? Did they live all their lives within the kind of Ṣūfī *ribāṭ* founded by Abū Najīb?[9] Or were the novices more akin to the tertiary (also called third order or secular) members of Roman Catholic mendicant orders of Friars like the Carmelites[10] and Franciscans, or the oblate members of the Benedictine order of monks.[11] In other words, did they live their spirituality out in the world? What clues does the text provide?

Certainly, we know that the last proposition was a possibility. Suhrawardī did this himself and notes that some Ṣūfīs 'when they had reached the state of stability, became commanders and administrators, and mixing with the people did not damage their religious position'.[12] But here the author refers to *experienced* Ṣūfīs. We also know that those *inexperienced* in the Ṣūfī life could nonetheless 'collect' affiliations to the great Ṣūfī orders with little effort, spiritual or otherwise. The great fourteenth century traveller Ibn Baṭṭūṭa is an excellent example of one who did just that.[13] Certainly, he never troubled with the formality of a novitiate as such.[14]

What then, was the status of those for whom Suhrawardī wrote his famous text? Quite simply, a cursory glance at the text shows that it is directed at two types of Ṣūfī; the amount of space devoted to each type however, is quite disproportionate and disparate. Overwhelmingly, Abū Najīb's text addresses the Ṣūfī who is able to live in community and, thus, as a novice (*murīd*) to 'choose only pure food, drink, and clothes',[15] 'render service to his brethren' and 'not leave his Shaykh before the eye of his heart opens',[16] 'to associate with people of his kind and those from whom he can benefit' and 'to undertake to serve his brethren and companions (*khidmat al-ikhwān*) and help them in obtaining their sustenance'.[17] These are just a few examples of the manner in which the good Ṣūfī, and aspirant or novice, should behave. It is clear that such actions are best, and most easily undertaken, within the context of a resident community.

Yet Suhrawardī does have a few words to spare in his text for those analogous to the tertiaries mentioned above.[18] These are the 'associate' or 'lay members' of the Ṣūfī Order or Brotherhood.[19] Abū Najīb calls them in one place in his text *muḥibbūn* (lovers, i.e. of God),[20] and Menahem Milson comments:

> Although the affiliation of lay members to Sufism was a phenomenon both very common and of great consequence to the Sufi orders, this subject is hardly discussed in the Sufi manuals. Abū al-Najīb seems to have been the first Sufi author to deal explicitly with this form of association with Sufism and to propose a doctrine of Sufi ethics that would accommodate it. To this effect, Abū Najīb uses . . . the concept of *rukhṣa*.[21]

Any examination of the structure of the *Kitāb Ādāb al-Murīdīn* must, therefore, be undertaken in the light of the *dual* constituency at whom the text is directed (and an awareness that some dispensations (*rukhaṣ*), originally designed just for the 'lay members' were adopted by full members of the Brotherhood as well).[22] It is clear, then, that the concept of 'dispensation' (*rukhṣa*) from some of the severer Ṣūfī practices is, in the view of Suhrawardī, a licit part of Ṣūfī *adab*. Bearing this in mind, we will now survey briefly the general structure of Suhrawardī's work, emphasizing in conclusion those areas which were particularly designed for, or reflect, 'lay member' practice. In what follows I have preferred not to adopt Milson's major fourfold division, nor his more extensive dissection of the text into 208 sections;[23] rather, as a *via media*, I have delineated a chronological sequence of *fifteen* discrete parts or sections which is intended to achieve a clearer presentation of the structure while at the same time incorporating sufficient detail for the purposes of this paper. Like Milson's my divisions or sections are not contained within the text but are imposed by myself according to what I believe are the *fifteen* principal sections of Suhrawardī's work.

After a very brief *Foreword* (Section 1), which begins by invoking a blessing on Muḥammad and his family, Suhrawardī moves to an *Outline of Islamic Dogmatic Theology* (Section 2), which stresses God's Oneness using an almost Neoplatonic negative terminology. Reference is made to such fundamentals of Islamic dogma and debate as God's attributes, the uncreatedness of the Qur'ān and various aspects of eschatology. Having set the scene in a traditionally orthodox fashion, the writer moves to an *Outline of Ṣūfī Belief and Ritual* (Section 3), surveying such aspects of this as Ṣūfī poverty, the love of God, the nature of miracles and the Ṣūfī ritual of *samā'*. Suhrawardī then turns to deal with *Ṣūfism within an Islamic Context* (Section 4), identifying three types of religious scholar: traditionists, jurists and Ṣūfī religious scholars. A further threefold division occurs in the following section on the *Ṣūfī Hierarchy and Character* (Section 5): there are three grades of Ṣūfī, namely the Novice, the Initiate and the Gnostic Master.[24] Suhrawardī then pursues his evident liking for classification in threes by identifying three classes of people and different kinds of *ādāb* which they espouse.

What might be termed the first major section on *Ṣūfī Spirituality* (Section 6) now appears. Here Suhrawardī deals with those classic aspects of the Ṣūfī journey, the stations (*maqāmāt*) and the states (*aḥwāl*) before turning to an extended discussion of *Ṣūfī Epistemology* (Section 7). It is after this that the real *Rule Book for Novices* (Section 8) *qua* Rule Book seems to begin with its frequent references to the proper and appropriate behaviour of the novice, whether that be from the point of view of food and drink, repentance, or service to his companions. The next section might conveniently be labelled *The Ṣūfī and the World I* (Section 9). Here the author deals with such areas of life (and possible hazards!) as companionship, association, visiting, entertainment, and travel. It is succeeded by a section on *The Ṣūfī and Himself* (Section 10) where such matters as dress, food and sleep are covered. Suhrawardī follows this by discoursing at some length on *The Ṣūfī Office and Ritual* (Section 11) and provides an illuminating account of correct behaviour during the *samāʿ*, with many apposite quotations. He then reverts to a previous theme of the Ṣūfī's external relations with the outside world and discusses the topics of marriage and begging. This section might neatly be called *The Ṣūfī and the World II* (Section 12), and it is followed by one dealing with *The Testing of the Ṣūfī* (Section 13). Here our author covers such matters as illness, death and other trials. Stress is laid on the spiritually beneficial results of illness and the way it can purge sin. The last major section deals with *Dispensations* (Section 14) and the whole work concludes with a *Prayer* (Section 15).

This brief survey of the contents and structure of Suhrawardī's *Kitāb Ādāb al-Murīdīn* shows that the regular Ṣūfī, who belonged to and lived within the kind of Ṣūfī brotherhood or convent envisaged by the author, was viewed as being very much a part of the classical Ṣūfī tradition: for example, he was an ascetic, traversing a spiritual path, following a defined code of *adab*, with a detachment from worldly things yet a courtesy towards people of the world. Mystical experience, in terms of *ahwāl*, may figure on the journey; and the Ṣūfī who travels the spiritual path is characterized as a seeker (*ṭālib*), a wanderer or voyager (*sā'ir*) or an arriver (*wāṣil*) according to whether he is respectively a novice, initiate or gnostic master.[25]

Thus far, in our survey of the structure and contents of the *Kitāb Ādāb al-Murīdīn*, we have concentrated on the role of the regular full-time member of the Ṣūfī brotherhood. Yet, as we noted above, it is clear that there was a genuine place and role for the 'affiliate', the 'lay member' or 'adherent', who was not able to undertake the full community life or rigors implicit in the full Rule, yet who wished, nonetheless, to share in the spirituality of the Brotherhood.[26] It is to these lay members we now turn in our survey of Suhrawardī's work.

Before his final discussion of the dispensations, and their primary orientation towards the lay membership of the Brotherhood,[27] Suhrawardī, in his text, draws attention to the lay members both as *providers* of hospitality and as *recipients* of one of the charisms of the Brotherhood. The Ṣūfī brother, on arrival at a town, should pay his respects to the local Ṣūfī Shaykh or, failing that, in the absence of such a Shaykh, he should go to the place where the Ṣūfīs congregate. However, it may be that the town lacks both a formal Ṣūfī brotherhood and place of meeting. If this be the case, the itinerant Ṣūfī is advised to lodge with one of these townspeople who loves the Ṣūfīs.[28] This is a clear reference to the lay members.[29] That this whole procedure is regarded as a formally meritorious and correct aspect of Ṣūfī *adab* and behaviour, is signalled in the text by the words which open the section, *wa min ādābihim* . . .[30] and it stresses that the provision of hospitality for fellow Ṣūfīs who were itinerant must have been one of the major offices of the lay members.

Yet these *providers* of hospitality also shared in some of the *privileges* of their full-time brethren. When Ṣūfī garments were torn up and distributed, and lay members (*muḥibbūn*) were present, they too were entitled to a share. However, the clothing of such lay members was not considered suitable for tearing and distribution, but was to be sold or given to the reciter instead.[31] There is clearly a division of Ṣūfīs here, from a hierarchical point of view, into the first and second class according to whether one is a regular or lay Ṣūfī; and, in view of the statements that 'they approve of tearing the "patched mantles" (*muraqqa'āt*) only for the purpose of deriving *baraka* from them' and that 'it is preferable to tear to pieces the *khiraq* of the regular Ṣūfīs, if they can be used for patching, so that each one can get his share', it is also clear that the degree of *baraka* judged to attach to the garb of the regular Ṣūfī was rather more than that deriving from the lay member's clothing. The latter for Suhrawardī thus shared in some of the privileges or fruits of his Brotherhood; but he did not share in the rank of the regular member nor have parity of esteem with him.

By way of interesting contrast, we may briefly compare the position of such a Ṣūfī lay member to that of the modern member of the (Roman Catholic) Secular Order of Discalced Carmelites, a group with sometimes striking similarities to those of the mediaeval lay Ṣūfīs. 'The Secular Branches of every Mendicant Order', comments Griffin, 'are truly part of the Order'.[32] Article 1 of the *Rule of Life of the Secular Order of Discalced Carmelites* states: 'The Secular Order forms an integral part of the Carmelite family; its members are therefore sons and daughters of the Order . . .'[33] However, Griffin again comments that it is clear 'that there is little similarity to the way the life is lived [by the Friars and Nuns]' and that 'the participation of the Lay Carmelite in the life of the Order is different because of their members living a different lifestyle . . . Today in the Order one hears of the *one family of Carmel* and of the three branches living the *same Teresian charism*'.[34] The implications are clear: though the Carmelite Order as a whole may comprise First, Second and Third Orders or Sections (i.e. Friars, Nuns and Seculars), the principal difference between them is one of type and lifestyle rather than rank. There is a total lack of stress on hierarchisation in both the Carmelite *Rule of Life of the Secular Order* which we have cited, and its principal *Commentary*.[35] But, by total contrast, hierarchy for Suhrawardī in his *Ṣūfī Rule for Novices* is clearly part of Ṣūfī *adab* and, as such, is 'enstructured' or encoded in the *Rule* in the manner outlined above.

In view of this, it is perhaps somewhat ironical – though extremely human! – that some of the regular Ṣūfis, proud as they must have been of their ascetical lifestyle and mortifications, clearly adopted, or availed themselves of, some of the dispensations (*rukhaṣ*) primarily designed for the lay membership.[36] Structurally, the section on 'Dispensations' in the *Kitāb Ādāb al-Murīdīn* occurs towards the end of the book. (In Milson's artificial division of 208 sections, it comprises Sections 166–207.)[37] Suhrawardī lists here a total of forty dispensations and Milson reminds us that forty was a favourite number among Arab authors.[38] (A memorable example of this is al-Nawawī's famous collection known as *Forty Ḥadīth*.) The forty dispensations listed by Suhrawardī in his text cover a wide variety of material ranging from permission to engage in business,[39] to permission to joke,[40] through permission to visit old women[41] and soothe poets with payment![42] The final *rukhṣa* listed is that which allows one 'to show annoyance and exasperation upon encountering that which is absurd and which should not be tolerated'.[43] At the end, however, Suhrawardī makes it very clear *who* is permitted such dispensations: it is the 'lay members' of the brotherhood, called here, *non-pejoratively*, in Arabic *al-mutashabbihūn* ('the simulators', or 'those who pretend to be Ṣūfis'), but qualified by the adjective *al-Ṣādiqīn*, 'the truthful'.[44] As Suhrawardī puts it in Milson's translation:

> He who adheres to the dispensations and accepts the rules which govern them is one of *the truthful simulators*, about whom the Prophet said: "Whoever makes the effort to resemble a group of people is one of them" . . . Whoever adopts the dispensations is one of the beginners, and he should strive to enhance his inner state and ascend to the heights of the *aḥwāl*. Whoever falls below the level of the "dispensations" thereby renounces Sufism and is forbidden to enjoy the gifts and endowments which are made for the Sufis, and the Sufi congregation should excommunicate him.[45]

The passage quoted clearly addresses two audiences: there are the 'lay members', or 'truthful simulators' according to Milson's translation, who are covered by the dispensations with no blame; and there are the regular members of low calibre who are classified as 'beginners' and who may yet, it is hoped, aspire and ascend to greater heights. Suhrawardī's Ṣūfī *adab* or courtesy here dictates that a measure of 'humanity' is built into the rigors of the *Rule*. While it is clear that such dispensations as the permission to engage in business were primarily and initially directed at the lay member[46] because of his family dependents, and equally clear that Suhrawardī believed the regular Ṣūfī should avoid marriage,[47] it is also clear from the passage we cited above that dispensations from a variety of strictures *were* available to the lowest grade of regular Ṣūfī who would not, however, advance very far in his spiritual journey until he had abjured such 'comforts' as these *rukhaṣ*.[48]

We have referred several times already in the course of what has preceded to the concept of *adab*. This is perhaps a useful point at which to pause and try to assess the real meaning and significance of that term for Suhrawardī, before going on to evaluate the parts played within that *adab*, and within his text, by other terms like *maqāmāt* and *aḥwāl*. It is a truism that the term *adab* has a multitude of different meanings;[49] only those which pertain to the field of *taṣawwuf* will be mentioned here. We have already suggested translations such as 'Ṣūfī correct behaviour' (modelled on Jo-Ann Gross's usage), 'manners' and 'courtesy'. The latter is particularly felicitous with its connotations both of mediaeval chivalry and an attitude of loving gentleness towards one's God and one's fellow man. Trimingham, we have noted above, defined *adab* as 'the *conduct and discipline* of the Ṣūfī in relation to his Shaykh and associate Ṣūfīs';[50] and Milson follows him, translating *ādāb* as 'rules of conduct',[51] 'ethical conduct'[52] and also just 'ethics'.[53] R.A. Nicholson's rendition of the term in his translation of Hujwīrī's Persian *Kashf al-Maḥjūb* stresses the aspects both of 'manners' and 'discipline' implicit in the word:

> The Apostle said: "Good manners (*ḥusn al-adab*) are a part of faith" . . . You must know that the seemliness and decorum of all religions and temporal affairs depend on rules of discipline (*ādāb*) . . .[54]

In *Kitāb Ādāb al-Murīdīn* Suhrawardī himself shows a considerable awareness of the nuances and the richness of the term *adab*. He says that from the point of view of *adab* people fall into three categories: there are the people of this world (*ahl al-dunyā*), the religious people (*ahl al-dīn*) and God's elite among the last group (*ahl khuṣūṣiyya min ahl al-dīn*). (Here we might note in passing that the usual contrast of *dīn* and *dunyā* is given a Ṣūfī gloss with the addition of a third category.) In Suhrawardi's eyes, the *ādāb* of the people of this world comprise such things as eloquence, rhetoric, preserving or memorizing the (traditional) sciences, (*ḥifẓ al-'ulūm*), history and poetry. The *ādāb* of the religious people include learning, discipline, refinement of character and eagerness to do good. But the *ādāb* of the final group, those whom I have translated as 'God's Elite', go far beyond such normative behaviour as is prescribed for the second group. This third group is clearly that of the Ṣūfīs: their *ādāb* are (mysteriously) characterized as the preservation of hearts (*ḥifẓ al-qulūb*) – a direct contrast with the previously cited *ḥifẓ al-ʻulūm* of the first group – as well as compliance with the secrets 'and being the same both secretly and outwardly'.[55]

Adab, then, as a term in the eyes of both modern translators and such mediaeval authors as Suhrawardī clearly has a variety of layers of meaning and carries a considerable weight of what might be termed 'cultural baggage'. However, I would like to suggest here that, apart from its obvious senses in *taṣawwuf*, already suggested, of 'discipline' and 'rules of conduct', there is another, perhaps more literary way of looking at the term. This is that *adab* is a useful *literary motif* which provides a convenient *structure* or *frame* within which may be articulated the whole of Ṣūfī life. Parallels with frame stories such as occur in the *Panchatantra, Kalīla wa Dimna* and *The Thousand and One Nights* are not hard to find. But I suggest that one comes even closer, in literary terms, if one looks at the genre of *Riḥla* literature and observes how that genre served as a notable vehicle or *frame* for, *inter alia*, descriptions both of the pilgrimage to Mecca and Medina, and surveys of those holy cities themselves.[56] For Suhrawardī, we can say that *adab* is both the context or frame of the internal literature of Ṣūfism as well as the context or frame of the external Ṣūfī life as it is lived and which it directs and moulds to itself. It is therefore Structure, Frame and Rule all at once.

It is thus from the primary perspective of *ādāb* as frame that I now wish to evaluate, within that frame, Suhrawardī's treatment of the *maqāmāt* and in particular the *aḥwāl*. These 'stations' (*maqāmāt*) and 'spiritual states' (*aḥwāl*) – the first 'to be effected by the individual's endeavour' and the second to be 'regarded as divine gifts' for they 'do not result from human action or volition but from God's favour'[57] – are specifically held by Suhrawardī in his text to be an integral part of Ṣūfism.[58] Suhrawardī shows, however, that he considers them to be a very special part of Ṣūfism, which possesses its own external and internal facets (*ẓāhiran wa bāṭinan*). The first consists in behaving ethically with regard to one's fellow man (*istiʻmāl al-adab maʻa al-khalq*), the second in engaging the *aḥwāl* and the *maqāmāt* with regard to God Himself, called here 'The True' or 'The Real', *al-Ḥaqq*.[59] As always, the *bāṭin* is to be elevated above the *ẓāhir*, in this statement as elsewhere. We note also, here the use of *adab* in the sense of 'code or rule of ethics' but perhaps even more significantly, the triple, and surely deliberate, contrast between *ẓāhir* and *bāṭin*, *adab* and *aḥwāl* plus *maqāmāt*, and the corporeal (i.e. man) and the divine (i.e. God).

Here, then, earthly *adab* is contrasted with the two progressions in the spiritual life of *maqāmāt* and *aḥwāl*. This is a very significant contrast for it serves to root *adab* among matters terrestrial and corporeal while it elevates the *maqāmāt* and *aḥwāl* by associating them with the Divine. Here, in a nutshell – and we shall return to this point later – is a mirror of what Suhrawardī attempts in his *Kitāb Ādāb al-Murīdīn*: the propagation of an earthly, or earth-bound and earth-designed Rule, which attempts to 'ground' within it, or encapsulate, in some way, whether it be by contrast or stress, the stations and states which properly belong to the divine world. Here, there is a *contrast* of *adab* in the sense of 'ethical rule' on the one hand, and *maqāmāt* and *aḥwāl* on the other. However, we may also present the latter two terms as *part* of *adab* if we adopt the suggestion which I formulated earlier of *adab* as 'literary' and 'life' *frame*. This idea finds some logical support within Suhrawardī's own text where he notes that 'it is said that the whole truth of Ṣūfism is *adab*; each moment (*waqt*), each state, and each station has its *adab*'.[60] We have stressed above that Suhrawardī specifically cites the *maqāmāt* and *aḥwāl* as part of Ṣūfism.[61] It is because the structure constitutes a frame such as I have described, and that frame is *adab*, that I have spent a considerable amount of time surveying this structure and the contents it encapsulates.

The discussion of the spiritual stations and mystical states in the *Kitāb Ādāb al-Murīdīn* is low-key and unsophisticated. The primary, *but not the only* constituency towards whom the work was directed was the Ṣūfī novice.[62] Nonetheless, though the material be lightweight, it is still of considerable interest. Definitions and lists of the stations and states are many. A useful and very early passage illustrating the distinction between a *maqām* and a *ḥāl* occurs in the *Kashf al-Maḥjūb* of Hujwīrī, who writes:

> "Station" (*maqām*) denotes anyone's "standing" in the Way of God, and his fulfillment of the obligations appertaining to that "station" . . . "State" (*ḥāl*), on the other hand, is something that descends from God into a man's heart, without his being able to repel it when it comes, or to attract it when it goes, by his own effort . . . *"Station" belongs to the category of acts, "state" to the category of gifts*.[63]

Seyyed Hossein Nasr has drawn attention to one of the oldest Persian Ṣūfī descriptions of the *maqāmāt*, the *Forty Stations* (*maqāmāt-i arba'īn*) ascribed to the fourth/eleventh century Persian Ṣūfī master Abū Sa'īd ibn Abī'l-Khayr. (We note in passing the stress again on the number "forty").[64] Abū Saʿīd begins with intention (*niyya*) as the first station, and concludes with a fortieth which is Ṣūfism (*Taṣawwuf*) itself.[65] Professor Nasr adds that some of the *aḥwāl* described by other Ṣūfis appear in Abū Saʿīd's list as *maqāmāt*.[66] Furthermore, for Abū Saʿīd, the station of "subsistence-in-God" (*baqā*), usually regarded by others as the highest 'because it is the station of the Union with God'[67] ranks only as the twenty-second station.[68]

If we turn now to examine Suhrawardī's own text, the *Kitāb Ādāb al-Murīdīn*, we find a similar lengthy list of mixed *maqāmāt* and *aḥwāl*; this particular list, however, lacks the descriptions attached to each item found on Abū Sa'īd's list of forty spiritual stations. However, Suhrawardī also has a slightly later, and shorter, list to which we will come, which does contain a brief definition of the mystical terms. We should note, firstly, that Suhrawardī makes it clear in his work that all questions about the spiritual stations and states are to be directed to 'the masters of Ṣūfism' (*a'immat al-Ṣūfiyya*).[69] For him, *'Maqām* signifies the position of man in worship before God . . . Junayd defines *ḥāl* as a form of inspiration which comes down to the heart but does not stay in it permanently.'[70]

Milson, in his introduction to the *Sufi Rule* makes several comparisons between parts of Suhrawardī's work and al-Kalābādhī's *Ta'arruf*.[71] By way of contrast, therefore, we will, instead, note Hujwīrī's *maqāmāt* and *aḥwāl* beside those listed in Suhrawardī's text (see Tables 1 and 2). We have already noted that Suhrawardī has two basic lists: since the first mixed listing of *maqāmāt* and *aḥwāl* does not, however, provide a useful definition in the text after each *maqām* and *ḥāl*,[72] we will not cite it here, although it should be noted that it is in this stark but lengthy listing that the key words *fanā'* and *baqā'* appear, while they do not appear in the listings given in Table 1. For the latter, Suhrawardī provides brief textual definitions, stresses the last spiritual station designated for novices and emphasizes which is the last of the mystical states, all clearly in a didactic and pedagogic fashion.

It is proposed now to present a few comparisons between the works of Suhrawardī and Hujwīrī with regard to the *maqāmāt* and *aḥwāl*, before turning for a further comparison, by way of complete contrast, to one mediaeval and one modern Christian *Rule*.

Of the two works, the *Kashf al-Maḥjūb* and the *Kitāb Ādāb al-Murīdīn*, the *Kashf* is considerably the longer, and it is directed to a much wider Ṣūfī audience. It embraces a wide body of material ranging from chapters on Poverty, important Imāms and Ṣūfis to a series of chapters characterized as the uncovering of various veils: there are eleven of the latter, and they constitute the primary formal frame within which discussion takes place in the latter part of the *Kashf*.[73] The section which perhaps best equates to the material of the *Kitāb Ādāb al-Murīdīn* is that entitled 'The Uncovering of the Ninth Veil: Concerning Companionship, Together with its Rules and Principles'.[74] This includes discussion of the rules of companionship, rules of discipline for resident Ṣūfīs, rules for travel, eating, sleeping, speech, silence, begging, marriage and celibacy. If only because of its length, and the wider intended audience, Hujwīrī's is inevitably the profounder of the two works.

Hujwīrī declines 'to enumerate every *ḥāl* and explain every *maqām*'[75] though it is clear that, as with Suhrawardī, both *aḥwāl* and *maqāmāt* have a major role to play in the Ṣūfī path. But it is instructive that with neither master do these stations and states become an end in themselves. Both their texts indicate levels of progress and spirituality beyond the *maqāmāt* and *aḥwāl*. Hujwīrī, for example, stresses the evanescent quality of such stations and states – 'the fleeting state (*ḥāl*) of the saint is the permanent station (*maqām*) of the prophet'[76] – and later notes:

> Now I, 'Ali b. Uthmān al-Jullābi, declare . . . that annihilation comes to a man through vision of the majesty of God and through the revelation of Divine omnipotence to his heart, so that in the overwhelming sense of His majesty this world and the next world are obliterated from his mind, *and "states" and "stations" appear contemptible in the sight of his aspiring thought* . . .[77]

Even on a formal level, Hujwīrī divides the 'Way to God' into the three kinds of *maqām*, *ḥāl* and *tamkīn* and, indicating that the latter is the highest of the three, defines it as 'the residence of spiritual adepts in the abode of perfection and in the highest grade . . .'[78] Indeed, there is a type of *tamkīn* in which God's influence so predominates that even such key terms as *fanā'* and *baqā'* cease to have real meaning.[79]

Suhrawardī likewise, has a triple division of levels of spirituality: *maqāmāt*, *aḥwāl*, *fawātiḥ*, etc. He however, prefers to talk of the grade above the *aḥwāl* as comprising such indescribable things as *fawātiḥ* (revealed signs), *lawā'iḥ* (appearances of light), and *manā'iḥ* (graces).[80] These last three, while by no means the same as Hujwīrī's *tamkīn*, constitute nonetheless Suhrawardī's own parallel grade of highest spirituality. Significantly, while the terms *fanā'* and *baqā'* appear in Suhrawardī's long list of *maqāmāt* and *aḥwāl*,[81], Hujwīrī in his *Kashf* makes it clear that such terms are distinct from the *maqāmāt* and *aḥwāl* and, indeed, beyond them.[82] There is thus some comparability, and some divergence in the use of terminology; but perhaps the highest divergence of all between the texts of Suhrawardī and Hujwīrī is structural: Suhrawardī's teachings fall within a text whose constant frame is *adab*. This is clearly signalled in several places by such phrases as *min ādābihim* but a reading of the entire text shows, as I have stressed above, that the whole work is set within a frame of *adab*. Hujwīrī, too, saw a role for *adab*[83] but not as an all-embracing frame: his *adab* is part of a broader fabric; his *rules* of Ṣūfī life figure as one aspect of that life.

Before moving to our conclusion, it is illuminating, briefly, to make one final comparison, between the Islamic *Rule* of Suhrawardī and two Christian *Rules* of spirituality: (i) the early mediaeval sixth-century monastic Rule of the Christian Saint Benedict, and (ii) the modern (1979 version) of the *Rule of Life of the Secular Order of Discalced Carmelites*.

Of the former, Benedictine Rule Henry Chadwick noted:

> [Benedict's] rule was one of simplicity and self-discipline, not of penitential austerity and self-inflicted mortification.[84]

The principle of restraint identified here and elsewhere[85] by Chadwick as a major facet of the Benedictine Rule is clear from any casual examination of the *Rule* itself.[86] It is full of sound common sense and ranges in its subject matter from 'Restraint of Speech' (*De Taciturnitate*)[87] through 'The Celebration of the Divine Office during the Day' (*Qualiter Divina Opera per Diem Agantur*)[88] to 'Brothers working at a Distance or Travelling' (*De Fratribus qui Longe ab Oratorio Laborant Aut in Via Sunt*)[89] and 'The Good Zeal of Monks' (*De Zelo Bono quod Debent Monachi Habere*).[90] From a structural point of view it seems that the shape of the *Benedictine Rule* is fairly clear 'even though the connections between parts are sometimes loose or unclear'.[91]

> The spiritual doctrine is first . . . followed by the regulations . . . After the Prologue and the opening chapter on the kinds of monks, the ascetical program is laid down in three successive articulations: the abbot and his advisers . . . a catalogue of good works . . . and the three capital virtues of the monk: obedience, silence and humility . . . The Second part of the *RB* prescribes the necessary elements of institutional structure and discipline.[92]

Parallel examination of the two texts, the *Benedictine Rule* and the *Kitāb Ādāb al-Murīdīn* of Suhrawardī, will clearly reveal that both manuals have points in common. We might loosely observe that perhaps the

Benedictine Rule concentrates rather more on the practical aspects of community life, though the author is always aware of the *spiritual* reasons for monastic observances.[93] Significantly, Chapter 73, the last of the *Benedictine Rule*, is entitled 'This Rule [is] only a Beginning of Perfection' (*De Hoc quod non Omnis Justitiae Observatio in hac Sit Regula Constituta*).[94] And though Benedict characterizes his 'little rule' as having been 'written for beginners' (*hanc minimam inchoationis regulam descriptam*),[95] there is no doubt that he intends by this phrase 'beginners in the monastic and spiritual life' (i.e. the majority of monks for, perhaps, most of their lives), rather than just the novices as with Suhrawardī's work. Indeed, St Benedict has only one separate chapter in his *Rule* devoted to novices out of a total of 73.[96]

While aspects of what Suhrawardī would regard as *maqāmāt* are clearly present in the *Rule* – for example, the two spiritual stations of *zuhd* (renunciation) and *faqr* (poverty) mentioned by Suhrawardī have their parallels in the renunciation of possessions by the would-be Benedictine monk[97] – it is clear that there is no formal concentration on a Suhrawardīan-type order of *maqāmāt* or *aḥwāl* as such, although the pages of the *Rule* are imbued with the 'character' of some of what the Muslim author might have characterised himself as 'states'. For example, monks are to show 'to God, loving fear' (*amore Deum timeant*).[98] (However, full discussion of such things as *baqā'* and *fanā'* is absent.) In other words, where with Suhrawardī the would-be-mystic is not to progress from one spiritual station to the next until the *ādāb* of the first have been mastered[99] (and these *maqāmāt* themselves form part of a formal and ordered structure of *maqāmāt*, *aḥwāl* and *fawātiḥ* etc), with Benedict, though the spirituality may sometimes be the same in essence, it is far less structured and much more practical. The Benedictine monk, it is true, does have some formal gradations or signposts on his spiritual journey but these are marked by the progression through simple and solemn vows and, for clerics, ordination, rather than a formal progression through *maqāmāt*, much less *aḥwāl*.

The *Benedictine Rule* was a merciful and generous *Rule* which made due allowance for the frailties of the sick and the elderly.[100] Such relaxations or dispensations in the *Rule* as were allowed are obviously paralleled by the much more extensive passages on the *rukhaṣ* in Suhrawardī's text. And this brings us briefly, and neatly, to our final point of comparison, that between the *Rule* as enunciated by Suhrawardī and the *Rule of Life of the Secular Order of Discalced Carmelites*. I have chosen Carmelite tertiaries as the point of comparison here, rather than, say, Benedictine Oblates, to provide a comparison with a fresh perspective and spirituality. The primary point of interest is in the *rukhaṣ* permitted by Suhrawardī and the 'easier' or rather *different*, lifestyle of the secular Carmelites.[101] Secular Carmelites, as the name implies, live *in* the world and, for example, recite a reduced Office of Lauds and Vespers and, if possible, Compline.[102] Secular Carmelites thus share the same spirituality as that of the Friars and Nuns but their lifestyle is quite different. Furthermore, and this is significant, the Carmelite Friars and Nuns of the Order are not expected, or indeed permitted, to adopt the 'dispensations' of the Secular Order. However, as we have seen from our study of Suhrawardī, the regular Ṣūfīs adopted elements of the *Rule* originally designed for the Ṣūfī tertiaries or lay members.[103]

How successful, then, was Suhrawardī in attempting to integrate earthly 'manners' and 'spiritual states' in a single document for novices. Certainly his frame of *adab* appears to work well at first sight. It is perhaps most successful on the practical level. But there is, inevitably perhaps, a tension between the written 'frame' and the material it encapsulates. The various *maqāmāt* and *aḥwāl* are mainly listed but hardly discussed in depth. There is little attempt to show the novice – or regular Ṣūfī for that matter – how to progress from station to station, beyond enjoining a proper achievement of each before progression to the next. The listings of *maqāmāt* and *aḥwāl* give the impression of having been incorporated for the sake of completeness. They have little real *didactic* value in the text especially for the novice or regular Ṣūfī who might aspire later to the higher reaches of the mystical path.

For Milson, apart from its *adab* orientation, the real significance of Suhrawardī's text lay in the fact that 'Abū al-Najīb believed that the Ṣūfī's sphere of activity is within society'.[104] As we have already noted, the high-flying Ṣūfī could indeed return to that society.[105] Both Suhrawardī and Abū Ḥāmid al-Ghazālī did just that in a literal way.[106] Milson thus suggests that 'Abū al-Najīb presents an ethical doctrine that is applicable to social reality'.[107] This is all true. We have, in other words, a *Rule* or guide which is not confined or applicable just to the fastness of the Ṣūfī house but one with a much broader area of action. The key to this, of course, lies primarily in the existence of the 'lay members', rather than just those 'regulars' who returned to society.

But I would like to go beyond Milson here by way of conclusion and suggest that the very existence of these 'lay members', with the *rukhaṣ* built into the *Rule* for them, posed a real problem or even a threat: it incorporated an *element of instability* into what was supposed to be a stable frame of spirituality. It represented moreover, in a very real way, a *decline* from the 'high ground' of a Hujwīrī, whose *Kashf al-Maḥjūb*

Table 1 Al-Suhrawardī (c. 490/1097–563/1168)

Maqāmāt[1]	*Aḥwāl*[2]
Intibāh (awakening out of carelessness)	*Murāqaba* (attentive observation)
Tawba (repentance)	*Qurb* (nearness)
Ināba (returning)	*Maḥabba* (love)
Wara' (moral scrupulosity)	*Rajā'* (hope)
Muḥāsabat al-nafs (examination of the soul)	*Khawf* (fear)
	Ḥayā' (diffidence)
Irāda (aspiration)	*Shawq* (yearning)
Zuhd (renunciation)	*Uns* (intimacy)
Faqr (poverty)	*Ṭuma'nīna* (serenity)
Ṣidq (veracity)	*Yaqīn* (certainty)
Taṣabbur (forbearance [the final station of novices])	*Mushāhada* (experience of vision [the final *ḥāl*])
Ṣabr (patience)	
Riḍā (satisfaction)	The *aḥwāl* are followed by such 'indescribable things' as:[3]
Ikhlāṣ (total sincerity)	
Tawakkul (trust in God)	*Fawātiḥ* (revealed signs)
	Lawā'iḥ (appearances of light)
	Manā'iḥ (graces)

1 The translations here follow Milson, *Sufi Rule*, p. 38; *Ādāb al-Murīdīn*, pp. 20–21.
2 For translations, see ibid.
3 Ibid.

had this to say on the subject of *rukhaṣ*, here translated as 'indulgences' by Nicholson: Speaking of al-Shāfi'ī and Ṣūfism, Hujwīrī notes: 'It is related that he said: "When you see a divine busying himself with indulgences (*rukhaṣ*), no good thing will come from him"'.[108]

Finally, the *rukhaṣ* in Suhrawardī's *Rule* represented, in one sense, a *return to 'society'*, an arena fled by many other Ṣūfīs including Suhrawardī himself, at various times. (By 'society' I mean the 'material', 'secular' world as opposed to the 'spiritual' world, in addition to the usual connotations of the term.)

The three concepts of *instability*, *decline* and *return to 'society'*, which I have extrapolated from the *Kitāb Ādāb al-Murīdīn*, herald – though it is not suggested here that they directly caused in any way – the later degeneration in some of the Orders and some areas of *taṣawwuf* which Arberry[109] and others have graphically described. These are the textual or exegetical semiotic indicators of an *adab*, or frame of manners or conduct for Ṣūfīs, *which has weakened itself from within* albeit with

Table 2 Al-Hujwīrī (d. between 465/1072–469/1077)

Maqāmāt[1]	*Aḥwāl*
Tawba (repentance): *Maqām* of Adam	No formal lists but we may include *inter alia*:
Zuhd (renunciation): *Maqām* of Noah	
Taslīm (resignation): *Maqām* of Abraham	*Maḥabba* (love)[5]
Ināba (contrition): *Maqām* of Moses	*Muḥādatha* (conversation)[6]
Ḥuzn (sorrow): *Maqām* of David	*Musāmara* (nocturnal discourse)[7]
Rajā (hope): *Maqām* of Jesus	
Khawf (fear): *Maqām* of John	Beyond the *ahwāl* lies the grade of *tamkīn* (see the text for definition)
Dhikr (praise): *Maqām* of Muḥammad	
Other *maqāmāt* cited in the text, not in the above list:	
Tawakkul (trust in God)[2]	
Faqr (poverty)[3]	
Riḍā (satisfaction), 'the end of the "stations", and the begining of the "states"'.[4]	

1 Translations here and below by Nicholson, *Kashf al-Maḥjūb*, p. 371. Al-Hujwīrī also provides a list of the 'ten stations of spirits' (p. 265) and a shorter list of stations (p. 181).
2 Ibid., p. 181.
3 Ibid., p. 58.
4 Ibid., p. 182; see also pp. 157, 176–77.
5 Ibid., p. 157; see also p. 309.
6 Ibid., pp. 380–81.
7 Ibid.

(N.B. These Tables do not claim to list all the *maqāmāt* and *aḥwāl* cited by al-Suhrawardī and al-Hujwīrī, but it is hoped that the most important ones are here.)

the best of intentions. The 'return to society' represents in some ways a 'flight from the desert' taking that word in both its spiritual and physical aspects. But a return to the eremitical tradition with its proverbial love of the 'desert' clearly characterised the mediaeval Christian Carthusian and Cistercian reformist Orders.[110] The relaxations by the Carmelites of the Ancient Observance, or Calced Carmelites, of their *Rule* were later followed by the reformist zeal of the discalced St John of the Cross (1542–1591) and St Teresa of Avila (1515–1582).[111] And for the Islamic mystical Orders, the degeneration in some areas of *taṣawwuf* down the centuries which was to follow the death of Abū Najīb al-Suhrawardī and other mystics, was halted by the rise of such Orders as the Sanūsiyya and Tijāniyya.[112]

NOTES

1 My italics.

2 Al-Subkī, *Ṭabaqāt*, (Cairo: al-Maṭba'a al-Ḥusayniyya, 1905–1906, repr. Beirut: Dār al-Ma'rifa, n.d.), vol. 4, p. 256, trans. by J. Spencer Trimingham, *The Sufi Orders in Islam*, (Oxford: Clarendon Press, 1971), p. 34. For a brief life of Abū Najīb al-Suhrawardī, see Menahem Milson, abridged trans. and introduction, *A Sufi Rule for Novices: Kitāb Ādāb al-Murīdīn of Abū al-Najīb al-Suhrawardī*, (Cambridge, Mass., and London: Harvard University Press, 1975), pp. 10–16. [This work is hereafter referred to as Milson, *Sufi Rule*.]

3 See Milson, *Sufi Rule*, p. 13, esp. n. 30.

4 For the Arabic text see Abū Najīb al-Suhrawardī, *Kitāb Ādāb al-Murīdīn*, edited by Menahem Milson, Max, Schloessinger Memorial Series, Texts 2, (Jerusalem: Hebrew University of Jerusalem, Institute of Asian and African Studies, 1977 [distributed by the Magnes Press]). [This work is hereafter referred to as *Ādāb al-Murīdīn*].

5 See above, n. 2.

6 *Adab* is an Arabic and Persian word with a wide variety of meanings. For a survey, see F. Gabrieli, art. '*Adab*', *EI*[2], vol. 1, pp. 175–6. *In a technical Ṣūfī sense* Trimingham defines it as 'the conduct and discipline of the Ṣūfī in relation to his Shaykh and associate Ṣūfīs.' (*The Sufi Orders in Islam*, p. 300). Perhaps one of the best renditions is 'proper behaviour'. This is the sense preferred by Jo-Ann Gross, 'Interpretations of Improper Behaviour in the Hagiographies of Khwāja Aḥrār', paper presented at the conference on 'The Legacy of Mediaeval Persian Sufism', SOAS, University of London, 1990. (A revised version of this paper, entitled 'Authority and Miraculous Behavior: Reflections on *Karāmāt* Stories of Khwāja 'Ubaydullāh Aḥrār' later appeared in L. Lewisohn (ed.), *The Legacy of Mediaeval Persian Sufism*, (London: KNP, 1992), pp. 159–71). As Ibn al-'Arabī shows, *adab* could be 'courtesy' extended towards the Deity Himself when it was a matter of allocating responsibility for good and evil deeds respectively. See William C. Chittick, *Ibn al-Arabi's Metaphysics of Imagination: The Sufi Path of Knowledge*, (Albany: SUNY Press, 1989), pp. 209–210. By contrast, for an excellent review of *Adab as a literary genre*, see S.A. Bonebakker, '*Adab* and the concept of belles-lettres' in Julia Ashtiany *et al.* (eds.), *The Cambridge History of Arabic Literature: 'Abbasid Belles-Lettres*, (Cambridge: Cambridge University Press, 1990), pp. 16–30. (This chapter also contains a brief survey of pre-literary usages, see ibid., pp. 17–19.)

The following valuable sources should also be consulted in any study of *adab*: Dj. Khaleghi-Motlagh and Ch. Pellat, s.v. '*Adab*' in *Encyclopedia Iranica*, vol. 1, pp. 431–44; J. Nurbakhsh, 'The Rules and Manners of the Khānaqāh', *In the Tavern of Ruin*, (New York: KNP, 1975); G. Makdisi, *The Rise of Humanism in Classical Islam and the Christian West*, (Edinburgh: Edinburgh University Press, 1989).

7 Milson, *Sufi Rule*, p. 16.

8 (My italics), ibid., pp. 16–17.

9 See Milson, *Sufi Rule*, p. 13.

10 See, for example, *The Rule of Life of the Secular Order of Discalced*

Carmelites, printed in Michael D. Griffin OCD, *Commentary on the Rule of Life*, The Growth in Carmel Series (Washington: Teresian Charism Press, 1981), pp. 156–167.

11 See 'Lay Affiliation with English Benedictine Monasticism' in Dom Gordon Beattie (ed.), *The Benedictine and Cistercian Monastic Yearbook 1991*, (York: Ampleforth Abbey, 1991), pp. 24–5.

12 Milson, *Sufi Rule*, p. 36, p. 13 n. 30; *Ādāb al-Murīdīn*, p. 17.

13 Indeed, Ibn Baṭṭūṭa was invested with the robe of the Suhrawardī Ṣūfī Order itself: see *Riḥlat Ibn Baṭṭūṭa*, (Beirut: Dār Ṣādir, 1964), pp. 200–202; see also Ian Richard Netton, 'Arabia and the Pilgrim Paradigm of Ibn Baṭṭūṭa: A Braudelian Approach' in Ian Richard Netton (ed.), *Arabia and the Gulf: From Traditional Society to Modern States*, (London: Croom Helm, 1986), p. 38, and idem., 'Myth, Miracle and Magic in the *Riḥla* of Ibn Baṭṭūṭa', *Journal of Semitic Studies*, vol. 29: 1 (Spring 1984), pp. 134–5. [The latter two articles are reprinted in this volume.]

14 Netton, 'Myth, Miracle and Magic', p. 135.

15 Milson, *Sufi Rule*, p. 41; *Ādāb al-Murīdīn*, p. 26.

16 Milson, *Sufi Rule*, p. 43; *Ādāb al-Murīdīn*, p. 31.

17 Milson, *Sufi Rule*, pp. 45–6; *Ādāb al-Murīdīn*, pp. 34–5.

18 See Griffin, *Commentary on the Rule of Life*.

19 See Milson, *Sufi Rule*, pp. 9, 18–20.

20 *Ādāb al-Murīdīn*, p. 68; Milson, *Sufi Rule*, p. 66, see also p. 19.

21 Milson, *Sufi Rule*, p. 19.

22 Ibid., p. 20.

23 See ibid., pp. 25–6. I do not follow, either, the manuscript's division of the *Kitāb Ādāb al-Murīdīn* into 26 unequal chapters (*fuṣūl*).

24 These are my renditions of the Arabic terms *murīd*, *mutawassiṭ*, and '*ārif* or *muntahin*: see Milson, *Sufi Rule*, p. 35; *Ādāb al-Murīdīn*, p. 16.

25 See *Ādāb al-Murīdīn*, p. 16.

26 See Milson, *Sufi Rule*, p. 19.

27 See Milson, *Sufi Rule*, pp. 19–20.

28 *Ādāb al-Murīdīn*, p. 50; Milson, *Sufi Rule*, p. 53.

29 See Milson, *Sufi Rule*, p. 19 n. 53.

30 *Ādāb al-Murīdīn*, p. 50; Milson, *Sufi Rule*, p. 53.

31 *Ādāb al-Murīdīn*, p. 68; Milson, *Sufi Rule*, p. 66.

32 Griffin, *Commentary on the Rule of Life*, p. 12.

33 See *The Rule of Life* in ibid., p. 158. See also Marie Janinek OCDS, 'Aspirants Knock, Seek, and Ask Questions', in *Welcome to Carmel: A Handbook for Aspirants to the Discalced Carmelite Secular Order*, The Growth in Carmel Series, (Washington: Teresian Charism Press, 1982), p. 74.

34 Griffin, *Commentary on the Rule of Life*, p. 13.

35 See ibid., *passim*.

36 See Milson, *Sufi Rule*, p. 20.

37 Ibid., pp. 72–82; *Ādāb al-Murīdīn*, pp. 80–99.

38 Milson, *Sufi Rule*, p. 20.

39 Milson, *Sufi Rule*, p. 73; *Ādāb al-Murīdīn*, p. 82.

40 Milson, *Sufi Rule*, p. 75; *Ādāb al-Murīdīn*, p. 85.

41 Milson, *Sufi Rule*, p. 79; *Ādāb al-Murīdīn*, p. 92.

42 Milson, *Sufi Rule*, p. 80; *Ādāb al-Murīdīn*, p. 95.
43 Milson, *Sufi Rule*, p. 81; *Ādāb al-Murīdīn*, p. 97.
44 Milson, *Sufi Rule*, pp. 18, 82; *Ādāb al-Murīdīn*, p. 98.
45 (my italics) Milson, *Sufi Rule*, p. 82; *Ādāb al-Murīdīn*, pp. 98–9.
46 Milson, *Sufi Rule*, p. 73; *Ādāb al-Murīdīn*, p. 82.
47 See Milson, *Sufi Rule*, p. 67; *Ādāb al-Murīdīn*, p. 69.
48 See Milson, *Sufi Rule*, pp. 81–2; *Ādāb al-Murīdīn*, p. 98.
49 See above, n. 6.
50 See ibid.
51 Milson, *Sufi Rule*, p. 16.
52 Ibid., p. 25.
53 Ibid., p. 45.
54 Reynold A. Nicholson, *The Kashf al-Muḥjūb: The Oldest Persian Treatise on Sufism by 'Alī B. Uthmān Al-Jullābī al-Hujwīrī*, new edn., trans. from the text of the Lahore edn., E.J.W. Gibb Memorial Series, vol. XVII, (London: Luzac, repr. 1970), p. 334.
55 Milson, *Sufi Rule*, pp. 36–7; *Ādāb al-Murīdīn*, p. 18.
56 See Netton, 'Myth, Miracle and Magic' and idem., 'Arabia and the Pilgrim Paradigm of Ibn Baṭṭūṭa'.
57 Milson, *Sufi Rule*, p. 5. One of the best treatments of the *aḥwāl* in English is to be found in Javad Nurbakhsh, *Spiritual Poverty in Sufism*, (London: Khaniqahi Nimatullahi Publications, 1984), see especially Chapter 4, pp. 63–80.
58 Milson, *Sufi Rule*, p. 81; *Ādāb al-Murīdīn*, p. 98.
59 Milson, *Sufi Rule*, p. 36; *Ādāb al-Murīdīn*, p. 17.
60 Ibid.
61 Milson, *Sufi Rule*, p. 36; *Ādāb al-Murīdīn*, p. 98.
62 Milson, *Sufi Rule*, pp. 16–17. See also pp. 20–21, however, where Milson remarks: 'It should be noted that although *Kitāb Ādāb al-Murīdīn* is intended primarily for novices, it presents, in fact, an ethical doctrine for Ṣūfis in general'.
63 (my italics), Nicholson, *Kashf al-Maḥjūb*, pp. 180–81; see also Seyyed Hossein Nasr, *Les Etats Spirituels dans le Soufisme*, (Rome: Accademia Nazionale dei Lincei, 1973), pp. 10–11.
64 Milson, *Sufi Rule*, p. 20.
65 See Nasr, *Les Etats Spirituels*, pp. 15–21.
66 Ibid., p. 21.
67 Ibid.
68 See ibid., pp. 18–19.
69 Milson, *Sufi Rule*, p. 35; *Ādāb al-Murīdīn*, p. 15.
70 Milson, *Sufi Rule*, p. 38; *Ādāb al-Murīdīn*, pp. 20–21.
71 See Milson, *Sufi Rule*, pp. 21–2; for the work of al-Kalābādhī (d. 390/1000), see his *Kitāb al-Ta'arruf li-Madhhab Ahl al-Taṣawwuf*, 2nd edn. (Cairo: Maktabat al-Kulliyyāt al-Azhariyya, 1980); and A.J. Arberry's English translation of the same as *The Doctrine of the Sufis*, (Cambridge University Press, 1977, repr. of 1935 edn.).
72 See Milson, *Sufi Rule*, p. 35 (which omits the translation of the list); *Ādāb al-Murīdīn*, p. 15.
73 See Nicholson, *Kashf al-Maḥjūb*, pp. 267 ff.

74 Ibid., pp. 334–366.
75 Ibid., p. 371.
76 Ibid., p. 236, see also p. 157.
77 Ibid., p. 246 (my italics); see also p. 243.
78 Ibid., p. 371. Nicholson translates the word *tamkīn* as 'steadfastness' (*Kashf al-Maḥjūb*, p. 371). It can also mean 'dignity' and 'authority' in Persian. Julian Baldick's preferred rendition is 'fixity'; see his *Mystical Islam: An Introduction to Sufism*, (London: Tauris, 1989), p. 63.
79 Nicholson, *Kashf al-Maḥjūb*, p. 373.
80 Milson, *Sufi Rule*, p. 38; *Ādāb al-Murīdīn*, p. 21.
81 See *Ādāb al-Murīdīn*, p. 15.
82 See Nicholson, *Kashf al-Maḥjūb*, pp. 242–6.
83 See ibid., pp. 334, 341.
84 Henry Chadwick, *The Early Church*, The Pelican History of the Church, vol. I (Harmondsworth: Penguin, 1967), p. 183.
85 See ibid., p. 179.
86 See *Regula Sancti Benedicti* [hereafter referred to as *RB*] in Timothy Fry OSB (ed.), *RB 1980: The Rule of St Benedict*, in Latin and English with Notes, (Collegeville: Liturgical Press, 1981), pp. 156–297. I am most grateful to Dom Benedict Couch OSB, Prior and Novice Master of Buckfast Abbey (in Buckfastleigh, Devon, England) for sending me a copy of the above edition of the *Rule* (which he uses with his own novices) together with a useful bibliography.
87 *RB*, pp. 190–1.
88 *RB*, pp. 210–11.
89 *RB*, pp. 252–5.
90 *RB*, pp. 292–5.
91 *RB*, ('Introduction'), p. 91.
92 *RB*, ('Introduction'), pp. 91–2.
93 *RB* ('Introduction'), p. 94.
94 *RB*, pp. 294–7.
95 See *RB*, pp. 296–7.
96 See *RB*, pp. 266–71: Chapter 58: 'The Procedure for Receiving Brothers' (*De Disciplina Suscipiendorum Fratrum*). See also pp. 442 ff.
97 See *RB*, pp. 268–9.
98 See *RB*, pp. 294–5.
99 See Milson, *Sufi Rule*, p. 43; Suhrawardī, *Ādāb al-Murīdīn*, p. 29; Compare Hujwīrī, *Kashf al-Maḥjūb*, p. 181.
100 See *RB*, pp. 234–7, 252–3.
101 Griffin, *Commentary on the Rule of Life*, p. 13.
102 See *The Rule of Life* in Griffin, *Commentary on the Rule of Life*, p. 159.
103 See Milson, *Sufi Rule*, p. 20.
104 Ibid., p. 17.
105 Ibid., p. 13 n. 30.
106 Ibid.
107 Ibid., p. 17.
108 Nicholson, *Kashf al-Maḥjūb*, p. 116.
109 See A.J. Arberry, *Sufism: An Account of the Mystics of Islam* (London: Allen & Unwin, 1950), pp. 119ff. Julian Baldwick (*Mystical Islam*, p. 72)

notes significantly: 'It is interesting that, although the Suhrawardī brotherhood became noted for its emphasis on severity, some of its members were also conspicuous for their self-enrichment, collaboration with temporal rulers and enjoyment of worldly pleasures'. However, this does not represent the whole picture and I am grateful to my colleague Dr Leonard Lewisohn for drawing my attention to the way in which scholars have taken other, opposing views regarding *rukhaṣ*. Dr Lewisohn (letter to the author, July 1992) adds the following important caveat to what I have written in this essay:

'Religious tolerance (in the form of *rukhaṣ*), was a dynamic and original element in Ṣūfism which actually prevented decay in the social fabric of mediaeval Islam. This viewpoint has been elaborated by many scholars; see, for instance, F. Meier ('Soufisme et Déclin Culturel' in *Classicisme et Déclin Culturel dans l'Histoire de l'Islam*, Actes du Symposium Internationale d'Histoire de la Civilisation Musulmane, organisé par R. Brunschvig and G.E. Von Grunebaum, [Paris, 1957], where he notes (p. 236, after translating *rukhṣa* as 'tolérance'): 'La disposition du Soufisme au compromis a donc servi ici à enrichir et à élargir la culture religieuse islamique'. *Rukhaṣ* might be as well interpreted as 'tolerance' as much as 'laxity' and 'indulgence' and thus not viewed as a decline from the high ideals of Ṣūfism: for although on the level of one's personal spiritual life, seeking after indulgences may be a decline in discipline, this seems to be less true when it comes to the particular social phenomenon of *rukhaṣ* described by Abū Najīb. And when Abū Najīb's nephew (and founder of the widespread Sufi Order which bears his surname), Abū Ḥafṣ 'Umar Suhrawardī, instituted the Orders of *Futuwwah* – those fraternities of chivalry during the reign of the caliph al-Nāṣir (r. 577/1181–620/1223) – he carried on his uncle's tradition of humanistic tolerance by declaring that 'according to the code of chivalry – unlike the religious Law which does not pardon the sinner who begs forgiveness – if a man commits a sin seventy times over and begs forgiveness seventy times over, he should be excused.' (from his *Treatise on Chivalry*, ed. M. Sarrāf, *Rasā'īl jawānmardān* [Tehran: French–Iran Institute, 1973], p. 133) . . . Western orientalists are at variance concerning the role of Sufism in the cultural decline of Islamdom. If we compare the views of M. Hodgson (see esp. *The Venture of Islam*, II, 455–67) or F. Meier with those of A.J. Arberry on this so-called decline of Sufism, there appears a vast difference of opinion.'

110 I am indebted to my good friend Professor C. Holdsworth, Emeritus Professor of History in the University of Exeter, for valuable advice on the significance of these Orders.

111 See 'Saints of Carmel' in *Welcome to Carmel*, pp. 133–47.

112 See Jamil M. Abun-Nasr, *The Tijaniyya: A Sufi Order in the Modern World*, Middle Eastern Monographs: 7, (London: OUP, 1965); Nicola A. Ziadeh, *Sanūsīya: A Study of a Revivalist Movement in Islam*, (Leiden: E.J. Brill, 1968).

Section Two

TRAVEL

6

IBN JUBAYR

Penitent Pilgrim and Observant Traveller

Abū 'l-Ḥusayn Muḥammad b. Aḥmad b. Jubayr al-Kinānī, known as Ibn Jubayr, was born in Valencia in 1145. His education was a fairly typical and traditional one and it enabled him to gain an appointment as secretary to the Almohad governor of Granada, Abū Sa'īd 'Uthmān b. 'Abd al-Mu'min. Yet Ibn Jubayr's fame in history rests neither upon a bureaucratic super-efficiency nor upon acting as an *éminence grise* behind his master, as many in similar positions did before and after. It was, instead, a by-product of his career, the result of an incident which a less pious and scrupulous man might have laughed away. One day he was called by the governor to write a letter and offered some wine to drink. Mindful of Islam's prohibition on the drinking of wine, Ibn Jubayr refused. This clearly angered the governor who then responded by insisting that his secretary should drink *seven* cups of the wine. Ibn Jubayr, obviously fearing for his life, drank the wine as he was told.

Strangely enough, the circumstances of his unwilling fall from grace are not related to us by Ibn Jubayr himself at the beginning of his journal or travelogue known simply as his *Riḥla*. We are obliged to consult such sources as the seventeenth century *Nafḥ al-Ṭīb* of al-Maqqarī to discover the details. Maqqarī goes on to imply that the governor seems to have regretted his impetuous and insensitive order, for he then filled the wine cup from which Ibn Jubayr had drunk, seven times with gold dinars and gave them to his scribe.

But the affair was not so easily concluded for the scrupulous Ibn Jubayr. He decided to make amends for his 'sin' by journeying to Mecca and using the money to fulfil that pilgrimage obligation incumbent upon every healthy Muslim of visiting the sacred city at least once in a lifetime. Ibn Jubayr's voyage or *riḥla* was thus a journey of expiation and, as such, it has parallels with mediaeval practice in Western Christendom. Just as Ibn Jubayr set out on his *riḥla* to expiate the specific fault of wine-drinking, so the Christian sinner, guilty perhaps of worse crimes like murder or adultery, was sometimes required to travel, even on foot, to Jerusalem to make physical amends for *his* sin. Of course, the moral theologian today, examining Ibn Jubayr's 'crime', might conclude that, since force was used, no subjective guilt can have been incurred by the wine-drinker, whatever the objective gravity of wine-drinking in Islamic ethics. But such a basic moral point does not seem to have occurred to Ibn Jubayr who was a pious rather than a subtle Muslim.

With Abū Sa'īd's permission, and in the company of a medical doctor from Granada, Ibn Jubayr left his native land on 3rd February 1183. He was not to return until 25th April 1185 and he was thus absent from Spain for a little over two years. This might appear a brief space of time if we compare his *riḥla* with that of Islam's *raḥḥāla* par excellence, Ibn Baṭṭūṭa (1304–1368/9 or 1377) who travelled in the fourteenth century; but Ibn Jubayr's *riḥla* was, nonetheless, a period of intense activity and insight for the traveller which the original, and rather bland, Arabic title of his travel journal, *Tadhkira bi'l-Akhbār 'an Ittifāqāt al-Asfār* (translated by Broadhurst as 'An Account of the Events that Befell upon Certain Journeys'), somewhat belies.

There are two interesting, almost curious, features which are worth stressing at the beginning of any account of Ibn Jubayr's *riḥla*. The first is that, though he journeyed in what might be loosely termed 'The Age of the Crusades', he had no apprehensions about travelling on Christian ships. Indeed, the extraordinary freedom of movement enjoyed by Christians and Muslims, especially merchants, in each other's lands was commented upon by Ibn Jubayr who noted that each side gave the other security upon payment of a tax, and he wryly concluded: 'The soldiers engage themselves in their war, while the people are at peace . . . ' (Broadhurst, p.301). And it was not a war which had lacked, or was to lack, ferocity. His *riḥla* was undertaken during a period of consolidation of Muslim power and at a time when the star of the great Ṣalāḥ al-Dīn (Saladin) was in the ascendant. This warrior is referred to in a variety of places by Ibn Jubayr who clearly held him in enormous veneration and admired his exploits. It is perhaps this, more than anything else, which led Ibn Jubayr to write of Ṣalāḥ al-Dīn's attack on the castle of Kerak, situated east of the Dead Sea, in 1184 as if it had been less of the failure that it actually was and to laud the following seizure of Nablus in terms that seem to try and disguise the prior failure at Kerak. Ṣalāḥ al-Dīn's finest hour, however, his overwhelming victory over the army of Jerusalem at the Battle of Ḥaṭṭīn on 4th July 1187, was still in the future and took place more than two years after Ibn Jubayr's return to Spain.

It was against this background, dominated by the shadow of Ṣalāḥ al-Dīn and the clashes of Muslim and crusading armies, that Ibn Jubayr travelled on Christian ships. Right at the beginning of his journey he tells us that he caught a Genoese ship from Ceuta to Alexandria, and later he sought to travel in a similar Christian merchant ship from Acre called a 'salibiyya' (a word deriving from the Arabic *ṣalīb*, a cross). Broadhurst explains that such vessels were so-called because 'the sails were set cross-ways to the mast, or, in other words, were square-rigged'. Ibn Jubayr's motives in such a choice of transport derived, of course, from necessity rather than a liking for Christianity: on the return journey from Acre we sense a kind of relief in Ibn Jubayr's comment that the Muslim passengers had managed to obtain berths which were apart from those of the Frankish travellers, and he sends up a prayer to be relieved soon of the company of more than two thousand Christian pilgrims who joined the ship. Elsewhere, he does not hesitate to inveigh against those Christians whom he dislikes: he describes the leper King Baldwin IV, who ruled both Jerusalem and Acre, as a pig and he curses the Franks. It is his fervent prayer that the city of Acre, in which 'unbelief and unpiousness . . . burn fiercely, and pigs [Christians] and crosses abound' (Broadhurst, p.318), will be returned to the fold of Islam.

The second noteworthy feature about the *riḥla* of Ibn Jubayr is that, though he travels much by sea, he is not a mariner at heart: he both fears and dislikes the sea. This is evident from his appalled descriptions of some of the storms which he encounters. On the outward voyage, having left Sardinia, he describes how a ferocious storm blew up which was so bad that it snapped the spar of one of the small sails. He and the other Muslims on board were filled with despair and spent much time in praying to God to deliver them from the storm. His relief and thankfulness at the eventual abating of the wind and the calming of the sea is vividly expressed in his paean of gratitude to God which follows. Later on, having embarked on a small Red Sea ship called a *jilaba* from 'Aydhāb to Jiddah, he is again filled with despair by another storm, but in the morning God, that Helper in every difficulty, brings relief. As Ibn Jubayr himself later says, the passengers lived and died many times on that voyage.

This was not, however, his worst encounter with the sea. The most traumatic experience of all took place off the coast of Messina on the return voyage when he was actually shipwrecked. Having entered the famous Straits, the flow of whose waters he compared to the bursting of the great South Arabian dam of Ma'rib in *circa* AD 542 (see *Qur'ān* 34:14–15) the ship was driven aground on the Sicilian shore by the powerful wind. Ibn Jubayr tells us that the ship, which had two rudders, 'stuck by its keel to the ground' (Broadhurst, p.336), and the captain of the vessel was unable to lower the sail because of the ferocious wind which continued to buffet the ship together with the waves. He was then obliged to cut it piece by piece. The Christian passengers gave in to despair while the Muslims 'submitted themselves to the decree of their Lord'. The captain then tried to make the ship fast with one of the anchors but to no avail. A long boat was able to make one single journey to safety with some of the men and women but it was then smashed to pieces on the beach. Finally, the storm ended and the terrified passengers were rescued by a number of small boats which came out from the city. King William II of Sicily himself came out to see what had happened and he generously gave some of the more indigent Muslims enough money to pay for their rescue. Ibn Jubayr was saved but, by the following day, the ship on which he had travelled had been shattered by the inclement weather. It will now be readily appreciated why Ibn Jubayr disliked and feared the sea!

His voyage stretched from Spain in the West to the holy cities of Mecca and Medina in the East. It embraced in its path many of the other great cities of Islam including Alexandria, Cairo, Baghdad and Damascus. For all of these he is a fascinating and informed source, and in much of what he describes he allows his own temperament, character and emotions – fear as well as joy, pity as well as choler – to shine through. Thus, on arriving in Alexandria on the outward journey he was particularly vexed by the treatment of the Muslims at the hands of the Egyptian customs officials. He describes the great confusion and the crowds in the customs area where the belongings of the Muslims were searched and piled by the customs men who even felt inside the travellers' waistbands to see if anything had been hidden there. In an added refinement of customs procedures – which today's modern customs officers have yet to adopt! – the owners of the luggage were then obliged to swear an oath that they had not concealed anything else. The confusion which reigned inevitably meant that much of the property disappeared forever from its owner's sight. Ibn Jubayr noted with disgust that the immigration procedure must have been unknown to his hero Ṣalāḥ al-Dīn who would surely otherwise have put a stop to it. But he was swift to add that this was the *only* criticism he would make of the lands ruled by Ṣalāḥ al-Dīn.

Ibn Jubayr is an extremely valuable source for the architecture which he saw in the Near and Middle East and he has placed students of mediaeval Islamic art and architecture perpetually in his debt. This is especially the case in his descriptions of such cities as Alexandria, Mecca and Medina. The great pharos or lighthouse of Alexandria, one of the wonders of antiquity, was still standing when he visited that city. He regarded it as one of the marvels of the city, a monument whose size defied description. It was very old, he says, and visible from a distance of more than seventy miles. He saw it from his own ship at a distance of some twenty miles. Ibn Jubayr tells us he was informed that it stood more than 150 *qāma* in height (1 *qāma* – a man's height) and he was amazed at the number of its stairways, entrances and rooms. He was delighted to find a mosque built in its summit, thereby consecrating a monument from pagan antiquity to Islam, and one Thursday he himself prayed in this room. His description does not hint at any physical decay in the fabric of the lighthouse; later, earthquakes took their toll, however, and when Ibn Baṭṭūṭa visited the same monument in 1326 he found one of its faces in ruins, and on another visit in 1349 he 'found that it [the lighthouse] had fallen into so ruinous a condition that it was impossible to enter it or to climb up to the doorway' (Gibb, p.19).

It is, however, for his description of Mecca and Medina that Ibn Jubayr has justly achieved most fame from his *Riḥla*. This should not surprise us: as A. Miquel points out in his *Encyclopaedia of Islam* article on that later traveller, Ibn Baṭṭūṭa, 'the traditional *riḥla* was centered round the visit to the Holy Places of Arabia'. And though Ibn Jubayr does not perpetually harp on the subject of expiation, those twin cities were, nonetheless, the whole object of his journey and focal point for his injured conscience. The quality of his descriptions was such that Ibn Baṭṭūṭa himself, and/or his editor Ibn Juzayy, did not hesitate to plagiarise some of them quite shamelessly and, up to our own day, Ibn Jubayr's *Riḥla* has constituted a valuable archive for much of the architecture and art which the traveller saw in the holy cities.

Much of the value of his account lies in its precision and detail, with considerable attention being paid to measurements, dimensions and distances, large and small. Thus the Well of Zamzam is twenty-four paces from 'the Black Corner'. The depth of the Well is eleven times the height of a man and the depth of the water itself is seven times. The Black Stone is said to penetrate two cubits in length into the wall of the Ka'ba. The *kiswa* or covering of the sacred Ka'ba comprises thirty-four pieces. Many other measurements like this are given in addition to the more usual ones which one might expect, like the dimensions of the Meccan mosque itself.

The worth of his writing is again apparent in his meticulous account of this Ka'ba: it has five stained glass windows of Iraqi provenance. One is set in the middle of the ceiling and the others are at each corner of the building. There are two chests with Qur'āns immediately inside the entrance below a pair of silver doors which resemble windows. And so on. It is, indeed, something of a euphemism to describe Ibn Jubayr as a precise observer, for he is much, much more. His whole narrative, moreover, is infused with a reverent joy which derived from all the sights and ceremonies which he witnessed in the holy city, and which must also have come from the realisation that his 'sin' was now expiated.

Ibn Jubayr spent nine months in Mecca and then, like many pilgrims before and after him, visited Medina where lay the tombs of Muḥammad and early *khulafā'* like Abū Bakr and 'Umar. He then turned for home, heading across the desert to Kufa. From Kufa he travelled to Acre via Baghdad, Mosul, Aleppo and Damascus; and it was on his voyage aboard a Genoese ship, caught in Acre for Messina, that the shipwreck described earlier in this essay occurred. He arrived back in Granada on 25th April 1185.

It is clear that this first *riḥla* gave Ibn Jubayr a taste for travel: he made two other journeys which we know about but, alas, have no account of: one from 1189 to 1191, and in 1217 a final voyage to Alexandria, where he died on 29th November 1217. The first period was contemporary with the siege of Acre which the Muslim garrison eventually gave up in 1191. Ibn Jubayr's great hero, Ṣalāḥ al-Dīn, died in February 1193 and the years 1213–1215 saw a fresh call to the Crusade by Pope Innocent III, followed by the capture of Damietta in 1219. But the whole crusading drive was in decline and other forces were emerging. In 1258, only forty-one years after the death of Ibn Jubayr, the Mongols sacked Baghdad and finally extinguished the moribund 'Abbāsid caliphate. In the light of all this it is a pity that Ibn Jubayr has left us no accounts of his second and third journeys which took place at times of great political flux.

Pellat has described the *Riḥla* of Ibn Jubayr as 'the first and one of the best of the works of this kind' which has 'served as model to many other pilgrims', and he is right. Not only is the work a mine of valuable information but, in J.N. Mattock's words, it 'is interesting, simply written and well-detailed; it does very well what it is intended to do: describe the places that he [Ibn Jubayr] visits, so that their main features are clear to his audience'. It established a genre in Arabic literature which would be pursued by other author-travellers, most notably Ibn Baṭṭūṭa, but which would not always make the cities of Mecca and Medina the centrepiece or focal point of the narrative. Yet for Ibn Jubayr they had to be: his 'sin' demanded it.

SOURCES AND FURTHER READING

R.J.C. Broadhurst, *The Travels of Ibn Jubayr*, translated from the original Arabic, (London: Jonathan Cape, 1952); A. Gateau, 'Quelques observations sur l'intérèt du voyage d'Ibn Jubayr', *Hespéris*, XXXVI (1949), pp. 289–312; H.A.R. Gibb, *The Travels of Ibn Baṭṭūṭa A.D. 1325–1354*, vol. I, translated with revisions and notes from the Arabic text edited by C. Defrémery and B.R. Sanguinetti, (Cambridge: Cambridge University Press for the Hakluyt Society, 1958); Ibn Baṭṭūṭa, *Riḥla*, (Beirut: Dār Ṣādir, 1964); Ibn Jubayr, *Riḥla*, (Beirut: Dār Ṣādir, 1964); J.N. Mattock, 'The Travel Writings of Ibn Jubair and Ibn Baṭṭūṭa', *Glasgow Oriental Society Transactions*, XXI (1965–6), pp. 35–46; A. Miquel, art. *Encyclopaedia of Islam*, 2nd edn., vol. III, 'Ibn Baṭṭūṭa'; Ian Richard Netton, 'Myth, Miracle and Magic in the *Riḥla* of Ibn Baṭṭūṭa', *Journal of Semitic Studies*, XXIX/1 (Spring 1984), pp. 131–140; Ch. Pellat, art. *Encyclopaedia of Islam*, 2nd edn., vol. III, 'Ibn Djubayr'. The best account of the crusading period in which Ibn Jubayr travelled is to be found in K.M. Setton (ed.), *A History of the Crusades*, (Madison, Milwaukee & London: University of Wisconsin Press): see especially vol. I. *The First Hundred Years*, ed. by M.W. Baldwin (2nd edn., 1969) and vol. II: *The Later Crusades, 1189–1311*, ed. by R.L. Wolff & H.W. Hazard (2nd edn. 1969).

7

MYTH, MIRACLE AND MAGIC IN THE *RIḤLA* OF IBN BAṬṬŪṬA

The *riḥla* in mediaeval Arabic literature is, perhaps, best regarded as an art form rather than a formal geography.* Indeed, Janssens believes that Ibn Baṭṭūṭa considered the actual travel as an art as well, one that had its own set rules and regulations including a canon not to retrace one's steps wherever possible.[1] But academic, scientific geography did not interest Ibn Baṭṭūṭa: he contributed nothing to its development though he assuredly profited from its knowledge.[2] Where he *is* of use to historians of geography, he is 'the supreme example of *le géographe malgré lui*' as H.A.R. Gibb elegantly put it.[3]

The itineraries and purposes of the travel, coupled with the interests and prejudices of the narrator, dictated the artistic format in which they were set down. Differences in the first created clear differences in the second, resulting in some variation in type within the *riḥla* genre itself. The most obvious illustration of this is seen in a brief comparison of the *Riḥlas*[4] of Ibn Jubayr (1145–1217; travelled mainly between 1183 and 1185) and Ibn Baṭṭūṭa (1304–1368/9 or 1377; travelled between 1325 and 1354).

Pellat has ranked Ibn Jubayr's *Riḥla* as 'the first and one of the best of the works of this kind' providing a model which many, including Ibn Juzayy (Ibn Baṭṭūṭa's scribe and editor), did not hesitate to plagiarise.[5] So it is not surprising the Ibn Jubayr's and Ibn Baṭṭūṭa's works should have a number of similar literary features.[6] In addition, they reveal several shared human interests and even a few worries held in common. Thus both men disliked the sea, though obliged to make much use of it.[7] Both were particularly interested in recording the many types and sources of water available.[8] Both were Mālikīs and they visited several of the same cities in the course of their travels.

Nonetheless, leaving aside the basic difference in the lengths of journey undertaken by each man and the difference in length of each narrative, it is clear that the *Riḥla* of Ibn Baṭṭūṭa represents a considerable development upon that of Ibn Jubayr. The latter's is a pilgrimage *riḥla* of expiation undertaken to make amends for the specific fault of wine drinking.[9] As such, it has the twin cities of Mecca and Medina as its focus and goal. The development in Ibn Baṭṭūṭa's work is characterised primarily by a turning away from the *ḥajj* as the focal point and motivation of the narrative[10] to the interests of the author himself, which assume a greater primacy than in the earlier work of Ibn Jubayr. The *riḥla* with Ibn Baṭṭūṭa becomes a vehicle or frame within which that author feels free to incorporate a multitude of prejudices,[11] interests and boasts, even to the extent of trying to impress his readers with stories of journeys which he could not possibly have undertaken.[12] It is being used, in other words, in a manner akin to that of the frame stories in *Kalīla wa-Dimma* and the *Panchatantra*.

This essay then, proposes to treat the *Riḥla* of Ibn Baṭṭūṭa as a 'frame' and examine, in that context, some of the mythical and miraculous tales to which the author refers. For in this sphere, as elsewhere, Ibn Baṭṭūṭa is very much 'a cataloguer and a compiler'.[13] Miquel has also characterised him as 'un merveilleux représentant du musulman de son temps'[14] and his *Riḥla* is not only an Arabic biographical and topographical source *par excellence* for the age but a marvellous compendium of anecdote, folklore, and descriptions of myths, miracles and magic, many of which derive from the author's infatuation with the Ṣūfī orders and holy men of the day.[15] It is worth recalling at this point that part of the formal title of his work was *Gharā'ib al-Amṣār wa 'Ajā'ib al-Asfār*, and there is far more incidental anecdote in Ibn Baṭṭūṭa's *Riḥla* than in that of Ibn Jubayr, which is also much more sparing in the number of myths and miracles which it describes. Furthermore, though Ibn Jubayr is mildly interested in Ṣūfism,[16] it is not a consuming passion as with Ibn Baṭṭūṭa.

There are two main kinds of myth in Ibn Baṭṭūṭa's *Riḥla*: firstly – using the word fairly loosely – that perpetrated by himself where he wishes us to believe that he has visited areas in which he has not, in fact, set foot. These myths are elaborated at greater length in the footnotes and need not detain us here.[17] The second kind is that which Ibn Baṭṭūṭa hears from others, and this variety frequently includes descriptions of miracles or magical events by Ṣūfīs or other holy men. A related area which must also be considered, particularly in any assessment of the traveller's gullibility or credibility, is his description of miracles and magic which he himself witnesses or claims to have witnessed.

The references in the *Riḥla* to the diverse Ṣūfī orders and to Ṣūfism provide some of the clearest evidence that Ibn Baṭṭūṭa's religious interests ranged far beyond the narrow legal confines of the Mālikī *madhhab* which he espoused as a *qāḍī*. Not only did he betray a kind of appalled fascination when he witnessed the excesses of orders like the Rifā'iyya, whose adherents near Wāsiṭ he saw indulging in fire-dancing and fire-eating during the *samā'*,[18] but he actually affiliated himself to some of the orders: for example, he had already joined this same Rifā'ī order in Jerusalem;[19] he was invested in the Suhrawardī order in Iṣfahān;[20] and he received yet another Ṣūfī robe of investiture from the Sharīf Quṭb al-Dīn Ḥaydar al-'Alawī in Ūja, Sind.[21] Trimingham has warned that not too much significance is to be read into these investitures of Ibn Baṭṭūṭa, who seems to have been able to collect such affiliations without under going any sort of formal novitiate.[22] Apart from on one occasion, which will be noted later, Ibn Baṭṭūṭa cannot, in his dealings with Ṣūfīs, be said to have fully embraced the Ṣūfī path. Even so, the orders remained a source of endless fascination for him.

Arising from this interest are what might be classified as Ibn Baṭṭūṭa's Ṣūfī or Ṣūfī-type myths: these are the miraculous or magical stories recounted to the traveller about a variety of holy men, pious *qāḍīs* and Ṣūfīs, encompassing a range of paranormal phenomena. Such accounts are sometimes prefaced with the phrase 'a miracle of this Shaykh' (*karāma li-hādhā al-Shaykh*) or something similar. Thus Ibn Baṭṭūṭa was told about the pious Shaykh Jamāl al-Dīn who lived in the cemetery of Damietta. During an exchange of words with the *qāḍī* Ibn al-'Amīd, in which the *qāḍī* derided him for having shaved off his beard, the Shaykh suddenly grew a fine black beard, then a white one and then caused his face to revert to its initial beardless state. The astonished *qāḍī* became a disciple of the Shaykh.[23]

In Shīrāz, Ibn Baṭṭūṭa heard about two episodes which both slightly recall the story of Androcles and the lion. In each case wild animals refrained from killing a holy man. The first concerned the *qāḍī* of Shīrāz Majd al-Dīn, who incurred the wrath of Sultan Muḥammad Khudābanda and was condemned to be thrown to a group of huge vicious dogs which had been specially trained to attack and devour human beings. But when the dogs were set on Majd al-Dīn, they became tame and friendly before him and did not harm him in any way.[24]

In the second episode, the Shaykh Abū 'Abdullāh b. Khafīf, who held 'a high rank among the saints', was spared from being killed by a herd of wild elephants in Ceylon while his companions, who in hunger had eaten the flesh of an elephant which the Shaykh refused, were all killed. This is another episode described by the *Riḥla* as miraculous.[25]

There are several other tales as well recounted by Ibn Baṭṭūṭa throughout the *Riḥla* similar in kind to these. None is particularly extraordinary in a Ṣūfi context and our traveller seems to have accepted many such stories as logical confirmations of the sanctity of the saint or saint's tomb he has visited or heard about. Thus in Delhi he notes that people endow the pious Maḥmūd al-Kubbā with the ability to produce food for all visitors and to conjure, from no apparent store of his own, gifts of gold, silver and clothing: 'Many miraculous graces have been operated through him and he has acquired a great reputation for them'.[26] But occasionally, a note of scepticism creeps in, as where Ibn Baṭṭūṭa says of the Shaykh Atā Awliyā', whom he encounters in the 'mountains of Pashāy' before reaching Parwān, and who claims an age of three hundred and fifty and the ability to grow new hair and teeth every hundred years: 'I had some doubts about him, and God knows how much truth there was in what he claimed'.[27]

Ibn Baṭṭūṭa's alleged credulity should only be partly assessed by reference to those miracles, extraordinary phenomena and examples of magic which he himself claims to have witnessed. Commentators have tended to stress this credulity but, as Gibb has pointed out, it was not unlimited.[28] It is true that he believed holy men could have foreknowledge of his dreams and could interpret them accurately.[29] The antics of a juggler in Khansā (Hang-Chow) made him feel physically ill: he claimed to have seen the juggler climb a rope after one of his apprentices and then, out of sight, dismember the boy and cast the limbs down to his audience. The act ended with the juggler putting the pieces of the dismembered corpse together and kicking the body into life again! It was left for a neighbouring *qāḍī* to tell Ibn Baṭṭūṭa: 'By God, there was no climbing or coming down or cutting up of limbs at all; the whole thing is just hocus-pocus'.[30]

If we add to such accounts Ibn Baṭṭūṭa's descriptions of his miraculous escape near Kūl (Koel) on the shoulders of a saint[31] and of the levitating yogi in Delhi, whose actions caused Ibn Baṭṭūṭa to faint,[32] it is small wonder that some have chosen to regard Ibn Baṭṭūṭa as an indiscriminate purveyor of fantasy.

Yet to hold such a view is somewhat one-sided and, indeed, misleading for there are other episodes in the *Riḥla* which serve as a balance for all this. Ibn Baṭṭūṭa remains 'prudently non-committal'[33] when informed by the terrified sailors manning his ship that they have witnessed the legendary rukh which, at first, they mistook for a mountain.[34] We have already noted his scepticism regarding the saint who claimed to be able to regenerate his teeth and hair every hundred years; and when he was told of yogis able to assume the shape of tigers, he refused to believe what he had heard.[35] If such expressions of scepticism and incredulity are placed alongside the episodes mentioned above where Ibn Baṭṭūṭa betrays a very real credulity, it can only be concluded that the traveller is highly selective in what he chooses to believe, though perhaps predisposed in favour of the miraculous by (a) his predilection for Ṣūfis and other holy men and (b) an inability to explain adequately the paranormal phenomena which he actually thinks he has witnessed. It is true that Ibn Baṭṭūṭa claims to have witnessed or experienced the episodes in the Khansā/Delhi examples cited above, and only to have heard about some of the next set: but one cannot argue from this that he is more disposed to believe what he thinks he sees than what he hears about. As has been shown earlier, he is inclined to believe many of the 'holy men' stories we have mentioned, even though they are received at second hand.

Ibn Baṭṭūṭa stands at the beginning of the age of decay in the Ṣūfī orders. His credulity, such as it was, would later be magnified a hundredfold in others with few of the caveats which pertain to him. A.J. Arberry sums up the situation as it developed in a nutshell: 'It was inevitable, as soon as legends of miracles became attached to the names of the great mystics, that the credulous masses should applaud imposture more than true devotion; the cult of saints, against which orthodox Islam ineffectually protested, promoted ignorance and superstition, and confounded charlatanry with lofty speculation. To live scandalously, to act impudently, to speak unintelligibly – this was the easy highroad to fame, wealth and power'.[36]

Ibn Baṭṭūṭa has been described as a theologian as well as an indefatigable *raḥḥāla*. Gibb noted: 'It was because he was a theologian and because of his interest in theologians that he undertook his travels at all'.[37] Aga Mahdi Husain believes that Gibb identified the roles and functions of *qāḍī* and *mutakallim*, and maintains that Gibb's statement supports his own conclusion that Ibn Baṭṭūṭa wished to become a *qāḍī* in China.[38]

There seems to be a slight confusion here. It is true that Ibn Baṭṭūṭa was a professional canon lawyer, but there is little evidence in the *Riḥla* that he was overwhelmingly interested in, or excited by, *kalām* as such, or even in sectarian theology. His dislike of Shī'ism, for example, did not lead him into long polemical discussions of Shī'ī theology which he dictated to Ibn Juzayy. On the contrary, on a minor note, he frequently showed considerable respect for many of the saints revered by Shī'ism like 'Alī and al-Ḥusayn.[39] He certainly sought out many of the leading scholars and jurists of his day, but he was motivated as much by his predilection for Islamic law and a desire to collect 'academic qualifications'[40] as by any interest in dogmatic or scholastic theology.

It is because he was much less a traditional theologian than a canon lawyer – and a clear distinction should be made between the two – that Gibb's surprise at finding him 'so deeply interested in and so sympathetic in general towards the darwīshes and Sūfis' is misplaced. His affectionate interest in the mystical was possible precisely because he had not become one of those 'average' theologians specified by Gibb who 'regarded [the Ṣūfis] with suspicion, if not with aversion, for various reasons, religious and secular'. And it is precisely because the mystics and holy men whom Ibn Baṭṭūṭa encountered did not in turn despise Ibn Baṭṭūṭa as a theologian armed with a rigorous 'formalism and cult of the letter' that the traveller's interest was sustained and, indeed, flourished.[41]

There is another way of viewing Ibn Baṭṭūṭa and that is as the orthodox *qāḍī* whose personal piety and interest in Ṣūfism and related subjects at one point – and one point only – in his life led him actually to embrace the ascetic path. In this there are parallels with the life of the great theologian and Ṣūfi al-Ghazālī (1058–1111). Al-Ghazālī, educated in his youth by Ṣūfis, among others, eventually turned his back on his professorship, and abandoned his students at the Niẓāmiyya College in Baghdad for the Ṣūfi life.[42] Though al-Ghazālī's embracing of Ṣūfism certainly lasted longer than Ibn Baṭṭūṭa's, this should not lead us to underestimate what that traveller did.

It was, Gibb believes, 'a genuine act of world-renunciation',[43] and the event tends to undermine, here, Trimingham's sweeping statement that no-one could possibly claim Ibn Baṭṭūṭa was a Ṣūfi.[44] Having been first befriended by the Sultan of Delhi, Muḥammad ibn Tughluq, Ibn Baṭṭūṭa then fell into disgrace. He was placed under armed guard but later unexpectedly released. He tells us that he then withdrew from the Sultan's service and entered that of a pious Shaykh Kamāl al-Dīn 'Abdullāh al-Ghārī. With him, Ibn Baṭṭūṭa for five whole months gave himself up to pious works and an austere life in which he even tried to emulate the severe fasts of his Shaykh and in which he dressed as a mendicant.[45]

There seems little reason to doubt the sincerity of Ibn Baṭṭūṭa's ascetic conversion at this point and, had he not been summoned back into the Sultan's service and sent as ambassador to China, it is most likely that it would have continued. For it is clear from the *Riḥla* that Ibn Baṭṭūṭa's narrow escape from death at the hands of the bloodthirsty ruler had made a deep spiritual impact on him: during his confinement by the Sultan he had fasted rigorously and recited the Qur'ān over and over again.[46] Is it fanciful to suppose that the embracing of the ascetic life on his unexpected release was the fulfilment of some vow which the captive Ibn Baṭṭūṭa had made? Whatever the truth of the matter, it is also clear that Ibn Baṭṭūṭa's flight to a life of poverty and hardship was not a political act designed to make him escape the notice of the ruler: he did not succeed in escaping the latter's capricious attention nor even try to. As Ibn Baṭṭūṭa states: 'When the Sultan was informed of my leaving the world he summoned me. . . I entered his presence dressed as a mendicant. . .' And a genuine devotion, rather than political calculation, prevented Ibn Baṭṭūṭa from re-entering the Sultan's service immediately.[47]

In this whole episode, Ibn Baṭṭūṭa, for the first and last time, emulated al-Ghazālī in the latter's flight from academe to a Ṣūfī retreat in Ṭūs. The text of the *Riḥla* as dictated by the traveller in middle age provided not only a framework in which he could freely parade the 'Berber's interest'[48] in Ṣūfīs and holy men which had haunted his travels, but an opportunity to display, as a jewel within that frame, the point at which his interest became transmuted into a genuine ascetic devotion. For a short period, the fascinated outside observer became an inside participant.

Beckingham has summed up Ibn Baṭṭūṭa's intentions in his *riḥla* very neatly: 'If one looks for the motive of his travel, or perhaps one should say the pretext, I think it was the accumulation of what in Arabic is called *baraka*, the blessings both in this world and the next which would come from visiting holy places and obtaining the blessings of saintly men'.[49] According to this, Ibn Baṭṭūṭa must have accumulated much *baraka* in India during his ascetic interlude.

NOTES

* The following abbreviations are used in the footnotes:

Broadhurst	*The Travels of Ibn Jubayr*, tr. R.J.C. Broadhurst, London, 1952.
Gibb, *Selections*	H.A.R. Gibb, *Ibn Battūta: Travels in Asia and Africa 1325–1354*, London, 1929.
Gibb, *Travels*	H.A.R. Gibb, *The Travels of Ibn Baṭṭūṭa A.D. 1325–1354*, translated from the Arabic text edited by C. Defrémery and B.R. Sanguinetti, 3 vols., Cambridge, 1958–71. [Vol. IV was published in 1994]
IB, *Riḥla*	Ibn Baṭṭūṭa, *Riḥla*, Beirut 1964 (follows the text of Defrémery and Sanguinetti).
IJ, *Riḥla*	Ibn Jubayr, *Riḥla*, Beirut, 1964.

1 Herman F. Janssens, *Ibn Batouta 'le Voyageur de l'Islam' (1304–1369)*, (Brussels, 1948), pp. 83–4; IB, *Riḥla*, p. 191; Gibb, *Travels*, II, p. 283.

2 Janssens, *op. cit.*, pp. 23, 25.

3 Gibb, *Selections*, p. 12. Gibb regards Ibn Baṭṭūṭa's *Riḥla* as 'first and foremost a human diary, in which the tale of facts is subordinated to the interests and preoccupations of the diarist and his audience' (ibid., p. 2); see also Janssens, *op. cit.*, p. 34.

4 The convention is adopted in this essay of referring to the work of each of these authors simply by the title *Riḥla*. The original title of Ibn Jubayr's work was *Tadhkira bi 'l-Akhbār 'an-Ittifāqāt al-Asfār* while that of Ibn Baṭṭūṭa's was *Tuḥfat al-Nuẓẓār fī Gharā'ib al-Amṣār wa 'Ajā'ib al-Asfār*. With regard to the latter, no attempt is made here in this essay to differentiate between the work of Ibn Baṭṭūṭa and that of his scribe and editor Ibn Juzayy.

5 Ch. Pellat, *EI*[2], art. 'Ibn Djubayr'.

6 The plagiarism of Ibn Juzayy/Ibn Baṭṭūṭa has been carefully documented by Gibb, e.g. see his *Travels*, I, pp. 178–9, 190 ff., for copied or abridged descriptions of the environs of Medina and Mecca; IB, *Riḥla* pp. 124–5, 131 ff. J.N. Mattock compares Ibn Juzayy's/Ibn Baṭṭūṭa's general style unfavourably with that of Ibn Jubayr: see his 'The travel writings of Ibn Jubair and Ibn Baṭṭūṭa', *Glasgow Oriental Society Transactions*, XXI (1965–6), pp. 38, 41.

7 E.g. IJ, *Riḥla*, pp. 9–11, 52, Broadhurst, pp. 26–8, 69–70; IB, *Riḥla*, pp. 321, 601, Gibb, *Travels*, II, pp. 468–9, *idem, Selections*, p. 261; see also Janssens, *op. cit.*, pp. 84–5, and the whole of M. Mollat's instructive article 'Ibn Batoutah et la Mer', *Travaux et Jours*, XVIII (1966), pp. 53–70. Interestingly, neither man was unwilling to travel aboard Christian ships: e.g. IJ, *Riḥla*, p. 271, Broadhurst, p. 313; IB, *Riḥla*, p. 283, Gibb, *Travels*, II, pp. 415–6; see also A. Gateau, 'Quelques observations sur l'intérêt du voyage d'Ibn Jubayr', *Hespéris*, XXXVI (1949), pp. 293–5; Gibb, *Selections*, pp. 25–6.

8 E.g. IJ, *Riḥla*, pp. 44–5, 49, 58, Broadhurst, pp. 63, 67, 75; IB, *Riḥla*, pp. 61, 203, 402, Gibb, *Travels*, I, p. 82, II, p. 299, III, p. 603.

9 See al-Maqqarī, *Nafḥ al-Ṭīb*, ed. Iḥsān 'Abbās, (Beirut, 1968), II, pp. 385–6.

10 A. Miquel, *EI*[2], art. 'Ibn Baṭṭūṭa'.

11 The prejudices of Ibn Baṭṭūṭa, like his antipathy to Shī'ism, are well-known and frequently derive from his Islamic upbringing and education. They have been carefully surveyed by A. Miquel, 'L'Islam d'Ibn Baṭṭūṭa', *BEO*, XXX (1978), pp. 75–83.

12 The two most suspect and notorious episodes are the journeys which Ibn Baṭṭūṭa claims to have made to Bulghār and to, or in, China: *Riḥla*, pp. 338, 627 ff, Gibb, *Travels*, II, pp. 490–1; *idem, Selections*, p. 282 ff. See also S. Janicsek, 'Ibn Baṭṭūṭa's journey to Bulghār: is it a fabrication?', *JRAS* (1929), pp. 791–800; Gibb, *Selections*, pp. 13–14, 368–9 n. 1; Janssens, *op. cit.*, pp. 101–3; Miquel, *EI*[2] art. 'Ibn Baṭṭūṭa'. There are other suspicious episodes as well and, as Ivan Hrbek reminds us in his magisterial article on the vexing problem of chronology in Ibn Baṭṭūṭa's *Riḥla*, '. . . it should be kept in mind . . . that [the *Riḥla*] contains many contradictory facts and

statements. . .'; see his 'The chronology of Ibn Baṭṭūṭa's travels', *ArO*, XXX (1962), p. 401. For Hrbek's views on the Bulghār episode, which he emphasises is the only example of proven fiction in the *Riḥla*, see ibid., pp. 471–3. T. Yamamoto believes that Ibn Baṭṭūṭa must have visited China; see his 'On Ṭawālisī described by Ibn Baṭṭūṭa', *Memoirs of the Research Department of the Toyo Bunko (the Oriental Library)*, VIII (1936), p. 103.

13 Mattock, *op. cit*, p. 38.

14 Miquel, 'Ibn Bat't'ût'a: trente années de voyages de Pékin au Niger', *Les Africains*, I, ed. Ch.-A. Julien *et alii*, (Paris, 1977), p. 128.

15 See below.

16 See, for example, his delight in the Ṣūfī *samā': Riḥla*, p. 256, Broadhurst, p. 297.

17 See n. 12 above.

18 *Riḥla*, p. 184, Gibb, *Travels*, II, pp. 273–4.

19 *Riḥla*, p. 59, Gibb, *Travels*, I, p. 80.

20 *Riḥla*, p. 201, Gibb, *Travels*, II, pp. 296–7.

21 *Riḥla*, p. 403, Gibb, *Travels*, III, p. 604.

22 J. Spencer Trimingham, *The Sufi Orders in Islam*, (Oxford, 1971), pp. 36, 185, 227; see also Gibb, *Travels*, I, p. 80, n. 47.

23 *Riḥla*, pp. 34–5, Gibb, *Travels*, I, pp. 38–9.

24 *Riḥla*, pp. 205–6, Gibb, *Travels*, II, pp. 303–4. This miraculous escape clearly made a deep impression on Ibn Baṭṭūṭa, for he refers to it again in connection with Muḥammad ibn Tughluq's generosity and mentions a gift sent by this Sultan of Delhi to Majd al-Dīn: *Riḥla*, p. 456, Gibb, *Travels*, III, p. 677.

25 *Riḥla*, pp. 213–4, Gibb, *Travels*, II, pp. 314–5.

26 *Riḥla*, p. 419, Gibb, *Travels*, III, p. 626.

27 *Riḥla*, pp. 391–2, Gibb, *Travels*, III, pp. 587–9.

28 See Gibb, *Selections*, pp. 35–6 and also Janssens, *op. cit*, p. 98.

29 *Riḥla*, p. 30, Gibb, *Travels*, I, pp. 31–2.

30 *Riḥla*, p. 641, Gibb, *Selections*, pp. 36, 296–7.

31 *Riḥla*, pp. 537–8, Gibb, *Selections*, pp. 36, 221–2.

32 *Riḥla*, pp. 544–5, Gibb, *Selections*, p. 226.

33 Ibid., p. 373, n. 1.

34 *Riḥla*, pp. 646–7, Gibb, *Selections*, pp. 301–2; but see Yamamoto, *op. cit.*, pp. 128–30, who believes that the 'story of the Rokh is a fabrication'.

35 *Riḥla*, p. 543, Gibb, *Selections*, p. 225.

36 *Sufism*, (London, 1950), p. 119.

37 *Selections*, p. 3. With regard to contemporary opinion of Ibn Baṭṭūṭa as a great traveller, the saintly Shaykh Jalāl al-Dīn al-Tabrīzī, who has never met Ibn Baṭṭūṭa before, tells him in Sylhet: *Anta musāfir al-'arab (Riḥla*, p. 613, Gibb, *Selections*, pp. 269, 366, n. 9), while Ibn Juzayy, right at the end of the *Riḥla*, observes of Ibn Baṭṭūṭa: *huwa raḥḥāl al-'aṣr . . . raḥḥāl hādhihi al-milla (Riḥla*, p. 701, Gibb, *Selections*, p. 339).

38 'Studies in the *Tuhfatunnuzzar* of Ibn Baṭṭūṭa and Ibn Juzayy', *Journal of the Asiatic Society of Bangladesh*, XXIII (1978), p. 27.

39 See Miquel, 'L'Islam d'Ibn Baṭṭūṭa', p. 78.

40 E.g. for those acquired in Damascus, see *Riḥla*, pp. 108–110, Gibb, *Travels*, I, pp. 154–7. The latter points out (ibid., p. 157, n. 338) that Ibn Baṭṭūṭa does

seem to have acquired an inordinate number of diplomas. He certainly was very qualification-conscious (see his remarks on an unqualified notary in *Riḥla*, pp. 73–4, Gibb, *Travels*, I, pp. 102–3), but there is surely a large element of exaggeration in what he claims to have acquired in Damascus. Miquel points out ('L'Islam d'Ibn Baṭṭūṭa', p. 75) that he is also not averse to collecting diplomas from jurists of law schools other than his own, such as the Shāfiʿīs.

41 Gibb, *Selections*, pp. 36–7.

42 See his *al-Munqidh min al-Dalāl*, ed. and tr. Farīd Jabre, (Beirut, 1969), pp. 35–40 (Arabic), pp. 95–102 (French).

43 *Selections*, p. 7

44 *Op. cit*., p. 227.

45 *Riḥla*, pp. 528–9, Gibb, *Travels*, III, pp. 765–7.

46 *Riḥla*, p. 528, Gibb, *Travels*, III, pp. 765–6.

47 *Riḥla*, pp. 529–30, Gibb, *Travels*, III, pp. 766–7.

48 *Idem, Selections*, p. 38.

49 'In search of Ibn Battuta', *Asian Affairs*, VIII (1977), p. 267.

8

ARABIA AND THE PILGRIM PARADIGM OF IBN BAṬṬŪṬA

A Braudelian Approach

The *Riḥla* of Ibn Baṭṭūṭa (1304–1368/9 or 1377) has been tackled over the years by a multitude of scholars in a variety of different ways.[1] Often, however, the various studies which have been published have concentrated – to use, loosely, a not inappropriate pair of Ismāʿīlī terms – on a *ẓāhir* exposition of the text and its problems rather than on an analysis of a *bāṭin* structure. I do not, of course, mean that the *Riḥla* might have a secondary meaning but that it has been analysed, for example, more often as a straight travelogue,[2] a problematic chronology,[3] a vehicle or mirror of Muslim institutions[4] and a focus for stylistic comparison.[5] The translation of three-quarters of it into English by H.A.R. Gibb for the Hakluyt Society series has placed it – at least for English non-Arabists – firmly within that type of travel genre or tradition in which the Hakluyt Society has always specialised. The essence or *raison d'être* of the genre was epitomised in the early resolution adopted in 1846 explaining that the Society was to be formed 'for the purpose of printing, for distribution among its members, the most rare and valuable voyages, travels and geographical records, from an early period of exploratory enterprise to the circumnavigation of Dampier'.[6] The emphasis, in other words, was to be on the voyage and on the data which might have resulted from original exploration. Finally, to provide a last illustration, the *Riḥla* has been examined recently by the present writer in terms of myth and magic,[7] and it is upon the approach used then that I would like to base that employed in the present essay.

In my essay 'Myth, Miracle and Magic in the *Riḥla* of Ibn Baṭṭūṭa' I put forward the proposition that Ibn Baṭṭūṭa used the *Riḥla* as a kind of frame story in a manner akin to the usage in *Kalīla wa Dimma* and the *Panchatantra*.[8] In other words, what was being stressed was the sheer *artificiality* of the art form employed by the author and/or his editor.[9] If we examine his *Riḥla* in these terms, we may go on to ask whether the whole is a frame for just a collection of disparate and, perhaps, unconnected places visited, episodes, interests, and prejudices, or whether there is some kind of identifiable structure upon which the *Riḥla* is built and some paradigm or pattern of widespread applicability by which it is ordered. Such tools of analysis need not, of course, have been present in the mind of the writer as he wrote or, rather, dictated his text. Indeed, it would be extraordinary if Ibn Baṭṭūṭa had thought in any kind of 'structuralist' way at all. What he did do, however, was to give vent to overriding interests and prejudices in the course of his text which we ourselves can now use as part of the meat of our analysis. It is therefore the purpose of this essay to assess what are the 'constants' at work within the frame which has been described. I propose to use, firstly, the three-level method of historiography established by that doyen of the French *Annales* school of history, Fernand Braudel (1902–1985), as a key to unlocking at least some of the structure of the *Riḥla* (*in particular, its Arabian section*) and identifying eventually what I will term the basic 'pilgrim paradigm' of Ibn Baṭṭūṭa.

Braudel's method, in which history is viewed and studied on three levels of (i) enduring geographic and economic structures, (ii) social structures and 'conjunctures',[10] and (iii) events, is best seen in operation in his magisterial three-volume *Civilization Matérielle, Économie et Capitalisme (XVe-XVIIIe Siècle)*.[11] But it also appeared earlier in his famous *La Méditerranée et le Monde Méditerranéen à l'Epoque de Philippe II*.[12] And it is precisely because of the Mediterranean orientation of the latter that I have decided to concentrate on it rather than on the former. In the preface to the first edition of *La Méditerranée* Braudel stressed that his book had three parts: the first studied the history of man 'dans ses rapports avec le milieu qui l'entoure; une histoire lente à couler, à se transformer, faite souvent de retours insistants, de cycles sans cesse'. The second part dealt with 'histoire sociale, celle des groupes et des groupements' and the way in which such forces as economic systems, civilisations and societies interacted in the field of warfare. For war, Braudel emphasised, was the product of more than purely individual responsibility. The last part of *La Méditerranée* was rather more traditional and dealt with the history of events or what had been termed by Paul Lacombe and François Simiand 'l'histoire événementielle'. Braudel summarised his efforts by saying that 'ainsi sommes-nous arrivés à une décomposition de l'histoire en plans étagés. Ou, si l'on veut, à la distinction, dans le temps de l'histoire, d'un temps géographique, d'un temps social, d'un temps individuel'.[13] And he entitled the three parts of his book respectively 'La Part du Milieu',

'Destins Collectifs et Mouvements d'Ensemble' and 'Les Événements, La Politique et les Hommes'.

It is instructive to try and apply the Braudelian categories to the Arabian section of Ibn Baṭṭūṭa's *Riḥla*. And although an *over-rigid* compartmentalisation of data is often unwise, none the less the Braudelian method can be valuable in highlighting aspects both of Ibn Baṭṭūṭa's own mind and the land and age through which he travelled, which might otherwise have been overlooked. Firstly, however, it is necessary to outline briefly the salient features of that first Arabian travelogue. Ibn Baṭṭūṭa made several pilgrimages to Mecca[14] but it is this first visit and first incursion into Arabia that will concern us here.

Ibn Baṭṭūṭa left Damascus with the pilgrim caravan on 1 September 1326. He passed by the great castle of al-Karak with its legendary crusading associations and entered the desert after passing through Ma'ān which the traveller described as the last of the Syrian towns. He then began to encounter places associated with the Prophet Muḥammad in one way or another: Tabūk to which the Prophet had led an expedition in 631; the well of al-Ḥijr from which the Prophet had refused to drink; and finally, and most notably, the City of Medina with its plethora of associations with the life of the founder of Islam. Relying much on the earlier work of Ibn Jubayr, Ibn Baṭṭūṭa describes in detail the Mosque of Medina where Muḥammad, as well as the two early Caliphs Abū Bakr and 'Umar b. al-Khaṭṭāb, lie buried. He retails, again in some detail, the circumstances of the building of this mosque and the way in which it was gradually enlarged over the centuries.[15]

Ibn Baṭṭūṭa tells us that he stayed four days in Medina and spent each night in the mosque.[16] After leaving the city, he donned the pilgrim garb and entered the state of *iḥrām* near the mosque of Dhū 'l-Ḥulayfa, about five miles away. The last major village through which he passed was Badr, site of the first notable battle between Muḥammad and the Meccans in 624. It is duly noted and eulogised by Ibn Baṭṭūṭa. Finally, with a full heart, the traveller reached Mecca.[17]

Mecca has been the object of his journeying and the importance of this city both for Islam generally, and for Ibn Baṭṭūṭa in particular, ensures that it is treated in page after page of almost fulsome detail. Not only does Ibn Baṭṭūṭa perform the familiar and age-old pilgrim rituals and traditions of *ṭawāf*, running between al-Ṣafā and al-Marwa, and drinking from the well of Zamzam, but he positively revels in every aspect of the city, describing its gates, the Sacred Mosque with the Ka'ba, the city cemetery and even the sanctuaries outside Mecca, and the Meccan mountains and caves significant for early Islamic history.[18]

Nor do the inhabitants of Mecca escape his curious attention: he praises the good qualities of the Meccan citizenry and, as is his wont, pays particular attention to the scholars and pious folk who inhabit the city and its environs, recounting several entertaining anecdotes about these people.[19]

Perhaps the kernel of Ibn Baṭṭūṭa's narrative of this, his first visit to Mecca for the pilgrimage, is his description of the *wuqūf* on the plain of 'Arafāt. The event clearly made an extraordinary impression on the young traveller for he notes not only the date of this *wuqūf* as a Thursday in AH 726 (= 6 November 1326)[20] but records in the same paragraph the names of the commanders of the Egyptian and Syrian caravans at that time and the names of some of the notables who made the pilgrimage that year. The 'Standing' at 'Arafāt is followed by the traditional rush to Muzdalifa, move to Minā, stoning of the pillars and celebration of 'Īd al-Aḍḥā.[21]

Ibn Baṭṭūṭa left Mecca with the Iraqi caravan on 17 November 1326 and travelled back to Medina, where he spent a further six days, before embarking on a quite different route from the inward one, which eventually brought the traveller to Kūfa in Southern Iraq. As he went he once again recorded the historical associations of the places through which he passed: Al-Ajfur, romantically connected with the lovers Jamīl and Buthayna; al-Qādisiyya, scene of one of the greatest early Arab victories over the Sassanians in 636 or 637, and Najaf with its Shī'ite heritage.[22]

The above paragraphs give the bare chronological bones of Ibn Baṭṭūṭa's first visit to Arabia for the purpose of making the pilgrimage to Mecca. And the value of the great quantity of material which he provides in his text (despite some obvious plagiarism)[23] has, of course, been much appreciated by scholars from a variety of disciplines, not least that of Islamic art and architecture. But what may have sometimes been neglected in the frequently indiscriminate mining of the *Riḥla* for information by scholars is a real appreciation and ordering of the several different *layers* of information provided by Ibn Baṭṭūṭa. Here the insights of Braudel can be of considerable value.

If we take first the *geographical* level in Braudel's methodology, we find that a vivid awareness of the harshness of the Arabian landscape permeates Ibn Baṭṭūṭa's narrative. This awareness is epitomised best in the constant search for, and references to, water.[24] Ibn Baṭṭūṭa is always delighted by the presence of water whether it be running as at Tabūk,[25] sweet from having been previously brackish as at the Well of Arīs,[26] or simply rain-water collected in tanks.[27] There are numerous references to water and Arabian watering places in his narrative: the principal problem associated with both seems to have been the usual one of continual supply[28] rather than the incidence of malaria.[29] And there are other references to the environment as well: secondary motifs in Ibn Baṭṭūṭa's Arabian section include the terrors of the desert where men can be lost[30] and the fearsome Samoom wind.[31] By contrast with all this, the cities of Medina and Mecca are positive oases of the good life – what Braudel calls 'minuscules points d'appui'[32] – with their mosques and well-stocked markets.[33] The exquisite importance of transport[34] – well-provisioned transport! – becomes excessively clear in such a desert-dominated milieu, and was a prime consideration of Ibn Baṭṭūṭa in Arabia as well as of every other sensible traveller.[35] It is factors such as the above that must have led Braudel to summarise Islam as 'la totalité de ce que le désert implique de réalités humaines, concordantes et discordantes . . .',[36] though he would be wrong if he intended to imply that Islam was *of* the desert, i.e. a desert faith in origin and essence.

In his second layer of analysis, which in *La Méditerranée* is encapsulated under the general rubric 'Destins Collectifs et Mouvements d'Ensemble', Braudel examined the role of interlocking factors such as the economy, trade and transport on the one hand, and social structures such as Empires, societies and civilisations, on the other. He concluded with an analysis of the forms of war.

All these elements are present or implicit, of course, in one form or another in the *Riḥla* of Ibn Baṭṭūṭa. On his first Arabian journey the author noted, for example, the role of the pilgrim caravan as a vehicle of trade.[37] Gibb comments: 'The pilgrim caravans were at all times occasions for trade, especially as they were often exempted from the ordinary transit and custom duties'.[38] Braudel cites the description of an anonymous Englishman who, a few centuries later in 1586, followed an extremely well-endowed caravan to Mecca from an assembly point outside Cairo. It allegedly had about 40,000 mules and camels and 50,000 people including many merchants. As the caravan travelled, it sold some of the rice, tin, grain, silk and coral destined to be exchanged in the markets of Mecca.[39] And, indeed, the caravans in which Ibn Baṭṭūṭa travelled in Arabia, although he gives us no figures, may well have been of a similar magnitude and luxurious nature. The Iraqi caravan in which he left Mecca was clearly a massive one: according to the traveller, the numbers of people were so large that they surged like the waves of the sea, and if anyone left the caravan to relieve himself, he was quite unable to find his place again. The caravan was also endowed, as we have observed, with many water-bearing camels as well as a massive supply of luxuries and food.[40] And Ibn Baṭṭūṭa like later[41] and earlier travellers, was not unaware of the dangers of a possible attack on the caravan.[42] In a sea-faring context, Braudel described piracy, 'industrie ancienne et généralisée', as a 'forme supplétive de la grande guerre'.[43] On land, raids on the Arabian caravan routes could serve similar or other purposes but were equally ancient and dangerous.[44] Ibn Baṭṭūṭa's caravans were not themselves attacked while he was in Arabia on his first pilgrimage, but his narrative betrays a distinct apprehension about the possibility.

The caravan trade described by the traveller reflected, in some small way, the larger economy of the states through which he travelled. Similarly, the larger empires and civilisations, with their mixtures of societies, which he encountered as he moved on his *Riḥla*, impinged upon him most clearly and obviously in the form of smaller social units or structures. Two important social groupings which he encountered in Arabia were those of the pilgrimage peer group and the '*Ulamā*'.

Ibn Baṭṭūṭa moved or worked, from the inside, with the one as a *ḥājj* and the other as a '*ālim*.[45] His narrative provides abundant evidence of the intricate 'group-ethos' which developed within the caravan with its customs and class structure: for example, it was customary for the Syrian pilgrims on arriving at Tabūk to charge the camp with drawn swords and smite the palm trees with those swords in emulation of the deeds of the Prophet Muḥammad on his expedition to Tabūk in 631.[46] Similarly the pilgrims made a point of drinking a mixture of barley meal and water or butter called *sawīq*, which was mixed with sugar, at the Pass of al-Sawīq. Again the action commemorated a previous one by the Prophet who, finding his companions to be without food in that place, changed sand into *sawīq* in a miracle which echoed that of the New Testament Cana.[47] The class structure of the pilgrim caravan is reflected in the fact that the Amīrs had their own tanks of water set aside for them at, for example, the spring of Tabūk, unlike the ordinary pilgrims;[48] and it was the Amīrs who assumed the responsibility for filling the water tanks with *sawīq* and doling it out to the people from them.[49] Wealth and/or high rank and a privileged access to water and associated beverages in the caravan are thus seen to be inexorably linked. Such divisions, to a certain extent, ought to have vanished with the group assumption of *iḥrām*.[50] But it was only in the rituals of the *Ḥajj* itself, communally celebrated in Mecca and 'Arafāt and its environs, that the pilgrims really merged with their peers and assumed a single corporate identity *par excellence*.

Ibn Baṭṭūṭa's interest in, and encounters with, his fellow-'*Ulamā*' is a constant *leitmotiv* throughout his *Riḥla*. It is thus no surprise to find the traveller noting by name during the account of his first pilgrimage such individuals as a Mālikī professor,[51] a Zaydī Qāḍī,[52] and the imāms of the four principal *madhāhib* at Mecca.[53] Though Ibn Baṭṭūṭa does not seem to have collected in Medina and Mecca the *ijāzāt* which he claims to have acquired in vast quantities in Damascus just before setting off on his first Arabian journey,[54] it is clear from his accounts of these cities that he enjoyed to the full the company of his academic peers.[55]

Braudel has described events as 'poussière'. For him 'ils traversent l'histoire comme les lueurs brèves; à peine naissent-ils qu'ils retournent déjà à la nuit et souvent à l'oubli'. But every event, 'si bref qu'il soit, porte témoignage . . .'[56] and Ibn Baṭṭūṭa's own first pilgrimage to Mecca and incursion into Arabia is much more than a single Braudelian event, or even a chain of connected events or journeyings, at a particular time. Because of its nature it is a celebration across time and space of a whole series of 'events', or alleged 'events', which took place long before in both the pre-Islamic pilgrimages and those of Muḥammad, and which function as a set of symbols in the present. It is *these* 'events' rather than what Ibn Baṭṭūṭa himself does, and where he goes, which constitute in a major sense the substance of his pilgrimage.

This three-level analysis based on the insights of Fernand Braudel enables us to marshal and present the data in Ibn Baṭṭūṭa's *Riḥla* in a particularly 'compartmentalised' fashion. The question may now be fairly asked: can we identify, through the medium of such a method, certain constants which have a function, relevance, or applicability throughout much of the *Riḥla*, and which may be said to constitute *in toto* a 'pilgrim paradigm' for the traveller? In other words, having achieved its most Islamically perfect form in Arabia because of the pilgrimage and Mecca – (although Mecca may not be the sole focal point of Ibn Baṭṭūṭa's journeyings as it was with Ibn Jubayr)[57] – is there a pattern of intentions which appears to operate in other cities and regions visited in the *Riḥla* as well?

An analysis of the *Riḥla* shows that this is the case. There are a certain number of constants which may be said to transcend, though they may be permeated by, or even a cause of, the traveller's more individual preoccupations or characteristics such as an interest in watering holes or uxoriousness. They transcend simply because of their breadth and the far-reaching nature of their significance for the narrative scope of the entire *Riḥla*; and they may thus be said to constitute a substrate or, better, an underlying 'pilgrim paradigm' for this work. The principal elements of the paradigm are four-fold. Firstly, we may derive from Braudel's generalised primary level of geographic constants the enduring religious geography of an Islamic sacred area, which in Arabia means primarily Mecca and its environs, and in which are celebrated, in a strictly ordered series of rituals, religious 'facts' from the past. Thus there is a linkage between Braudel's first and third levels. Religious geography and the 'facts' such geography has witnessed and absorbed engender a *primal and focal search or journeying to a shrine*, which in the case of Mecca is the Ḥajj to the sacred Ka'ba itself.

Secondly, bearing in mind Braudel's second level of social structures generally, and the grouping of the Islamic *'Ulamā'* in particular, we may note Ibn Baṭṭūṭa's *search for knowledge*. The *'Ulamā'* as a social and educational group personified and institutionalised knowledge; and travellers like Ibn Baṭṭūṭa implemented the mediaeval saw which instructed Muslims to seek knowledge even as far as China. This has two facets in the *Riḥla*: Ibn Baṭṭūṭa's desire to associate with, or meet, as many scholars as possible, a feature which is clear in his Arabian narrative, and his almost childlike eagerness to acquire as many of such scholars' *ijāzāt* as possible, a feature which is, however, lacking in this first Arabian account but prominent elsewhere.[58] Ibn Baṭṭūṭa may be said to have obeyed the saw to the letter in that he actually claims to have visited China and conversed with its academics.[59]

Thirdly, related to and deriving from this second Braudelian level of social structures is our traveller's *search for personal recognition and/or power and massive interest in those who hold power*. The isolation and loneliness felt by the youthful and inexperienced traveller as he sets out[60] are soon replaced by the satisfaction of scholarly converse, recognition in the form of the grant of an *ijāza* or ṣūfī robe,[61] personal fulfilment in marriage,[62] or the attainment of politico-religious power as in his appointments as Ambassador of Sulṭān Muḥammad ibn Tughluq of Delhi to China,[63] or Qāḍī to the Maldive Islands.[64] Ibn Baṭṭūṭa's predilection for recognition by the pious and the powerful appears on his Arabian journey not only in his dropping of the names of jurists and scholars whose converse he clearly enjoyed, but in the way, for example, that he persuades the Commander of the Iraqi caravan himself, Muḥammad al-Ḥawīh to take him under his wing, even to the extent of having the said Commander pay out of his own pocket the cost of hiring half a double litter as far as Baghdad, for Ibn Baṭṭūṭa.[65] Elsewhere, his interest in the great and the powerful is never far below the surface.[66]

Finally, as a species of Braudelian 'fact' occurring in the present, there is the *search for what might be characterised as the satisfaction of the raḥḥāla impulse*, that inquisitive 'itch' to travel for its own sake, shared to a greater or lesser degree by all real travellers, as opposed to mere tourists, whether they be the ancient, and anonymous, author of the *Periplus of the Erythraean Sea*[67] or the modern Tim Severin.[68] The urge is encapsulated in our mediaeval traveller's express wish never to travel the same route twice if it be possible.[69]

Ibn Baṭṭūṭa's 'pilgrim paradigm' thus comprises a series of four searches: for the shrine and/or its circumambient religious geography; for knowledge; for recognition and/or power; and for the satisfaction of a basic wanderlust. To test whether such a paradigm really exists, it is useful to look at some of the other cities and regions to which he travels and see if it is applicable there as well. Its various features are not, of course, always totally present and they may, at times, be permeated or changed by the traveller's other interests and prejudices, his vivid imagination and, indeed, his capacity for invention. But let us briefly take five cities or regions which are mentioned elsewhere in the *Riḥla* and see whether the pattern which has been posited holds true.

In *Najaf*, one of the great Shī'ite centres of culture and learning, Ibn Baṭṭūṭa takes a considerable interest in the alleged tomb of 'Alī[70] and eagerly soaks up information from 'trustworthy individuals' as well as three cripples hailing from Byzantium, Iṣfahān and Khurāsān, about healing miracles occurring every year on a certain 'night of life' (*laylat al-Maḥyā*) at the mausoleum.[71] The power and rank of the *Naqīb al-Ashrāf*, who governs Najaf, exercise the usual fascination over the traveller's mind and Ibn Baṭṭūṭa devotes some space to anecdotal material about a former incumbent of the office, Abū Ghurra.[72] On leaving the city, Ibn Baṭṭūṭa's wanderlust clearly transcends his justified fear of the inhabitants and highwaymen of the area between Najaf and Baṣra.[73]

In *Iṣfahān* Ibn Baṭṭūṭa chooses to stay in a convent much visited by people seeking *baraka* because it is associated with an ascetic disciple of al-Junayd. The traveller is warmly welcomed and honoured by the Convent Shaykh who ultimately invests him with the robe of the Suhrawardī Ṣūfī Order, thereby satisfying in the one action Ibn Baṭṭūṭa's constant yearning for recognition, fascination with *taṣawwuf*, and love of arcane knowledge and lore. The latter is particularly apparent in the way he records in the *Riḥla* after describing the investiture, what he now considers to be his own ṣūfī *silsila* which he has clearly attempted to memorise from the Shaykh himself or his learned associates in the Convent.[74] After Iṣfahān a ten-day journey, with a view to visiting a certain Shaykh in Shīrāz, is contemplated with equanimity or, at least, without comment.[75]

Ibn Baṭṭūṭa's one month and six days' sojourn[76] in *Constantinople* is marked by a similar collection of features: he is intrigued by the Christian places of prayer, whether they be the great church of Hagia Sophia or the city's monasteries.[77] He converses at length with the Qāḍī of Constantinople,[78] meets the ruler of the city[79] and also a monk named Jirjīs whom he believes to have been the former ruler.[80] Ibn Baṭṭūṭa's '*raḥḥāla* impulse' is clearly indulged to the full in his roaming about the city every day.[81] And the same pattern manifests itself all over again in and around *Delhi*: he provides a vivid description of the great Mosque of Delhi[82] and lauds the power possessed by the much-venerated tomb of the Shaykh Quṭb al-Dīn Bakhtiyār al-Ka'kī of the Chistī Order.[83] Ibn Baṭṭūṭa has his ample share of contact with the scholarly and the pious in Delhi,[84] as well as welcome and unwelcome recognition and power. The unstable and bloodthirsty ruler of Delhi, Sulṭān Muḥammad ibn Tughluq, showers him with gifts[85] and ultimately invests him with the Qadiship of Delhi[86] and an ambassadorship to China.[87] In between holding the latter two offices, however, he suffers the indignity of being placed under guard by the Sulṭān, having incurred the latter's displeasure.[88] Finally, his wanderlust surfaces readily in his eagerness to go hunting with the Sulṭān[89] and his (thwarted) attempt to go out on an expedition organised to fight the Sulṭān's enemies as well.[90]

It is, perhaps, in our fifth and final example, Ibn Baṭṭūṭa's sojourn in *Ceylon*, that we come closest to finding articulated the original Meccan paradigm. On Adam's Peak is a shrine or better, place of religious visitation *par excellence*: this is the footprint of Adam[91] and the visit to it has its own peculiar customs and pilgrim rituals.[92] The traveller absorbs (though he does not necessarily believe) the stories of the Yogis,[93] and he finds his lust for proper recognition sated in full measure by the hospitable and kindly reception which he receives from the infidel ruler whom he calls Sulṭān Ayrī Shakarwatī (Arya Chakravarti).[94] The enthusiasm with which Ibn Baṭṭūṭa seeks permission from the latter to undertake the difficult journey to the 'Foot of Adam' is yet a further simple indication of the traveller's innate wanderlust combined with curiosity.[95]

The five examples which we have provided above may not rigidly reflect, or adhere to, what has been termed 'the pilgrim paradigm' in every tiny detail. None the less, that paradigm is sufficiently present in each case: in other words, the illustrations chosen from a number of disparate cities and areas *do* show that there is an underlying, and therefore unifying, set of constants, in the narrative of each visit. The Arabian section of the *Riḥla* does, therefore, present a paradigm of features which are coherent, relevant and applicable to other areas of the text.

Ibn Baṭṭūṭa's work, of course, constitutes a particular development of the *Riḥla* form:[96] it is, so to speak, a canonisation of that form. If we turn back briefly to an earlier, and almost equally famous, *Riḥla*, that of Ibn Jubayr (1145–1217),[97] with which it is logical to make a comparison, we find a much more fluid travelogue: this is the record of a pilgrim journey undertaken for a different purpose, much shorter in terms of both time and distance travelled and not so much a frame story as a simple narrative of a voyage undertaken and experienced.[98] We may conclude with a, perhaps not inappropriate, gardening analogy: if Ibn Jubayr's work resembles the somewhat disordered 'swampy, treeless land about Versailles' in the days before the advent of Louis XIV's master-gardener André Le Nôtre (1613–1700), then Ibn Baṭṭūṭa's paradigmatic frame is akin – without too much exaggeration – to the ordered formalism of that gardener's great achievement at Versailles when he had finished.[99] The 'pilgrim paradigm' which we have proposed is both a 'way of seeing' or examining the age in which Ibn Baṭṭūṭa himself operated as well as a broader representation of some of the primary impulses of that which, for the sake of convenience, we describe loosely as 'Islam' itself.[100]

NOTES

1 I am indebted to the writings of my colleague Professor Aziz Al-Azmeh for suggesting to me a 'paradigmatic' approach to the *Riḥla* of Ibn Baṭṭūṭa. See M. Masterman, 'The Nature of a Paradigm' in I. Lakatos and A. Musgrave (eds.), *Criticism and the Growth of Knowledge*, Proceedings of the International Colloquium in the Philosophy of Science, London, 1965, vol. 4 (Cambridge: Cambridge University Press, 1970), pp. 59–90. (I owe this reference to Professor Al-Azmeh.) See especially p. 62, n. 5 and p. 63, n. 11.

2 E.g. by Herman F. Janssens, *Ibn Batouta 'le voyageur de l'Islam' (1304–1369)*, (Brussels: Office de Publicité, 1948).

3 Ivan Hrbek, 'The Chronology of Ibn Baṭṭūṭa's Travels', *Archiv Orientální*, vol. 30 (1962), pp. 409–86.

4 G.-H. Bousquet, 'Ibn Baṭṭūṭa et les Institutions Musulmanes', *Studia Islamica*, vol. 24 (1966), pp. 81–106.

5 J.N. Mattock, 'The Travel Writings of Ibn Jubair and Ibn Baṭṭūṭa', *Glasgow Oriental Society Transactions*, vol. 21 (1965–66), pp. 35–46.

6 Dorothy Middleton, 'The Hakluyt Society 1846–1923' in *Annual Report and Statement of Accounts for 1984* (London: Hakluyt Society, 1985), p. 14. The relevant Hakluyt volumes are H.A.R. Gibb, *The Travels of Ibn Baṭṭūṭa AD 1325–1354*, trans. from the Arabic text ed. by C. Defrémery and B.R. Sanguinetti, 3 vols. (Cambridge: Cambridge University Press for the Hakluyt Society, 1958–71). [Translation completed with the publication of vol. IV in 1994].

7 Ian Richard Netton, 'Myth, Miracle and Magic in the *Riḥla* of Ibn Baṭṭūṭa', *Journal of Semitic Studies*, vol. 29:1 (1984), pp. 131–40.
8 Ibid., p. 133
9 For references to Ibn Baṭṭūṭa's editor, Ibn Juzayy, see my 'Myth, Miracle and Magic', p. 132, nn. 4, 6.
10 For a discussion of the word 'conjuncture', see his *La Méditerranée* (1966), vol. 2, pp. 213–20. (Full bibliographical details appear below in n. 12).
11 (Paris: Librairie Armand Colin, 1979).
12 (Paris: Librairie Armand Colin, 1949; 2nd rev. edn. 1966); trans. of 2nd rev. edn. by Siân Reynolds, *The Mediterranean and the Mediterranean World in the Age of Philip II*, 2 vols. (London: Collins, 1972).
13 *Méditerranée*, vol. 1, pp. 16–17.
14 E.g. in 1326, 1332, 1349.
15 *Riḥlat Ibn Baṭṭūṭa* hereafter referred to as *Riḥla*, (Beirut: Dār Ṣādir, 1964), pp. 110–20.
16 Ibid., p. 126.
17 Ibid., pp. 128–30.
18 Ibid., pp. 130–46.
19 Ibid., pp. 148–68.
20 Gibb, *Travels of Ibn Baṭṭūṭa*, vol. 1, p. 245, n. 225.
21 *Riḥla*, pp. 169–71.
22 Ibid., pp. 172–218.
23 See my 'Myth, Miracle and Magic', p. 132, n. 6.
24 Ibid., p. 132.
25 *Riḥla*, pp. 111–12.
26 Ibid., p. 126.
27 Ibid., p. 173.
28 E.g. ibid., p. 174. See also the story recounted on p. 112 in which a caravan's water supplies dried up.
29 See Braudel, *Méditerranée*, vol. 1, pp. 56–9.
30 *Riḥla*, p. 111; see also the reference to the awful wilderness between Tabūk and al-'Ulā, p. 112. For deserts and oases see Braudel, *Méditerranée*, vol. 1, pp. 156–65, 169–70.
31 *Riḥla* pp. 112–13. See Braudel, *Méditerranée*, vol. 1, p. 223 for the impact of the sirocco and ibid., pp. 229, 231 for that of the mistral.
32 *Méditerranée, vol. 1*, p. 169.
33 *Riḥla*, pp. 132, 164.
34 *Méditerranée*, vol. 1, p. 158.
35 E.g. see the references to provisions and transports, including water-carrying camels for the foot pilgrims, in the Iraqi caravan, *Riḥla*, p. 172.
36 Braudel, *Méditerranée*, vol. 1, p. 171.
37 *Riḥla*, pp. 113, 175.
38 Gibb, *Travels of Ibn Baṭṭūṭa*, vol. 1, p. 159, n. 10.
39 Braudel, *Méditerranée*, vol. 1, pp. 165–6.
40 *Riḥla*, pp. 172–3; see n. 35 above.
41 Braudel, *Méditerranée*, vol. 1, p. 165.
42 *Riḥla*, p. 174.
43 Braudel, *Méditerranée*, vol. 2, pp. 190–1.

44 Compare the Cossack attacks on caravans along the Volga, *Méditerranée*, vol. 1, p. 178.
45 See my 'Myth, Miracle and Magic', pp. 138–9 for an assessment of the kind of '*ālim* that Ibn Baṭṭūṭa was.
46 *Riḥla*, p. 112.
47 Ibid., p. 129. See John 2:1–11.
48 *Riḥla*, p. 112.
49 Ibid., p. 129.
50 Ibid., p. 128.
51 Ibid., p. 110.
52 Ibid., p. 127.
53 Ibid., pp. 150, 151.
54 See my 'Myth, Miracle and Magic', p. 138, esp. n. 40.
55 See, for example, his sharing of the content of a dream with the Imām of the Malikites at Mecca, Abū 'Abdullāh Muḥammad, *Riḥla*, pp. 150–1.
56 *Méditerranée*, vol. 2, p. 223.
57 See my 'Myth, Miracle and Magic', pp. 132–3.
58 For *ijāzāt* acquired in Damascus, see *Riḥla*, pp. 108–10.
59 E.g. *Riḥla*, pp. 633, 637–8.
60 E.g. see ibid., p. 17.
61 E.g. ibid., p. 201.
62 E.g. ibid., pp. 19–20.
63 Ibid., p. 530.
64 Ibid., p. 588.
65 Ibid., p. 172.
66 E.g. see his account of the two Amīrs of Mecca, ibid., p. 148.
67 See the trans. by Wilfred H. Schoff (New Delhi: Oriental Books Reprint Corporation, 1974, [repr. from the New York: Longmans, Green & Co., 1912 edition]), and the more recent trans. by G.W.B. Huntingford, (London: The Hakluyt Society, 1980).
68 See his *The Brendan Voyage*, (London: Hutchinson, 1978) and *The Sindbad Voyage*, (London: Hutchinson, 1982). See also his more recent volume *The Jason Voyage: The Quest for the Golden Fleece*, (London: Hutchinson, 1985).
69 *Riḥla*, p. 191.
70 Ibid., pp. 176, 182.
71 Ibid., pp. 176–8.
72 Ibid., pp. 179–82.
73 Ibid., pp. 182–3.
74 Ibid., pp. 200–2. See Ibn Juzayy's somewhat snide commentary on this *silsila*, p. 202.
75 Ibid., p. 202.
76 Ibid., p. 356.
77 Ibid., pp. 351–4.
78 Ibid., p. 355.
79 Ibid., pp. 349–50.
80 Ibid., pp. 349, 354–5.
81 Ibid., p. 350.
82 Ibid., pp. 416–7.

83 Ibid., p. 419.
84 Ibid., pp. 419–20.
85 E.g. ibid., pp. 453, 507.
86 Ibid., p. 512.
87 Ibid., p. 530.
88 Ibid., p. 528.
89 Ibid., p. 517.
90 Ibid., p. 522.
91 Or the footprint of Shiva or Buddha depending on one's religious affiliation! See H.A.R. Gibb, *Ibn Battūta: Travels in Asia and Africa 1325–1354*, The Broadway Travellers, (London: Routledge & Kegan Paul, 1929), p. 365, n. 5.
92 *Riḥla*, pp. 598–600.
93 Ibid., pp. 597, 600.
94 Ibid., p. 594.
95 Ibid.
96 See my 'Myth, Miracle and Magic', p. 133.
97 *Riḥla*, (Beirut: Dār Ṣādir, 1964).
98 See my article 'Ibn Jubayr: Penitent Pilgrim and Observant Traveller', *UR*, No. 2 (1985), pp. 14–17. [Reprinted in this volume].
99 See Lucy Norton, *The Sun King and his Loves*, (London: The Folio Society, 1982), pp. 39–41.
100 See Masterman, 'The Nature of a Paradigm', pp. 76–7.

9

BASIC STRUCTURES AND SIGNS OF ALIENATION IN THE *RIḤLA* OF IBN JUBAYR

In a previous essay I identified in the *Riḥla* of Ibn Baṭṭūṭa (1304–1368/9 or 1377) what I termed his 'pilgrim paradigm'.[1] Using insights garnered from the three-tier approach to history devised by the great French scholar Fernand Braudel (1902–85), doyen supreme of the French *Annales* school of history, I maintained that this paradigm comprised 'a series of four searches: for the shrine and/or its circumambient religious geography; for knowledge; for recognition and/or power; and for the satisfaction of a basic wanderlust'.[2] Now it is frequently – and rightly – claimed that the *Riḥla* of Ibn Jubayr (1145–1217) constituted a prototype for several others of the genre including that of Ibn Baṭṭūṭa.[3] Indeed the debt of the former to other authors like Ibn Jubayr and al-'Abdarī[4] becomes ever more apparent, as recent scholarship continues to show.[5] To what extent then, it may be asked, may a similar (prototype) pilgrim paradigm be identified in the *Riḥla* of Ibn Jubayr? As an aid to answering this question, it is proposed first in this essay to analyse this *Riḥla* in terms of (1) its basic *structures*, and (2) some of its relevant semiotics.

The concept of *ṭalab al-'ilm* is a noteworthy factor in the *riḥlatayn* of Ibn Jubayr and Ibn Baṭṭūṭa,[6] but it is one which should be handled with care. We see, for example, that Lenker has stressed the general relationship between pilgrimage and study: he notes that in certain Andalusian works after the middle of the eighth century 'both the pilgrimage and study are two essential components of each biographical entry';[7] and, he goes so far as to maintain that 'as a motive for travel [*ṭalab al-'ilm*] surpassed in significance all other incentives including the pilgrimage itself'.[8] While this statement may well have been true, however, ultimately of Ibn Baṭṭūṭa with his unquenchable wanderlust,[9] it must be something of an exaggeration if applied *unreservedly* to Ibn Jubayr, despite his advice to the youth of the Maghrib [*I.J.* p. 258; see further in this essay]: Ibn Jubayr's *Riḥla* was undertaken for a specific *religious* purpose which had the pilgrimage to Mecca as its heart and goal. Indeed, his *riḥla was* a pilgrimage undertaken to make expiation (*kaffāra*) for the specific fault of wine-drinking: even though he had been forced to drink the wine by the Almohad governor of Granada, Abū Sa'īd 'Uthmān b. 'Abd al-Mu'min, to whom he was secretary, his delicate conscience bade him to make amends.[10] This motive of *kaffāra*, rather than pure *ṭalab al-'ilm*, must have been the driving force on his journey, and omnipresent to him, though it is indeed strange that Ibn Jubayr nowhere refers directly in his *Riḥla* to the real reasons for his journey. The details must be gleaned from other sources such as the seventeenth century *Nafḥ al-Ṭīb* of al-Maqqarī.[11]

Despite, however, the basic difference in motivation behind each of the *riḥlatayn* under discussion, there is no doubting the exuberant delight which *'ilm*, and the experiences deriving from the search for *'ilm*, produced in both Ibn Jubayr and Ibn Baṭṭūṭa. The energetic visiting by both of mosque, tomb, shrine, college, saint and scholar bears ample witness to that.

Apart from their respective motivations, perhaps the other major essential difference between the works of Ibn Jubayr and Ibn Baṭṭūṭa lies in their basic structures. Ibn Jubayr's *Riḥla* encompasses a much shorter timescale from the point of view of actual travel recorded (between 1183–1185), and consequently, far fewer cities and countries are visited than, for example, in the more wide-ranging *Riḥla* of his successor, Ibn Baṭṭūṭa. Ibn Jubayr's work is much less a frame story like the latter's (which was designed for the propagation of myths which might enhance a returning traveller's reputation and massage an already large ego,[12]) and much more "a simple narrative of a voyage undertaken and experienced".[13] Mattock has divided the content of Ibn Jubayr's work into two basic categories of description and narrative.[14] Having observed that "[the *Riḥla*] is a straightforward, non-technical work, written in a simple style",[15] Mattock remarks:

> Ibn Jubair's descriptive writing seems to me to be good but unremarkable. It is interesting, simply written and well detailed; it does very well what it is intended to do: describe the places that he visits, so that their main features are clear to his audience.[16]

The *structure* of Ibn Jubayr's *Riḥla* may, therefore, also be conceived in a simpler fashion than the more elaborate frame of Ibn Baṭṭūṭa's, and I propose to do so here by concentrating upon three very simple elements which seem to me to be the quintessential blocks upon which Ibn Jubayr's work is structured and founded. These elements are, respectively, a trinity of time, place and purpose as expressed in (a) the author's precise, almost neurotic, use of the Islamic calendar, (b) the travel or *riḥla* impulse and associated 'sense of place' which imbues the entire narrative, and (c) the primary orientation towards, or focus on, Mecca, goal of the Islamic pilgrimage.

It is useful, in any examination of Ibn Jubayr's usage, to examine first the later practice of Ibn Baṭṭūṭa, as far as dating is concerned. The latter author certainly deploys some dates in his text but what he provides certainly do not constitute a kind of textual punctuation or frame as happens in the earlier *Riḥla* of Ibn Jubayr. Indeed Gibb has noted, succinctly, of Ibn Baṭṭūṭa's practice, which may, in any case, have been that of his scribe and editor Ibn Juzayy: 'Many of the dates give the impression of having been inserted more or less at haphazard, possibly at the editor's request, but the examination and correction of them offers a task so great that it has not been attempted in this selection'.[17] Dunn confirms this observation: 'In composing the book, Ibn Baṭṭūṭa (and Ibn Juzayy, the literary scholar who collaborated with him) took far less care with details of itinerary, dates, and the sequence of events than the modern 'scientific' mind would consider acceptable practice for a travel writer'.[18] And while we *do* find formal dates at, for example, the beginning of the entire *Riḥla* [*I.B.*[19] p. 14] and scattered infrequently elsewhere in the text [e.g. *I.B.* pp. 53, 110, 172, 339, 393, 529], we find that Ibn Baṭṭūṭa's more usual narrative punctuation consists of such phrases as 'I went next to . . .'[20] (*thumma tawajjahtu ilā . . .) [I.B.* p. 31], 'I travelled next through . . .'[21] (*thumma sāfartu fī* . . .) [*I.B.* p. 33] and 'We came to . . .'[22] (*waṣalnā ilā . . .) [I.B.* p. 277].

By acute contrast, Ibn Jubayr uses his precise dating, in a surely conscious fashion, as a method of punctuating and dividing up his text. The entire *Riḥla* is laid out, *month by month*, according to the Islamic lunar calendar, [e.g. *I.J.*[23], pp. 13, 122, 190 and *passim*]. Each section, thus precisely, carefully and, apparently accurately,[24] introduced by date then at once contains a statement or description of the traveller's exact present location and often a description of, or reference to, his next projected destination(s), and the journeying involved. Ibn Jubayr's convention in his dating is to refer to the rising of the new moon, and also to provide Christian calendar equivalents; thus two typical diary entries, encapsulating all the above, read:

> *The Month of Rabīʿ al-Awwal of the Year [5]80, may God acquaint us with His blessing*
>
> Its new moon rose (*istahalla hilāluhu*) on the night of Tuesday,

> corresponding to the 12th June, while we were in the previously mentioned village.
>
> Then we set out from there at dawn on that Tuesday and arrived at Niṣībīn before midday of the same day [*I.J.* p. 214]
>
> *The Month of Jumāda al-Ūlā, may God acquaint us with His blessing.*
>
> Its new moon rose on the night of Friday, corresponding to the 10th August in foreign dating.
>
> A Descriptive Survey of Conditions in the City [of Damascus], may God make it thrive in Islam [*I.J.* p.254].

The formula occasionally varies as where Ibn Jubayr refers to the new moon being obscured (*ghumma hilāluhu 'alaynā*), [*I.J.* pp. 286, 318]. It is clear, furthermore, that the provision by the traveller of dating equivalents from the Christian calendar reflects the eclectic milieu in which he travelled, often, as is well known, using Christian ships [e.g. *I.J.* pp. 8, 317]. It was a strange age of real intercultural *travel and trading*, produced by centuries of co-operation, on the one hand, co-existing beside very real intercultural *military* strife produced by the Crusades, on the other, an apparent paradox upon which Ibn Jubayr himself felt moved to comment and rank among the '*ajā'ib* of his narrative [*I.J.* p. 260, see also pp. 271–3].

There is no doubt that, from a literary point of view, Ibn Jubayr's passion for dating can seriously slow down his narrative, making his text appear sometimes more ponderous and monotonous than that of Ibn Baṭṭūṭa which is less obviously subject to formal considerations of strict chronology, though also less fluid in other respects. Nonetheless, the precision of the former can also have distinct advantages: it is clear that, while Ibn Baṭṭūṭa claims to have lost some of his very few notes. [*I.B.* p. 369],[25] Ibn Jubayr must have been a frequent, careful and punctilious diarist (or had an extraordinary memory). Furthermore the chronological problems encountered in any study of the *Riḥla* of Ibn Baṭṭūṭa[26] are mercifully absent in that of Ibn Jubayr though, in fairness to the later traveller, it may be stressed that this is due as much to his predecessor's comparative shortness of voyage as the methodological nature of Ibn Jubayr's notetaking.

If attention to precise dating constitutes an obvious initial foundation for the *Riḥla* of Ibn Jubayr, then a 'sense of place',[27] and the travel impulse ineluctably associated with that sense, constitutes a second.

Here Ibn Jubayr is much more in harmony with Ibn Baṭṭūṭa. The former, like the latter, visited many of the great cities of Islam. And where Ibn Baṭṭūṭa expressed a wish to avoid, if at all possible, travelling over the same route twice [*I.B.* p. 191] Ibn Jubayr's own, admittedly smaller, *raḥḥāla* impulse is concretely expressed in *his* advice to the youth of the Maghrib to travel East to such great cities as Damascus, in search of success and knowledge (*fī ṭalab al-'ilm*) [*I.J.* p. 258]. Though there *is*, from a quantitative point of view, less anecdotal and fantastic material in Ibn Jubayr's *Riḥla* than that of Ibn Baṭṭūṭa,[28] nonetheless, there is sufficient to identify some genuine examples or aspects of such broad literary genres as *'ajā'ib*[29] or *nawādir*.[30] [It will be recalled that the full title of Ibn Baṭṭūṭa's own *Riḥla* was *Tuḥfat al-Nuẓẓār fī Gharā'ib al-Amṣār wa 'Ajā'ib al-Asfār*].[31] But the genuine in Ibn Jubayr is mixed in with much unnecessary rhetoric.

A few examples of what appears really to interest and intrigue Ibn Jubayr, not necessarily to be classified under either *'ajā'ib* or *nawādir*, may be provided here: he is amazed (lit: *shāhadnā 'ajaban*) at the bitumen well on the Tigris whose bitumen is dried out so that it congeals and can then be removed [*I.J.* p. 209]; he is enchanted by the sight of a Christian wedding in Tyre attended by both Christians and Muslims [*I.J.* pp. 278–79]; and he *is* fascinated by the strange story of an allegedly royal youth at the court of King William of Sicily [*I.J.* pp. 310–11]. But Ibn Jubayr's is basically a tourist vocabulary which becomes rapidly debased in its addictive use of superlatives. Mattock has already commented elsewhere on Ibn Jubayr's prose style: '. . . it employs a certain amount of unnecessary rhetoric . . . This verbal flatulence and empty praise after a while fails in its effect. It is irritating to the reader, and eventually turns him from his admiration for the author's ingenuity to consideration of his choice of words, and consequently to doubt of the sincerity of his description'.[32] His point may be briefly underlined and reiterated here: the almost 'baroque' and overblown nature of much of Ibn Jubayr's prose style sometimes makes the distinction between genuine elements of the *'ajā'ib* and *nawādir* genres on the one hand, and mere rhetoric, on the other, somewhat blurred, at least at first sight.[33]

His effusive style particularly invades his sense of place, producing false echoes of that early time when the *'ajā'ib* 'were correctly situated in geographical space'.[34] Indeed, Ibn Jubayr may be likened in intention to a prototype Roberts (1796–1864) or even Delacroix (1798–1863), trying to put into words what those Orientalist painters later produced so much more successfully on canvas.[35] Of the latter artist's work it has been observed: 'His vision of a living, sublime Antiquity in these countries [of North Africa] enabled him to strike a balance between the romantic and classical elements in his work'.[36] What Ibn Jubayr's prose style often lacks is a sense of *linguistic* or stylistic balance.

Thus the city of Damascus is described as 'the Paradise of the East' (*Jannat al-Mashriq*) [*I.J.* p. 234]; its hospitals and colleges are ranked among 'the great glories of Islam' (*mafkhar 'aẓīm min mafākhir al-Islām*) [*I.J.* p. 256]; and Ibn Jubayr enthusiastically informs his reader that 'one of the greatest and most amazing sights in the world' (*lit: wa min a'ẓam mā shāhadnāhu min manāẓir al-dunyā al-gharīb al-sha'n),* which is held to be indescribable, is that to be gained after the ascent to the top of the Lead Dome which crowned the Cathedral Mosque in Damascus [*I.J.* p. 264].

His immediate and insistent tourist delight in the *places* which he visits, however, does not preclude an interest in the diverse *people* of those places. In this, too, Ibn Jubayr resembles Ibn Baṭṭūṭa. Like the latter he is interested, though to a less passionate degree, in the ascetics of Islam[37] [e.g. *I.J.* pp. 220, 256–7]; and Ibn Jubayr also manifests a particular interest in, or veneration for, imams and notables, for example, of the Shāfi'ī *madhhab* whom he mentions frequently [e.g. *I.J.* pp. 22, 122–3, 177, 195, 224].

The third and final foundation upon which the *Riḥla* of Ibn Jubayr rests is its literal, as well as spiritual, orientation towards Mecca. Though, as we have previously noted, the purpose of the *Riḥla* is nowhere in the text precisely articulated in expiatory terms, it should never be forgotten by the reader of the *Riḥla* that its primary motor is the expiation of the 'sin' forced upon him in Granada. Whether this desire for penitence and expiation unconsciously informs the occasional virulence of his writing about sectarian Islam, or Christianity, in an excess of zeal, remains a matter for speculation. It must surely be responsible, however, in part at least, for the extended narrative about, and description of, the Cities of Mecca and Medina: by laying such conscious stress on their physical description and the pilgrimage ceremonies, Ibn Jubayr, at least unconsciously, manifests to all, including the Almohad governor of Granada, that his purpose is accomplished, expiation is made and forgiveness from Allah surely achieved. [See *I.J.* pp. 58–160, 167–81].

The semiotics of the *Riḥla* of Ibn Jubayr may next be considered. It is a truism that everything signifies;[38] the Qur'ān itself identifies an entire world, apparent and hidden, conceived of in terms of signs: 'We shall show them Our signs in the horizons and in themselves . . .' (*Sa-nurīhim āyātinā fī 'l-āfāq wa fī anfusihim*)[39] So it would be perfectly valid to say here that the *Riḥla* of Ibn Jubayr is also a world of signs, whose examination would be sufficient to fill a major thesis in itself. Our analysis will, therefore, be restricted to an identification of some of those signs which contribute, in some way, towards illuminating or assessing the primary question posed at the beginning of this essay: to what extent, if any, may a pilgrim paradigm, prototype to that identified in the *Riḥla* of Ibn Baṭṭūṭa, be identified in the *Riḥla* of Ibn Jubayr?

In the first place, his *Riḥla* is interesting for what is *not* signified: while Ibn Jubayr, like Ibn Baṭṭūṭa [*I.B.* p. 14], at the beginning of his work, makes a formal expression of intent to perform the pilgrimage (*lit: li- 'l-niyya al-ḥijāziyya al-mubāraka, I.J.*, p. 7), the intention *behind* the pilgrimage intention, as we have emphasised, remains hidden. Ibn Baṭṭūṭa's *Riḥla* unfolds at length as the ultimate satisfaction of a primary and insistent wanderlust which takes *that* traveller far beyond the Cities of Mecca and Medina. Ibn Jubayr's *Riḥla* once the Holy Cities are visited, is the narrative of a much briefer, return voyage to Spain, mission accomplished. Ibn Jubayr's work, then, signifies a search 'for the shrine' and wallows in the 'circumambient religious geography'.[40] But it provides little evidence that Ibn Jubayr's wanderlust, such as it was, approached in any way the magnitude of Ibn Baṭṭūṭa's.

What Ibn Jubayr's text *does* signify, most clearly, throughout, is an Islamic world already divided upon itself by religious faction and suspicion. A deeply riven sectarian milieu in the whole of *dār al-Islām* is apparent from Ibn Jubayr's view of and comments upon the state of Islam in Arabia, whose entire peninsula might be said to constitute a species of 'religious geography'[41] for the holy City of Mecca. This City, one of the profoundest symbols of the Islamic faith, and its theoretical and yearned-for unity, is thus, paradoxically, for Ibn Jubayr the focus of a voyage which sometimes instructs that traveller in a variety of aspects of Islam at its most *disunited*. His disillusionment and rage are only exacerbated and compounded by the strife of the Crusades and the conflicting and ambivalent attitudes which those wars generate about Christianity and Christians within his heart.[42] Broadhurst, writing of the age and milieu of Ibn Jubayr, observes: 'The eastern Muslim world was now one; the Frankish kingdom was enveloped, and its death-knell had sounded. If the opponents of the Cross were at last united, all within the Christian realm was anarchy and alarm. King Baldwin IV was a dying leper . . .'[43] Broadhurst's rhetorical intention is clearly to contrast Ṣalāḥ al-Dīn with such Christian figures as Baldwin. For Broadhurst, 'it was the role and achievement of Saladin to unite Islam'.[44] But this translator of Ibn Jubayr's *Riḥla* into English only provides an exaggerated and partial picture, drawing primarily upon the *politics* of the age: Ibn Jubayr himself, in what is a lengthy, and clearly deeply-felt passage, articulates his disgust at the 'events'[45] which have currently become associated with the eternal 'religious geography' of Arabia and Mecca. He writes:

> The lands of God which most deserve to be cleansed by the sword and have their filth (*lit: arjāsahā*) and uncleanness purged in blood shed in Holy War are these lands of the Ḥijāz. This is because they have untied the bonds of Islam and regarded as fair game both the wealth and the blood of the pilgrim [to Mecca]. Those among the jurists of al-Andalus who believe that [people] should be released from this religious obligation [of pilgrimage] are correct in their belief for this reason and because of the way in which the pilgrim is handled, which displeases God Almighty. He who travels this path exposes himself to danger and certain hazard. God intended His franchise in that place to be bestowed in quite another manner. So how is it that the House of God is now in the hands of people who seek a forbidden subsistence from it and make it a way to plunder wealth and unlawfully lay claim to [that wealth] and seize pilgrims because of it: in consequence the latter are humiliated and brought to dire poverty. May God soon remedy this in a cleansing which will remove these ruinous heresies from the Muslims with the swords of the Almohads, who are the Followers of the Faith , the Party of God, the People of Truth and Sincerity, Defenders of the Sanctuary of God Almighty, solicitous for His taboos, making every effort to exalt His name, manifest His mission and support His religion. God can do what He wishes. He is indeed a wonderful Lord and Ally. Let there be absolutely no shadow of doubt about the fact that there is no Islam except in the lands of the Maghrib . . . [*I.J.* p. 55].

While this stream of biased invective from Ibn Jubayr is clearly provoked, in the first instance, by his outrage at the treatment of pilgrims in Arabia, there is little doubt that it also reflects much more: it signifies a real deep-seated religious malaise and division within the Islamic world and reflects genuine sectarian squabbles, rather than simply the righteous anger expressed in a somewhat overblown fashion by one irate pilgrim at the cruel treatment of his fellows, and the unfair exactions levied against them, and himself.

This is confirmed by Ibn Jubayr in a typically exaggerated comment which appears in the text of the *Riḥla* shortly before the lines quoted above and which deserves to be cited here:

> Most of [the people of] these Ḥijāzī regions and other areas are sectarians (lit. *firaq*) and Shī'ites who have no religion (*lā dīn lahum*) and have split into diverse schools of thought (*madhāhib*) [*I.J.* p. 54].

We may safely conclude that Ibn Jubayr's *Riḥla* betokens a certain lack of enjoyment, in Arabia especially, as he strove, finally successfully, to reach his goal of Mecca and all that this City held for the pious pilgrim in terms of shrine and ritual.[46]

If the first *major* set of signals thrown up by the text reveals a divided Islamic world which itself inhibits or, at the very least, intrudes upon the search 'for the shrine',[47] then a second, which provides a significant contrast, is that which betokens the intrusive Christian presence in the Middle East. The signs and symbols of Christianity, embedded in many parts of the text, would have reminded Ibn Jubayr's reader of the contemporary crusading wars between Muslim and Christian, and also served as overt indicators to that reader of the author's Almohad 'orthodoxy' [see *I.J.* pp. 55–6] which he felt constrained to champion and proclaim. This was particularly the case when such signs and symbols of the Christian faith were linked to dirt and filth and some examples of this will be cited shortly. A semiotic examination of all this highlights Ibn Jubayr's occasionally ambivalent attitude to Christianity in a particularly vivid way. Such an examination also reveals a semiotics of cultural-religious alienation in which, paradoxically, the exotic (represented for Ibn Jubayr by certain aspects of Christianity), plays some role.[48]

We may identify in the *Riḥla* at least five basic 'signs' of alienation for Ibn Jubayr: several are tinged by aspects either of the 'exoticism' or the ambivalence referred to above. These signs recur to a greater or lesser degree in the text and may be enumerated briefly as follows: (i) *The Christian cross*, (ii) *The Christian ship*, (iii) *Christian regal power*, (iv) *Christian taxation*, and (v) perhaps most oddly and paradoxically, *Christian chivalry, courtesy and mores*. Each will be surveyed here.

(i)*The Christian cross* for Ibn Jubayr is not so much a sign or message of folly[49] as a sign of oppression, a sign of what impedes the search for the shrine. It is the arch-symbol of an invader who has stolen away some of the most precious sites of the Muslim peoples like, for example, Acre [See *I.J.* pp. 276–7]. Of the latter City Ibn Jubayr writes: 'The Franks wrested it from the hands of the Muslims . . . Islam wept grievously (*lit: mil'a jufūnih*) for it. It was one of [Islam's] griefs' [*I.J.* p. 276]. Little wonder, then, that the cross in Ibn Jubayr's text is linked with dirt and filth, or deliberately devalued in an equally derogatory association: Acre 'burns with unbelief and tyranny, boiling over with pigs and crosses. [The City is] filthy and squalid and all of it is filled with dirt and shit' [*I.J.* p. 276]; the City of Messina is 'overcast through unbelief; no Muslim resides there. It is laden with cross worshippers (*'abadat al-Ṣulbān*) . . . [and] is full of stench and dirt' [*I.J.* p. 296]. Elsewhere 'the cross worshippers' are described (somewhat resentfully?) as living a life of comfort and ease on the island of Sicily and though Muslims *do* share to a degree in this comfort, it is subject to a tax levied by the Christians twice a year [*I.J.* p. 297]; by severe contrast, the Muslim populace is said to suffer painfully under 'the cross worshippers' (*'ubbād al-Ṣalīb*) in the Sicilian town of Trapani [*I.J.* p. 313]. The cross is an exotic sign of prosperity and wealth among the Christians of Palermo where Ibn Jubayr remarks upon the numerous churches with gold and silver crosses [*I.J.* p. 305]; and a symbol of apostasy *par excellence* when it is trampled by a Christian convert to Islam [*I.J.* p. 312]. All these examples demonstrate the multivalent symbolism of the cross in Ibn Jubayr's text and the derogatory associations with which it is endowed.

It is tempting to try and tease out the semiotic connotations of the *hilāl* to which Ibn Jubayr always refers in his dating at the beginning of each chapter, and contrast it as an Islamic symbol with the semiotics of the Christian cross elaborated above. But such a superficially promising and attractive idea seems doomed to failure: Ibn Jubayr's own usage of the word *hilāl* is purely for dating purposes, rather than any latent or overt Islamic religious symbolism. In any case, recent research seems to conclude that, in mediaeval times, and later,

> there cannot have been a strong religious association with the *hilāl* in the Muslim world, as the emblem occurs also on secular buildings . . . and on military flags and textiles as well . . . There are also many renditions of mosques and other buildings dating from the 10th/16th century to the 12th/18th century which lack the crescent finial, and the motif plays no role on prayer rugs or on tiles applied to the walls of mosques . . . This indicates that in Muslim eyes, and in particular during the Ottoman period, the *hilāl* was not of great importance. It certainly does not seem to have had a major religious significance and was apparently applied mostly for decorative purposes.[50]

The most that we can say then is that, while the *hilāl* certainly had *some* cultural and religious symbolism in the Islamic Middle Ages,[51] it was by no means as dominant a motif in purely symbolic religious terms as the cross: this difference in emphasis, at least in mediaeval times, is reflected in Ibn Jubayr's own text. Where, of course, the *hilāl* did have real significance in Islam, from a religious point of view, in mediaeval times as in modern, was in the area of religious law because of the need to date the pilgrimage and the start and finish of Ramaḍān.[52] Ibn Jubayr himself, not surprisingly, took an interest in the new moon from this point of view and, on at least two occasions in his text, he draws particular attention to the vital necessity of using the new moon to date such important events in the Islamic religious calendar [see *I.J.* pp. 117–121, 146–7] and how rumour, falsehood, eclipse or cloud could confuse the reckoning.

(ii) It might be thought at first sight that the *Christian ship* as well as being a symbol of wanderlust *par excellence*, would be a symbol or sign of unity, harmony and friendship, traversing as it did the boundaries of *dār al-ḥarb* and *dār al-Islām* and bearing, as it did, a mixed cargo of Christians and Muslims. And, as we have already seen, Ibn Jubayr himself sailed in Christian ships [e.g. see *I.J.* pp. 8, 317] while being perfectly aware of the anomalous situation created by Christian and Muslim travellers such as himself, and especially merchants, moving freely in each other's lands while their respective armies fought each other [*I.J.* p. 260]. Ibn Jubayr certainly appreciated the travel facilities thus extended to him by ships from Christendom but there is a clear ambivalence in his attitude and a latent prejudice and resentment never seem to be far from the surface: he admires the nautical skill of a Genoese Christian sea captain [*I.J.* p. 285] but clearly dislikes the fact that captain inherits the possessions of both the Christian and Muslim pilgrims who die on the voyage [*I.J.* p. 287]. On this large boat from Acre Ibn Jubayr notes how the Muslims secure berths separate from the Christians and his obvious approval of this is mixed with considerable resentment at the later boarding of more than two thousand Christian pilgrims from Jerusalem, from whose company Ibn Jubayr uncharitably prays to be speedily delivered! [*I.J.* p. 283] During his description of the events which lead up to the shipwreck off Messina, Ibn Jubayr unfavourably contrasts the griefstricken behaviour of the Christians with the more pietistic and fatalistic attitude of the Muslim passengers [*I.J.* p. 294]. Yet the salvation from the wreck of many impecunious Muslim passengers, unable to pay their rescuers' fee, is freely attributed to the generosity of the Christian King of Sicily, William II [*reg.* 1166–1189] [*I.J.* p. 295]. Indeed, Ibn Jubayr goes so far as to state, in a manner that has some significance for the semiotics of the ambivalent Muslim-Christian relations of the age, that the (almost miraculous) presence of the Christian king at this shipwreck was an example of God's kindness towards the Muslim passengers [*I.J.* p. 295].

The previous examples of Ibn Jubayr's description of his dealings with Christian ships, and the Christian section of the passengers and crew who sailed in them, constitute a microcosm of the broader frame of Muslim-Christian relations. Elements of trust, gratitude, appreciation and indeed, occasional admiration, mingle with disapproval, deep-seated hostility, suspicion and fear.

(iii) There are few areas in the *Riḥla* of Ibn Jubayr where the author's frequent bias against Christianity is more pronounced and manifest than in his succinct characterisation of those who hold *Christian regal power*. For example, Baldwin IV (*reg.* 1174–1185), King of the Latin Kingdom of Jerusalem and 'Lord of Acre' (*Ṣāḥib 'Akka*) is bluntly characterised by Ibn Jubayr as 'this pig' (*hādhā 'l-khinzīr* [*I.J.* p. 282; see also p. 274]; his mother, Agnes of Courtenay, is called a 'sow' [*I.J.* p. 274]; William II of Sicily, despite the good things said about him, as noted above, in connection with the shipwreck – and despite also the existence of a treaty or truce between him and the Almohad ruler Abū Ya'qūb Yūsuf b. 'Abd al-Mu'min [*reg.* 1163–1184][53] – is still brusquely deemed to be 'this polytheist' (*hādhā 'l-mushrik*) [*I.J.* p. 299], capable of considerable harshness towards the Muslims of Sicily, including forced conversion [*I.J.* p. 313]. Of him, Ibn Jubayr further notes: 'He is about thirty years old. May God save the Muslims from his misdeed[s] and his extension [of power]' [*I.J.* p. 298]. Count Raymond of Tripoli [1152–1187] is described as 'a man of great importance among the cursed Franks'. He is 'the cursed Count, Lord of Tripoli and Tiberias' [*I.J.* p. 282].

Of course, the ideal paradigm of the just ruler, and 'Mirror' for all other princes, Muslim as well as Christian, in the view of Ibn Jubayr was the redoubtable Ṣalāḥ al-Dīn. Not only was he a renowned Muslim champion in the crusading wars [see *I.J.* p. 270] but he was a model of rectitude as well: Ibn Jubayr states that the confusion and dishonesty of the Egyptian customs would certainly have been sorted out by Ṣalāḥ al-Dīn, had he known about it [I.J. pp. 13–14]; indeed, Ibn Jubayr states that Sālāḥ al-Dīn abolished several iniquitous taxes levied in Egypt, including a pilgrim tax and one on drinking Nile water! [*I.J.* pp. 30–31]. The theme of Ṣalāḥ al-Dīn's justice is a constant one throughout the *Riḥla* (see, for example, *I.J.* pp. 14, 30, 55–6, 270–1). It is small wonder that, by contrast, the Christian rulers surveyed above receive little but opprobrium from Ibn Jubayr's pen.

(iv) Taxation by one's own government is an obvious irritant and an often alienating feature in most societies! It is not surprising, then, that in the milieu in which Ibn Jubayr travelled, he should have found the imposition of *Christian taxation* a source of some annoyance. This annoyance would have been clearly exacerbated in his mind by the generosity and justice perceived from his great hero, Ṣalāḥ al-Dīn. We have just noted above the abolition by the latter of several taxes in Egypt and other examples are admiringly recorded in the *Riḥla* of Ṣalāḥ al-Dīn's generosity as far as taxation was concerned [see *I.J.* p. 16].

All this contrasts with examples cited in the text of taxes imposed by Christians: some, because of the element of reciprocity involved, are clearly not too irksome: 'The Christians levy a tax on the Muslims in their country which guarantees the Muslims full protection; in a similar fashion Christian merchants pay a tax on their goods in Muslim countries' [*I.J.* p. 270]. Others, however, rouse Ibn Jubayr's resentment to a greater degree: in Sicily the Muslim populace is subjected to a twice-yearly tax by the Christians which thus bars them from a full exploitation and enjoyment of the land [*I.J.* p. 297]. Ibn Jubayr prays for a full restoration of their rights. At the fortress of Tibnīn it is the itinerant Maghribis who are subject to taxation as punishment for a previous attack. Ibn Jubayr notes: 'When the Maghribis pay this tax, they are happily reminded of how they annoyed the enemy: this makes it easier for them and softens their hardship for them' [*I.J.* p. 274]. In the light of all this, Ibn Jubayr's acute embarrassment – which shines through the text – may be imagined when he discovers on the road from Tibnīn that there are Muslims living under Frankish occupation who are taxed and threatened far *less* harshly than some Muslims living under Muslim rule [*I.J.* pp. 274–5]. As Ibn Jubayr wryly remarks: 'Muslims complain of the tyranny of their own kind and praise the conduct of their Frankish enemy' [*I.J.* p. 275].

(v) Basically, for Ibn Jubayr, Christianity, with all it entails of *Christian chivalry, courtesy and mores*, is a snare and an exotic delusion from which Ibn Jubayr is perpetually praying to be delivered, the more he gains in knowledge about that faith. He has a natural curiosity about Christianity, especially what he perceives to be its 'exotic' elements; but he also seems to sense a seduction, and the potential for a fall from the true faith of Islam, behind every Christian smile and courtesy. Certainly, as we have seen, he is grateful to King William of Sicily for his help and generosity towards distressed Muslim passengers. This is freely acknowledged by the author. Credit is given elsewhere in the text to Christians where it is due. But, when all is said and done, Ibn Jubayr fervently prays for Muslims to be delivered from King William's 'enticement' or 'temptation' (*fitna*) [*I.J.* p. 298]. He is extremely wary of the courteous Christians whom he meets in Sicily: 'We perceived in their conduct and gentle demeanour (*lit: maqṣid*) towards the Muslims something which might cause temptation (*fitna*) in the souls of ignorant people' [*I.J.* p. 302; see also p. 304]. He prays that the people of Muḥammad may be protected from such a *fitna*. The exotic beauty of some of the decoration in the Christian Church of the Antiochian in Palermo creates temptation (*fitna*) in the souls from which the priggish Ibn Jubayr prays to be delivered [*I.J.* p. 306]. The author is similarly enchanted *and* disturbed by the exotic spectacle of the Christian wedding which he witnesses in Tyre. He admits to its being a spectacular sight, admires the finery of the bride and yet prays to be preserved from any temptation (*fitna*) arising out of the sight, a prayer which is repeated again, with the use of the same word *fitna* at the end of his description of the wedding [*I.J.* pp. 278–9, compare p. 307].

Ibn Jubayr's insistent usage of the word *fitna* is interesting. As is well-known, the Arabic word can mean 'civil strife' as well as 'temptation'. We can only speculate about the degree to which Ibn Jubayr surveyed a world divided upon itself religiously and politically and linked the two meanings in his own mind. What we can say is that Ibn Jubayr's usage of the word *fitna* often signals, or reinforces, a certain sense of the strange, the alien or the exotic which may deviate, or cause others to deviate, from the *ṣirāṭ al-mustaqīm* as he knows it and, in consequence, lead the soul to perdition.

Taken altogether, this fivefold semiotic survey of the principal elements of cultural-religious alienation in the *Riḥla* of Ibn Jubayr, imbued as they are with a certain authorial ambivalence on the one hand and aspects of the exotic which can both please and frighten on the other, leads inexorably to one conclusion which comes as no surprise. We may identify in the person of Ibn Jubayr a basic gut reaction: Ibn Jubayr did not really like Christians or Christianity. It is true that he may, on occasion, admire individual Christian people or their actions, but the Crusading milieu and his own religious upbringing and environment prove too strong to disguise Ibn Jubayr's fundamental attitude: Christianity is intrinsically the enemy from every point of view, whether it be moral, spiritual or physical.

We are now in a position to attempt an answer to the question posed at the beginning of this essay: to what extent may a prototype pilgrim paradigm, similar to that identified in the *Riḥla* of Ibn Baṭṭūṭa, be identified in the work of Ibn Jubayr? The answer must be that a *partial* paradigmatic prototype *does* exist which is in neat accordance with the idea of Ibn Jubayr's *Riḥla* being a general prototype for much else in the

Riḥla genre: thus, Ibn Jubayr *does* undertake a search for the shrine and traverse its religious geography; he *does* seek knowledge from people and places where he can find it, being directly familiar with the concept of *ṭalab al-'ilm* [see *I.J.* p. 258]; he *is* interested in the exercise of power though usually by others, e.g. Ṣalāḥ al-Dīn, William of Sicily, rather than himself: in this respect, at least, he is a rather humbler figure than that of Ibn Baṭṭūṭa. There remains, then, the question of a basic wanderlust: here, as we have noted, there *is* some divergence between Ibn Jubayr and Ibn Baṭṭūṭa. This is not to say that Ibn Jubayr is *totally* devoid of the travel urge but simply to note that his illustrious successor was beset by that urge to a sublime degree.

In conclusion, then, it is the contention of this essay that, in the matter of a pilgrim paradigm, as in so many other areas, Ibn Jubayr's *Riḥla* foreshadows, or acts as a precursor to, the *Riḥla* of Ibn Baṭṭūṭa, and acts as worthy forbear of that later work.

NOTES

[This essay was originally a paper presented to the Fourth International Colloquium of the Department of Arabic and Islamic Studies, University of Exeter, on *Hijra, Ḥajj and Riḥla*, 19–22 September, 1989. It also appeared in Ian Richard Netton (ed.), *Golden Roads: Migration, Pilgrimage and Travel in Mediaeval and Modern Islam*, (Richmond: Curzon Press, 1993), pp. 57–74; and *Journal of Arabic Literature*, vol. XXII:1 (March 1991), pp. 21–37.]

1 See my 'Arabia and the Pilgrim Paradigm of Ibn Baṭṭūṭa: A Braudelian Approach' in Ian Richard Netton (ed.), *Arabia and the Gulf: From Traditional Society to Modern States*, (London: Croom Helm, 1986), pp. 29–42.

2 Ibid., pp. 37–8.

3 See, e.g. Ch. Pellat, art. 'Ibn Djubayr', *EI*², vol. III, p. 755; and Michael Karl Lenker, 'The Importance of the *Riḥla* for the Islamization of Spain', unpublished PhD thesis, University of Pennsylvania, 1982, p. 34.

4 Muḥammad b. Muḥammad al-'Abdarī was the author of a notable *Riḥla* entitled *al-Riḥla al-Maghribiyya*. His birth and death dates are unknown but he commenced the travels which he describes in December 1289. His *Riḥla* has been edited twice in recent times in 1965 and 1968: Algiers/Constantine, 1965, ed. by Aḥmad b. Jadū; and Rabat: Jāmi'at Muḥammad al-Khāmis, 1968, ed. by Muḥammad al-Fāsī. See Muh. Ben Cheneb-W. Hoenerbach, art. 'Al-'Abdarī', *EI*², vol. I, p. 96 and Amikam Elad, 'The Description of the Travels of Ibn Baṭṭūṭa in Palestine: Is it Original?', *Journal of the Royal Asiatic Society* (1987), no. 2, esp. pp. 259, 269, nn. 27, 28.

5 See the aforementioned latest article to appear on the subject, dealing with the Palestinian material in the works of al-'Abdarī and Ibn Baṭṭūṭa, by Elad, pp. 256–72; see also Muh. Ben Cheneb-W. Hoenerbach, art. 'Al-'Abdarī', p. 96. See my remarks on Ibn Baṭṭūṭa's plagiarism of Ibn Jubayr in my article 'Myth, Miracle and Magic in the *Riḥla* of Ibn Baṭṭūṭa', *Journal of Semitic Studies*, vol. XXIX: 1 (1984), p. 132, esp. n. 6; and also Pellat, art.

'Ibn Djubayr', p. 755; J.N. Mattock, 'The Travel Writings of Ibn Jubair and Ibn Baṭūṭa', *Glasgow Oriental Society Transactions*, XXI (1965–6), pp. 35–46, esp. pp. 38–9; idem, 'Ibn Baṭṭūṭa's use of Ibn Jubayr's *Riḥla*', in Rudolph Peters (ed.), *Proceedings of the Ninth Congress of the Union Européene des Arabisants et Islamisants (Amsterdam 1st–7th September 1978*, Publications of the Netherlands Institute of Archaeology and Arabic Studies in Cairo, no. 4, (Leiden: E.J. Brill, 1981), pp. 209–218.

6 See Lenker, 'The Importance of the *Riḥla*', pp. 189–91 for more on this concept.

7 Ibid., p. 103.

8 Ibid., p. 189.

9 See my 'Arabia and the Pilgrim Paradigm of Ibn Baṭṭūṭa', p. 37.

10 See my article 'Ibn Jubayr: Penitent Pilgrim and Observant Traveller', *UR*, 2, 1985, pp. 14–17.

11 *Nafḥ al-Ṭīb*, ed. Iḥsān 'Abbās, (Beirut: Dār Ṣādir, 1968), vol. 2, p. 385.

12 See my 'Myth, Miracle and Magic', *passim.*

13 Netton, 'Arabia and the Pilgrim Paradigm of Ibn Baṭṭūṭa', p. 40.

14 'The Travel Writings of Ibn Jubair and Ibn Baṭṭūṭa', p. 36.

15 Ibid., p. 35.

16 Ibid., p. 36.

17 H.A.R. Gibb (trans.), *Ibn Battūta: Travels in Asia and Africa, 1325–1354*, The Broadway Travellers, (London: Routledge & Kegan Paul, 1929), pp. 12–13.

18 Ross E. Dunn, *The Adventures of Ibn Baṭṭūṭa: A Muslim Traveller of the 14th Century*, (London: Croom Helm, 1986), p. x., see also p. 313.

19 *I.B.* = the Arabic text of the *Riḥla* of Ibn Baṭṭūṭa as contained in the edition edited by Karam al-Bustānī: *Riḥlat Ibn Baṭṭūṭa*, (Beirut: Dār Ṣādir, 1964).

20 Trans. by H.A.R. Gibb, *The Travels of Ibn Baṭṭūṭa A.D. 1325–1354*, (Cambridge: Pub. for the Hakluyt Society at the University Press, 1958), vol. I, p. 34.

21 Ibid., p. 36.

22 Trans. by H.A.R. Gibb, *The Travels of Ibn Baṭṭūṭa A.D. 1325–1354*, (Cambridge: Pub. for the Hakluyt Society at the University Press, 1962), vol. 2, p. 405.

23 *I.J.* = the Arabic text of the *Riḥla* of Ibn Jubayr in the following edition: *Riḥlat Ibn Jubayr*, (Beirut: Dār Ṣādir, 1964).

24 William Wright, in his early edition of the *Riḥla* (*The Travels of Ibn Jubayr*, ed. from a Ms. in the University Library of Leyden by William Wright, 2nd edn. rev. by M.J. de Goeje, [Leiden: E.J. Brill/London: Luzac, 1907; repr. New York: AMS, 1973]), has the following comments in his 'Preface': 'The dates are, I believe, with the alterations I have made, everywhere correct, though perfect uniformity with calculations according to the method laid down in the *Art de vérifier les dates* is not to be expected' (p. 16). See the important comments on Ibn Jubayr's prose style and his fetish for dating by John Mattock. 'The Travel Writings of Ibn Jubair and Ibn Baṭūṭa', p. 43.

25 What he lost were details which he had copied down from scholars' tombs in Bukhārā. Whether he made any *other* notes is highly debatable: see Gibb, *Ibn Baṭṭūṭa: Travels in Asia and Africa, 1325–1354*, p. 10; Dunn, *The Adventures of Ibn Baṭṭūṭa*, pp. 312–13. John Mattock does seem to believe that some notes were made by Ibn Baṭṭūṭa: see his 'Ibn Baṭṭūṭa's use of Ibn

Jubayr's *Riḥla*', p. 217 and idem. 'The Travel Writings of Ibn Jubair and Ibn Baṭūṭa', p. 42.

26 See my 'Myth, Miracle and Magic', p. 133, n. 12, and Ivan Hrbek, 'The Chronology of Ibn Baṭṭūṭa's Travels', *Archiv Orientální*, XXX (1962), pp. 409–86.

27 A phrase used here by me to designate specifically both the delight in, and curiosity about, *new* places visited by a *raḥḥāla.*

28 See my 'Myth, Miracle and Magic', p. 134.

29 See C.E. Dubler, art. ''Adjā'ib', *EI*², vol. I, pp. 203–4 for a description of the genre. The author notes the degeneration of the concept of *'ajā'ib* from early times when they 'were correctly situated in geographical space' to a later type which 'transport us from tangible reality to the realm of fancy constituted by the oriental tales' (p. 204). Both types are apparent in Ibn Jubayr's work. See also Ibn al-Khaṭīb, *al-Iḥāṭa fī Akhbār Gharnāṭa*, vol. 2, ed. Muḥammad 'Abdallāh 'Inān, (Cairo: Maktabat al-Khānjī, 1974), p. 232.

30 For a lengthy example of this genre, see M.T. Magūz, 'A Critical Edition of the 14th Part of *Kitāb an-Nawādir wa az-Ziyādāt* by Ibn Abī Zayd al-Qayrawānī 310 A.H.-386 A.H.', unpublished PhD thesis, University of Exeter, 1989.

31 See Karam al-Bustānī's 'Preface' (p. 6) to the 1964 Beirut edition of Ibn Baṭṭūṭa's *Riḥla* cited above at n. 19; see also my 'Myth, Miracle and Magic', p. 132, n. 4.

32 Mattock, 'The Travel Writings of Ibn Jubair and Ibn Baṭūṭa', p. 36; see also Pellat ('Ibn Djubayr', p. 755) who writes: '[Ibn Jubayr's] style, though in certain narrative passages lively and vivid in a way which recalls the manner of modern reporters, is over-florid . . .'

33 This may, of course, have been a deliberate consequence of the magpie instinct with which many an author collected and reiterated phenomena in terms such as *'ajā'ib* and *nawādir*. However, Rosenthal's remarks on another 'minor branch of Muslim literature with affinities to *Adab*, historical and theological literature', namely the *awā'il* literature, are, in general, equally true of the *'ajā'ib* and *nawādir* genres: they 'are brilliant expressions of the cultural outlook and historical sense of their authors, and they are full of valuable material and interesting insights' (F. Rosenthal, art. *'Awā'il', EI*², vol. 1, p. 758). This is not, of course, always the case in Ibn Jubayr's *Riḥla*, as we can see. However, for a specimen of writing in Ibn Jubayr's text which may genuinely, and usefully, be classified under the *'ajā'ib* genre, and where the fantastic nature of the marvel cited is confirmed by others, see his enthusiastic description of the temple architecture at Ikhmīm in Upper Egypt [*I.J. pp. 35–8*]. See S. Sauneron, 'Le Temple d'Akhmīn Décrit par Ibn Jobair', *Bulletin de l'Institut Français d'Archéologie Orientale*, vol. 51 (1952), pp. 123–35, esp. p. 125. For Ibn Jubayr the temple which he describes at Ikhmīm is one of 'the wonders of the world' (*'ajā'ib al-dunyā*) [*I.J* p. 37].

34 See above, n. 29.

35 See Mary Anne Stevens, (ed.), *The Orientalists: Delacroix to Matisse: European Painters in North Africa and the Near East*, (London: Royal Academy of Arts/Weidenfeld and Nicolson, 1984), esp. pp. 42–5, 52–5, 122–8, 223–5.

36 Ibid., p. 122.
37 See my article 'Myth, Miracle and Magic', for Ibn Baṭṭūṭa reference. See also Ibn al-Khaṭīb, *al-Iḥāṭa*, vol. 2, pp. 232–33.
38 See Umberto Eco, *A Theory of Semiotics*, Advances in Semiotics, (Bloomington and London: Indiana University Press, 1976), pp. 6–7.
39 Q.XLI: 53, trans. by A.J. Arberry, *The Koran Interpreted*, (London: Allen & Unwin/New York: Macmillan, 1971), vol. 2, p. 191.
40 See my 'Arabia and the Pilgrim Paradigm of Ibn Baṭṭūṭa', p. 37.
41 For the term 'religious geography', see my article'Arabia and the Pilgrim Paradigm of Ibn Baṭṭūṭa', esp. p. 36.
42 Ibn Jubayr's attitudes to Christians and Christianity will be surveyed at a later stage in this essay. He was not the only one to wrestle with the problems generated by the presence of Christianity and the Crusades in the Middle East. For the attitudes of some of the Muslim jurists, for example, towards those Muslim pilgrims etc. who travelled in Christian ships, see A. Gateau, 'Quelques Observations sur l'Intérêt du Voyage d'Ibn Jubayr', *Hespéris*, vol. XXXVI: 3–4, (1949), pp. 293–5.
43 R.J.C. Broadhurst, (trans.), *The Travels of Ibn Jubayr*, (London: Jonathan Cape, 1952), p. 18.
44 Ibid., p. 17.
45 See my 'Arabia and the Pilgrim Paradigm of Ibn Baṭṭūṭa', p. 36.
46 Ibid.
47 Ibid., pp. 36–7.
48 For a reverse picture in which elements of Islam were perceived as exotic by Europeans, see my article 'The Mysteries of Islam', in G.S. Rousseau and R. Porter (eds.), *Exoticism in the Enlightenment*, (Manchester: Manchester University Press, 1989), pp. 23–45.
49 See 1 Corinthians 1:18, 23.
50 J. Schacht/R. Ettinghausen, art. 'Hilāl', *EI²*, vol. III, p. 383.
51 See ibid. where Ettinghausen notes: 'The *Hilāl* was also used in religious settings. W. Barthold states after N. Marr that when in the 5th/11th century the Cathedral of Ani was converted into a mosque the cross on its dome was replaced by a silver crescent, which could imply a symbolical value or at least a cultural identification for this emblem'. The same author notes the usage of the crescent on Arab-Sāsānian coinage 'including one probably struck for 'Abd al-Malik in Damascus in 75/695' (ibid., p. 381); and, in connection with the mosaics of the Qubbat al-Ṣakhra in Jerusalem, Ettinghausen believes that the Sāsānian-type crowns, to which the crescent constitutes 'the customary finial', and the Byzantine-type crowns from which the *hilāl* is suspended, are reflective 'of a pre-Islamic usage now introduced into a Muslim context' (ibid., p. 381).
52 See ibid., p. 379.
53 See Broadhurst, *The Travels of Ibn Jubayr*, p. 387, n. 171; Helene Wieruszowski, 'The Norman Kingdom of Sicily and the Crusades' in Robert Lee Wolff and Harry W. Hazard, *A History of the Crusades: Volume II: The Later Crusades 1189–1311*, 2nd edn., (Madison, Milwaukee & London: University of Wisconsin Press, 1969), pp. 32–33; A. Huici Miranda, art. 'Abū Ya'ḳūb Yūsuf B. 'Abd al-Mu'min', *EI²*, vol. I, pp. 160–62.

10

TOURIST *ADAB* AND CAIRENE ARCHITECTURE

The Mediaeval Paradigm of Ibn Jubayr and Ibn Baṭṭūṭa

There is a tourist paradigm or classic itinerary of visits which may be derived from any great city. This is as true of visits made in antiquity and the Middle Ages as it is in the late twentieth century. Constraints of time usually ensure that the visitor to – as opposed to the resident in – a chosen city undertakes a limited itinerary embracing a few major, much-traversed sites, which recur over and over again in every tourist programme, often at the expense of many others. We think, for example, of Stonehenge in England, the Acropolis in Athens, and the Taj Mahal in India. Cairo is – and was– no exception. A brief glance at a modern travel brochure, selected at random, promises from the glories of Ancient Egypt, visits to Memphis, Saqqara, the Pyramids and Sphinx at Giza, and the Egyptian Museum of Antiquities, if we confine our glance just to that part of the programme dealing with the City of Cairo and its environs. Of the glories of Islamic Cairo we are promised a 'fascinating tour' which 'starts with a visit to the 12th century citadel of Salah-El-Din, includes the Mohammed Ali Alabaster Mosque and the Sultan Hassan Mosque, both outstanding examples of Islamic architecture, and ends with a stroll round the pulsating Khan el-Khalili bazaar'.[1]

These details, drawn from a description of a 15-day tour entitled 'The Magnificent Nile', are fairly typical of tourism in Egypt, and its capital, today. There is, after all, much else to be seen and time is at a premium. This particular tour went on to visit Aswan, Luxor (with its Valley of the Kings and tomb of Tutankhamun), and Tel El Amarna among a number of other places in what was literally a packed itinerary. The participant in this tour would have remembered Cairo by a somewhat garishly decorated Turkish mosque (the Mohammed Ali),[2] the Citadel, a noisy bazaar, but also, fortunately, by one of the great mosques of mediaeval Mamlūk Cairo, the Sultan Hassan[3] Mosque. Much else of Islamic Cairo will frequently and inevitably be ignored by today's modern tour operators and that neglect may or may not even encompass some of the great mosques and mausolea in the *Qarāfa* (the cemetery or 'City of the Dead'), perhaps the Azhar itself and probably the Mosque of Sayyidnā 'l-Ḥusayn; though if the tourist is lucky a few relics of *Coptic* Cairo may be cast his way in the shape of the Coptic Museum and its environs. My main point in all this is that, in our late twentieth century, it is often *time which dictates and constitutes* the shape of the modern tourist paradigm in a major city like Cairo.

This brief essay attempts to show that in mediaeval Islam, as in our own age, there was a tourist paradigm for the visitors to the city of Cairo: naturally it would have differed somewhat – but not totally – from its modern counterpart – the Mosque of Muḥammad 'Alī, for example, did not exist in the age of Ibn Jubayr and Ibn Baṭṭūṭa – and the constraint of time, as a formulating principle in the paradigm, might have been replaced by the factor of the ultimate goal on which the traveller had set his heart: in other words, there might have been more, but not unlimited, time within which to go on and visit Mecca, if it were that city which was the ultimate goal, whether for pilgrimage or other reasons. But Cairo and its environs still, yesterday as today, had its classic places to be visited, people to be seen and shrines and graves at which homage and respect were to be paid. And this gave rise in several cases, notably in the *riḥlatayn* of Ibn Jubayr and Ibn Baṭṭūṭa, to what may neatly be termed a 'tourist *adab*' genre of literature.[4]

Ibn Baṭṭūṭa (1304–1368/9 or 1377) called Cairo the 'mother of cities' (*umm al-bilād*)[5] and with good reason. It had everything that the mediaeval – or modern – scholar and tourist or traveller could desire; and it has always been a tourist trap like most of the world's famous cities boasting major historical and cultural artefacts. While the accounts of Ibn Baṭṭūṭa, and Ibn Jubayr (1145–1217) before him, vary in their detail, it is interesting that a number of major sites are referred to in both their *riḥlatayn*. Now whether or not Ibn Baṭṭūṭa (or his scribe) is indulging in one of his favourite academic pastimes of plagiarizing Ibn Jubayr[6] and simply copying Ibn Jubayr in the emphasis which the latter places on certain sites, does not matter. What is clear is that certain sites in Cairo in the Islamic Middle Ages were obviously regarded as worthy of note and/or visit and it is these sites, whether or not actually visited by both Ibn Jubayr and Ibn Baṭṭūṭa, which this essay maintains constitute the *mediaeval tourist paradigm* which gave rise to – or rather, continued – a species of tourist *adab*. What is also interesting is that at least some of these sites have a good claim to being part of the *modern tourist paradigm* of visits today, dependent, of course, on the constraints of time – and the tour operator! Finally, the *riḥlatayn* of Ibn Jubayr and Ibn Baṭṭūṭa are sufficiently important in the history of Arab travel literature for us to rely on them in trying to establish any kind of mediaeval paradigm of visits and places to be visited by the visitor or traveller to Cairo.

Six *major* sites, geographical features, or areas of interest either stand out in, or are at least common to, the accounts of Cairo by both Ibn Jubayr and Ibn Baṭṭūṭa. They constitute together what I am terming 'the mediaeval tourist paradigm' which may be derived from their writings. They may be enumerated as follows and will each be considered briefly in this essay: (i) The Mosque of 'Amr b. al-'Āṣ; (ii) The Mosque-Shrine of al-Ḥusayn; (iii) The Tomb-Mosque of al-Shāfi'ī; (iv) The *Qarāfa*; (v) The Pyramids; and (vi) The River Nile.

Ibn Baṭṭūṭa (or possibly his scribe Ibn Juzayy) arriving for his first visit to the city of Cairo, later recorded his impressions as follows in a typically magniloquent style:

> [It is the] mistress of broad provinces and fruitful lands, boundless in multitude of buildings, peerless in beauty and splendour, the meeting-place of comer and goer, the stopping-place of feeble and strong. Therein is what you will of learned and simple, grave and gay, prudent and foolish, base and noble, of high estate and low estate, unknown and famous; she surges as the waves of the sea with her throngs of folk and can scarce contain them for all the capacity of her situation and sustaining power. Her youth is ever new in spite of length of days, and the star of her horoscope does not move from the mansion of fortune; her conquering capital (*al-Qāhirah*) has subdued the nations, and her kings have grasped the forelocks of both Arab and non-Arab. She has as her peculiar possession the majestic Nile, which dispenses her district from the need of entreating the distillation [of the rain]; her territory is a month's journey for a hastening traveller, of generous soil, and extending a friendly welcome to strangers.[7]

It is amusing and instructive to compare this encomium of the city of Cairo with the modern grandiloquence, flawed rhetoric, and deathless prose of the modern tour operator when he comes to describe either that same city or the land of Egypt itself. Here are just three examples:

> Egypt is an extraordinary, never to be forgotten country with a richness of sights, colour and sounds which makes a visit here unquestionably a holiday of a lifetime. Visit the fascinating capital,

> Cairo and dip into the riches of the Egyptian Museum or visit the colourful, bustling bazaar and barter for a bargain![8]
>
> And what an experience it is! Along the Nile you'll see the pulsating life of Egypt today – the colourful throng in the bazaars, villages where (as Kipling said) 'Time has stood still since the Ptolemies'. You'll witness scenes of breathtaking natural beauty – haunting sunsets over the Nile, warm moonlit desert nights. Above all you'll be captivated by the marvellous relics of the first great civilisation, monuments whose unimaginable grandeur and unfathomable time-scale still have their power to awe.[9]
>
> Cairo, the largest city in Africa is a unique blend of ancient and modern. From the wonders of the Sphinx and the Pyramids, to the modern luxury hotels on the banks of the timeless Nile, Cairo offers an abundance of delights to every visitor. Cairo is a city of contrasts, a place where East meets West, Christianity meets Islam, where past meets present.
>
> Old Cairo, where Saladin built his great citadel in 1160 AD is a place of hundreds of Mosques, Minarets and bazaars and locals thronging the streets in traditional dress – the men in their flowing galabiahs and the women clad in long black dresses.
>
> A week in Cairo offers the perfect opportunity to capture these contrasts and listed below are some ideas for exploring this exciting metropolis.[10]

It is true, of course – and this is clear in both the *riḥlatayn* of Ibn Baṭṭūṭa and Ibn Jubayr – that there was a certain rhetorical convention which employed exaggeration as a normative descriptive technique in much Arabic travel literature. We note, for example, the *'ajā'ib* and *nawādir* genres which often infused such literature. And as we have seen, this mediaeval practice bears comparison with that of the modern tour operator, or, indeed, estate agent! However, even allowing for such traditional exaggeration in the kind of tourist *adab* like the piece by Ibn Baṭṭūṭa cited above, it is clear that both he and his itinerant predecessor Ibn Jubayr were also deeply and *genuinely* impressed by the city of Cairo and its wonders. It is thus within what may be termed here 'a structure of necessary awe' that Ibn Jubayr and Ibn Baṭṭūṭa viewed the six features of the city whose description now briefly follows.

(i) The Mosque of 'Amr b. al-'Āṣ

Ibn Jubayr, who lodged next door to this mosque,[11] was clearly impressed with its income.[12] He notes that there is another Mosque named after 'Amr in Alexandria.[13] Ibn Baṭṭūṭa was also impressed by this ancient Cairene Mosque describing it as 'a noble mosque, highly venerated and widely celebrated'.[14] Of this mosque, Gibb noted, thus explaining perhaps why it was on the itinerary of both Ibn Jubayr and Ibn Baṭṭūṭa: 'The original mosque, the first in Egypt, was built by the Arab conqueror 'Amr b. al-'Āṣ in 641, but even by this time successive enlargements and restorations had left nothing of the primitive building. (In its present form it dates only from 1798.) After the destruction of the first Arab city of Fusṭāṭ in 1168, however, it was deserted and fell into disrepair . . . *In spite of all, it retained a reputation for special sanctity, owing to its associations with the Companions of the Prophet.*'[15] We might note also the comments of Parker, Sabin, and Williams about this mosque which also underline its importance from a *social* point of view: 'In addition to being the site of the first mosque in Egypt and the starting point of the country's conversion to Islam, it was for centuries the religious and social center of the thriving and cosmopolitan city of al-Fusṭāṭ'.[16] It is small wonder then, that this mosque should figure in both the *riḥlatayn* of Ibn Jubayr and Ibn Baṭṭūṭa.

(ii) The Mosque Shrine of al-Ḥusayn

In 'A note on Misr and Cairo and some of their wonderful monuments'[17] Ibn Jubayr describes in some detail 'the great tomb in Cairo in which is kept the head of Ḥusayn'.[18] He observes that 'it is in a silver casket and over it has been built a mausoleum so superb as to be beyond description and beyond the powers of the mind to comprehend'.[19] Ibn Jubayr concludes that 'I do not believe that in all existence there is a more superb work or more exquisite and wonderful building'.[20] Ibn Baṭṭūṭa betrays a similar, though more restrained, 'tourist' enthusiasm for this shrine, encapsulated within a briefer description: 'Among the celebrated sanctuaries [in the city of Cairo] is the imposing holy shrine where rests the head of al-Ḥusain . . . This shrine is paid its full meed of respect and veneration'.[21] Given the great reverence in Islam for al-Ḥusayn, none of this is surprising, What *is* of interest is the kind of 'tourist *adab*' spouted by both travellers as a by-product of their 'necessary awe' in the face of what had become one of the great shrines of the Islamic world.

(iii) The Tomb-Mosque of al-Shāfiʿī

Ibn Jubayr describes the tomb of Islam's great jurisprudent al-Shāfiʿī as 'a shrine superb in beauty and size' and continues: 'Over against it was built a school [*madrasa*] the like of which has not been made in this country, there being nothing more spacious or more finely built. *He who walks around it will conceive it to be itself a separate town*'.[22] Ibn Baṭṭūṭa also marvels at the construction of the shrine: 'The Mausoleum enjoys an immense revenue and is surmounted by the famous dome, of admirable workmanship and marvellous construction, an exceedingly fine piece of architecture and exceptionally lofty . . .'[23] However, Ibn Baṭṭūṭa refers to an adjacent large ṣūfī dwelling (*ribāṭ kabīr*)[24] rather than a large *madrasa* as in the case of the *Riḥla* of Ibn Jubayr. But Gibb believes that Ibn Baṭṭūṭa indicates by *ribāṭ* here the same *madrasa* as that described by his predecessor.[25] Of this Tomb-Mosque, Parker, Sabin, and Williams have noted: 'Although this mausoleum is of considerable architectural interest and is the largest Islamic mortuary chamber in Egypt, its historical and religious significance is perhaps even more interesting. It was here that Salah al-Din founded the first *madrasah* in Egypt as part of his effort to combat the Fatimid Shiʿa. This was a center of a successful missionary effort based on the Shāfiʿī rite . . . The Imam himself is revered as one of the great Muslim saints . . . One of the holiest shrines in Cairo, since the medieval ages it has been regarded as a source of healing emanations, of baraka. Visitors flock here from all over the Muslim world . . .'[26] In the light of this, further comment on the interest of Ibn Jubayr and Ibn Baṭṭūṭa in this famous Tomb-Mosque is unnecessary.

(iv) The Qarāfa

This great cemetery, in which, in fact, lies the above-mentioned Tomb-Mosque, is characterised by Ibn Jubayr in typical fashion as 'one of the wonders of the world' (*iḥdā 'ajā'ib al-dunyā*) because of the plethora of sacred tombs which it contains.[27] (Significantly Ibn Jubayr insists that he describes in his *Riḥla* only those tombs which he actually visited in the *Qarāfa*).[28] Ibn Baṭṭūṭa is equally glowing in his assessment of the sacred nature and content of the *Qarāfa*, describing it as 'a place of vast repute for blessed power' and citing a tradition which links it ultimately to 'the gardens of Paradise'.[29] The modern-day visitor to the *Qarāfa*, like the mediaeval, cannot fail to be impressed by the size of, and architectural treasures contained within, this great Cairene cemetery and it is thus sad that few formal visits are made as a matter of course by tour groups and operators.

(v) The Pyramids

As we have noted above, we have Ibn Jubayr's word that he personally visited those tombs which he describes in the *Qarāfa*. But did he *personally* visit the Pyramids? As might be expected, he enthuses over them: 'Near to these new bridges are the ancient pyramids, of miraculous construction and wonderful to look upon, four-sided, like huge pavilions rearing into the skies'.[30] There is a consciousness that these are indeed one of the wonders of the ancient world. But, as Broadhurst points out, he gets it wrong: 'Ibn Jubayr is uncharacteristically careless in his description of the pyramids. For example there are six not five smaller pyramids, and the Sphinx faces the Nile not the pyramids'.[31] Similar and much greater doubt may be cast upon Ibn Baṭṭūṭa's account which, unlike Ibn Jubayr's, does not even mention the Sphinx. While being just as admiring as his predecessor,[32] Ibn Baṭṭūṭa unaccountably and strangely describes the Pyramids as 'an edifice of solid hewn stone',[33] i.e. as if they all constituted one building. Because of this Gibb believes that Ibn Baṭṭūṭa did not make a personal visit to the Pyramids and Sphinx.[34] Whatever the truth of the matter, it is clear that both our travellers felt that they *should* have visited the Pyramids and they *may* have doctored their accounts accordingly. They may have been somewhat in the position of the modern tourist in Egypt who, struck by sudden illness or delay, is unable to visit what appears on every tourist itinerary, but who boasts that he has in fact done so, on his return home.

(vi) The River Nile

It only remains to mention that feature of Cairo which no visitor, whether mediaeval or modern, can avoid seeing, the omnipresent River Nile, whose gift, according to the cliché, the whole land of Egypt is. Both Ibn Jubayr and Ibn Baṭṭūṭa are duly respectful. Ibn Jubayr is perhaps the more practical in his description here, concentrating on its bridges constructed by Ṣalāḥ al-Dīn and the Nilometer.[35] Ibn Baṭṭūṭa plays the herald by announcing that 'the Egyptian Nile surpasses all rivers of the earth in sweetness of taste, breadth of channel and magnitude of utility . . . There is no river on earth but it which is called a sea . . . The Nile is one of the five great rivers of the world.'[36]

To conclude, it is the argument of this essay that, just as in the modern age certain aspects and sites of Cairo figure prominently on any tourist itinerary, so too there was a similar body of important sites, constituting what I am terming 'the mediaeval paradigm' of tourists' and travellers' visits. I have tried to identify this paradigm – or at least some of its principal features – by reference to the *riḥlatayn* of two of Islam's best-known and most seasoned travellers. The paradigm of places to be visited as established here is by no means, of course, exclusive. There were surely many other sites. The *riḥlatayn* of Ibn Jubayr and Ibn Baṭṭūṭa point us, however, in the direction of some of what was considered important to visit in mediaeval Cairo. In so doing, the two travellers often allowed their[37] prose styles, deliberately and as a result of their 'necessary awe', or even unconsciously, to run away with them and they created or continued in their works, a species of prose which I have chosen to characterise in this essay as 'Tourist *Adab*'. The modern tourist brochure then, when it describes the wonders of Cairo and Egypt in typically grandiloquent and flowery prose, may be said to participate in a 'great tradition', which, though it would hardly be recognised by F.R. Leavis, goes back to Ibn Baṭṭūṭa, Ibn Jubayr, and beyond.

NOTES

1 Thomas Cook, *Egypt and Nile Cruising . . . Escorted Journeys May 1990–December 1991*, [Tourist Brochure], p. 12.

2 I have retained here the spelling from the tourist brochure cited above.

3 See above, n. 2.

4 See my essay 'Basic Structures and Signs of Alienation in the *Riḥla* of Ibn Jubayr', which constitutes Chapter 9 of this volume.

5 *Riḥlat Ibn Baṭṭūṭa*, (Beirut: Dār Ṣādir, 1964) [hereafter referred to as I.B., *Riḥla*], p. 36, trans. H.A.R. Gibb, *The Travels of Ibn Baṭṭūṭa A.D. 1325–1354*, (Cambridge: Cambridge University Press, for the Hakluyt Society, 1958), I [hereafter referred to as Gibb, *Travels*, I] p. 41. Of Cairo in the age of Ibn Baṭṭūṭa, Ross E. Dunn, *The Adventures of Ibn Battuta: A Muslim Traveller of the 14th Century*, (London: Croom Helm, 1986), p. 45, observes: 'For all their teeming life, the market towns lining the lower Nile were but petty reflections of what the wayfarer beheld on reaching Cairo, the greatest bazaar of them all. *Travellers of the time, whatever their origin, stood bedazzled at the city's overpowering size*' (my italics).

6 For further comments on Ibn Baṭṭūṭa's plagiarism of Ibn Jubayr, see my 'Myth, Miracle and Magic in the *Riḥla* of Ibn Baṭṭūṭa', (Chapter 7 of this book), especially n. 6.

7 Trans. Gibb, *Travels*, 1, p. 41; see I.B. *Riḥla*, p. 36.

8 *Thomson Winter Sun, Spain . . . Egypt . . . Gambia*, 2nd edn. (October 1990–April 1991) [Tourist Brochure], p. 188.

9 Cook, p. 4.

10 *Bales in Egypt, 1990–1991* [Tourist Brochure], p. 18.

11 *Riḥlat Ibn Jubayr* (Beirut: Dār Ṣādir, 1964), [hereafter referred to as I.J., *Riḥla*], p. 19; trans. R.J.C. Broadhurst, *The Travels of Ibn Jubayr*, (London: Jonathan Cape, 1952), [hereafter referred to as Broadhurst, *Travels*], p. 36.
12 I.J. *Riḥla*, p. 24; Broadhurst, *Travels*, p. 42.
13 I.J. *Riḥla*, p. 29; Broadhurst, *Travels*, p. 46.
14 Trans. Gibb, *Travels*, 1, p. 43; see I.B., *Riḥla*, p. 37.
15 (My italics) Gibb, *Travels*, 1, p. 43, n. 125.
16 Richard B. Parker, Robin Sabin, and Caroline Williams, *Islamic Monuments in Cairo: A Practical Guide*, 3rd rev. and enl. edn. (Cairo: American University in Cairo Press, 1988), pp. 50–51.
17 Trans. Broadhurst, *Travels*, p. 36; see I.J. *Riḥla*, p. 19.
18 Ibid.
19 Trans. Broadhurst, *Travels*, pp. 36–7; see I.J., *Riḥla*, p. 19.
20 Trans. Broadhurst, *Travels*, p. 37; see I.J., *Riḥla*, p. 20.
21 Trans. Gibb, *Travels*, pp. 46–7; see I.B., *Riḥla*, p. 39.
22 (My italics) trans. Broadhurst, *Travels*, p. 40; see I.J., *Riḥla*, p. 22.
23 Trans. Gibb, *Travels*, 1, p. 47; see I.B., *Riḥla*, p. 39.
24 I.B., *Riḥla*, p. 39.
25 See Gibb, *Travels*, 1, p. 47, n. 143.
26 Parker, Sabin, and Williams, *Islamic Monuments in Cairo*, p. 149.
27 Trans. Broadhurst, *Travels*, pp. 37–8; see I.J., *Riḥla*, p. 20. For another usage of *iḥdā ʻajā'ib al-dunyā*, see ibid., p. 37.
28 Ibid.
29 Trans. Gibb, *Travels*, 1, pp. 45–6; see I.B., *Riḥla*, p. 39.
30 Trans. Broadhurst, *Travels*, p. 45; see I.J., *Riḥla*, p. 28.
31 Broadhurst, *Travels*, p. 46, n.
32 See I.B., *Riḥla*, p. 41; Gibb, *Travels*, 1, p. 50.
33 Trans. Gibb, *Travels*, 1, p. 51; see I.B., *Riḥla*, p. 42.
34 Gibb, *Travels*, 1, p. 51, n. 161.
35 I.J., *Riḥla*, pp. 27, 29–30; Broadhurst, *Travels*, pp. 45, 47.
36 Trans. Gibb, *Travels*, 1, pp. 48–9; see I.B., *Riḥla*, pp. 40–41.
37 For the sake of clarity of argument, I have, by and large, avoided reference to the role of Ibn Baṭṭūṭa's scribe, Ibn Juzayy, in the writing of the famous *Riḥla*, and the prose style which was created thereby. Clearly, some of the remarks which I have directed at Ibn Baṭṭūṭa in this matter may also – or even solely – apply to Ibn Juzayy.

INDEX

In this Index the Arabic definite article ('al-'/'el-') has been omitted at the *beginning* of an entry.